# Pomona's Lost Children

## A Book of Uncommon Antique Fruits

# Pomona's Lost Children

## A Book of Uncommon Antique Fruits

by

Jay T. Stratton

with illustrations
by the author

Westfield, New York

Chautauqua Gorge Press

2017

Jesse Cornplanter's drawing of the Seneca Frost Spirit ("Cornplanter drawing # 1") reproduced courtesy of the New York State Museum, Albany, New York.

Cover and author photos by Jim Turner.

Chautauqua Gorge Press logo designed by Trish Stratton.

Editing and production of print book, ebook and cover by Mary Kim.

Back cover: detail from Gooseberries on a Stone Plinth, 1701 (Adriaen Coorte, Dutch, active 1683–1707. In the collection of the Cleveland Museum of Art.)

Unless otherwise noted, all illustrations are by the author.



Printed in the United States of America.

ISBN: 978-0-9991051-0-8

10 9 8 7 6 5 4 3 2

Pomona's Lost Children, A Book of Uncommon Antique Fruits
Chautauqua Gorge Press, 121 Union Street, Westfield, New York, 14787

This is a work of creative nonfiction. Events of the author's life are portrayed to the best of memory.

*Blessed be Idunna*

*Goddess of Fruit*

# Contents

Reaper and Partridge Nest, 1797, Thomas Bewick (1753–1828)

# Introduction

This book is not just a cookbook. It is also somewhat of a personal memoir and a horticultural resource that tells the stories of a dozen minority fruits—how to grow them, harvest them, prepare them and cook with them, as well as bits of fruit lore from ancient mythology and from more modern times. So many of these fruits which humankind first grew have fallen into near oblivion today. I have spent the last thirty years of my life growing and cooking with these fruits. In the process I've become somewhat of an antique fruits missionary. I enjoy introducing people to fruits and flavors which their grandparents and great-grandparents cherished.

My love for plants began as a child, as witness the many childhood stories in this book. It was honed by my years as a botany major at the State University of New York College of Forestry, although I never graduated, and then furthered as a life-long member of the Bergen Swamp Protection Society and the Chautauqua Watershed Conservancy. Much of this lore was learned and many of these recipes were tried at gatherings through the years at Blue Heron Farm, Lavender Hill, Temenos Farm, Ganowungo and the Faërie Herbal Collective. I was a member of NAFEX (North American Fruit Explorers) before it became a computer group and I've long been a member of NOFA (Northeast Organic Farming Association) and of the Abundance Cooperative Market in Rochester. I have also enjoyed many permaculture meet-ups over the years organized by Patty Love's "Barefoot Permaculture." This book is also informed by my long career as a school teacher and linguist, as well as by my heathen and radical faërie spiritual beliefs.

In 1990 I purchased sixteen acres of abandoned farmland in Forsyth, New York, in the so-called "fruit belt" of the Lake Erie plain (zone 6). The farm had been abandoned in 1951, which I note with some irony is also the year of my birth. My life as a teacher in a city a hundred miles away was rewarding, but not enough. I decided that I wanted to become something of a farmer as well.

"Why do you want to buy that land? You'll never be able to grow anything there except frogs!" an old neighbor cajoled me.

Most of the "frog farm" had indeed reverted to shrub swamp and marsh, but I worked the two dry acres up by the road to create my fruit farm. I made most of my livelihood in the city during the academic year but during the summers and weekends I kept bees and grew most all of the fruits mentioned in this book. The farm has enriched my life immeasurably in ways I couldn't even imagine when I began this project. It has not enriched my pocketbook enough for me to be considered a "real farmer," whatever that is, but I continue to sell berries at the Westfield farmers' market and to produce all sorts of rare commodities for gifts and for home consumption.

Idunna carrying her apples, 1882, Carl Emil Doepler (1824–1905)

My farm (and this book) is dedicated to Idunna, the Nordic goddess of fruits. I take the broad interpretation that Idunna is the goddess of all fruits and that all are needed for us to have good health. She is not as widely known as she ought to be among those of us who are trying to revive and strengthen the old ways of our cultures. Here is a description of her taken from Padraic Colum's book *The Children of Odin*:

> In Asgard there was a garden, and in that garden there grew a tree, and on that tree grew shining apples. . . Everyday that passes makes us older and brings us to that day when we will be bent and feeble, gray-headed and weak-eyed. But those shining apples that grew in Asgard—they who ate of them every day grew never a day older, for the eating of the apples kept old age away.
>
> Idunna, the Goddess, tended the tree on which the shining apples grew. None would grow on the tree unless she was there to tend it. No one but Idunna might pluck the shining apples. Each morning she plucked them and left them in her basket and every day the gods and goddesses came to her garden that they might eat the shining apples and so stay forever young.
>
> Idunna never went from her garden. . . .

Now just what was Idunna growing? Her apples are said to be yellow or "golden." Did they have "Golden Delicious" apples in ancient times? In many other myths about golden apples these are thought to be that ancient Roman health food, the quince. Could this myth be the origin of our old saying "an apple a day keeps the doctor away"?

It is interesting to consider what an "apple" is. Must it be red or yellow? Certainly our words are older and less specific than the Linnaean system of scientific names which presumes a fruit to be one and only one thing. In the expression "the apple of your eye" it can be anything desirable. The French consider potatoes (*pommes de terre*) to be apples. In Italy tomatoes are "golden apples." In America we have "May apples," those yellow-green fruits of a forest wildflower. I've even heard of "road apples," which are neither red nor yellow nor desirable—except as fertilizer.

As time goes on I'll need more and ever more of those anti-oxidants in black currants to keep my eyesight keen and my mind healthy. If I eat enough quince and medlar, it may save me from getting an unfavorable colonoscopy. Pawpaw might one day save me from cancer. It is up to us to continue our customs of using these uncommon antique fruits.

Please don't imagine that this book is any quirky kind of health food cookbook. The recipes herein are old-fashioned ones filled with sugars, flours, fats, butter and cream. There is a lack of vegan and gluten-free recipes, but don't let that deter you. If you come to like these uncommon fruits, you will find new recipes waiting for you to invent them.

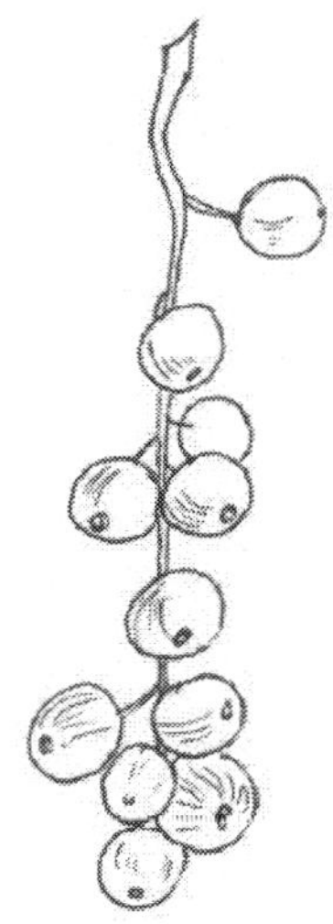

# Currants

*Ribes sativum*

When we were young everyone was eating currant jelly. Mother used to make our own special "Bar-le-Duc" jelly that combined the tart flavor of currant with red raspberry. Fruit jellies were often served with meat. Mint jelly for lamb, currant jelly for pork, those were the rules of the times. Cranberry was reserved for the turkey at Thanksgiving.

Currants are very much a part of the Swedish-American tradition. "*Vinbär*" means "wine berries" in Swedish. It is a hardy plant that grows in the far north all the way to the Arctic Circle, which grapes do not. The Vikings drank beer made from barley, mead made from honey and wine made from currants.

So what do Mother and Aunt do with ten little yammering Swedish-American children over a long, hot July? Something that builds character, encourages industry, enriches the family and acts as a free baby-sitting service. So they took all of us, siblings and cousins, down to a farm to work in the fields during the currant harvest.

I remember the field seemed to stretch for a mile along the railroad tracks to the distant vineyards. Half the kids in town seemed to be there! We were issued small cards on which the bosses noted our names. The cards were pre-printed with columns of numbers from one to one hundred. They had a special paper punch to punch out the number of pounds which we had picked. Supposedly one kid had been caught trying to get credit for pounds not picked by using a razor blade to cut a similar hole. It was easy to tell a counterfeit hole, we were warned. Each card, if properly punched, could turn into a five dollar bill. We got paid five cents a pound in the 1960s. This was my first real, paying, everyday job. The season lasted for two to three weeks.

We sat on upside-down wooden grape crates in the boiling hot sun picking into peck baskets. At first we were excited at the prospect of working for a berry farm. "Berries!" we said, the way a hungry Yogi Bear might have said it. Unfortunately these miniscule, seedy bunches of sour red "grapes" tasted nothing like the sweet currant jelly we were used to eating.

"Berries!" My little brother ran eagerly to our row of bushes and stuffed his mouth full. As he began to chew the look in his eyes changed and he began to spit them out.

"Yuck! These are too sour!"

The "bitter" truth began to hit us. Here we were in a beautiful field of ripe red berries but none of them were fit to eat. We'd been tricked! Berry bushes indeed! We hated fresh currants.

The ground was well cultivated. We got in trouble for throwing dirt clods at people. We liked to see the puff of "smoke" as the clods broke. The idea was not to injure people but to throw the clods in front of people so that they'd break on the ground and send up dust onto the victim. This was a subtle distinction totally lost on the boss, who said this was no time for play.

Back to the bushes. We worked two kids to a bush. That way we had somebody to talk to. We were about as tall as a currant bush back then, and little hands were good for harvesting little berries. Maybe it really was easier to have children pick the berries, if not for the discipline problems. It seemed to take hours to fill that basket. Then the boss lady would weigh it, punch the card, dump the basket into a larger crate and send us back to pick more. When the wagon filled with currant crates, the boss man hauled it off and returned with an empty one.

The only other break in the monotony was when a train went by. Everyone would look up at the engine and wave, and then wave again for the caboose. At lunch time we ate our peanut butter and jelly sandwiches in the patches of shade along the tracks. After a thirty-minute lunch the bosses returned and again set up the weighing station. We resumed work, though not quite as enthusiastically.

# Currants

It is easy to get lost in that green world down inside a currant bush, talking with one's favorite cousin. There is intense competition for the easily picked large clusters of berries on top of the bush, but of course we had to pick the berries down inside the bush as well. We pretended to fight over the larger clusters. "You thieving vulture! You get your hands off of *my* berries!"

The boss inspected our bushes as we completed each row and often made us go back. We got in trouble if we picked too many green currants or if we left too many red ones. Green currants could seriously depress the sugar levels of the crop. Every now and then there was a bush of white currants. At first we left them, thinking they were unripe green currants, so we got yelled at for that too. Sometimes a kid just can't win! The boss lady took us aside and showed us a white currant bush. "You can tell that it's ripe because the berries are soft and sweet," she said, and popped some into her mouth. We winced. Then she compared these with a bunch of green currants which were as hard as rocks and slightly different in color.

Adults worked all around us, doing two or three rows to our every one. The currants had an upright growth pattern and were grown to be harvested by the ton. Great gobs of fruit hung all along the branches, especially at the tops, so you could pick a whole handful at one time. They were production currants, the reds.

White currants are more appealing, reputedly sweeter. They have a more drooping growth pattern. They are used as "table currants" for fresh eating. The strigs are longer and the berries, larger. Table currants can be white, red, pink ("champagne") or yellow in color. The fields we worked in were mostly "production currants," but every here and there were planted a few white currants to enhance pollination. All these different-colored currants are considered to be the same species, except black currants which I discuss in the next chapter.

Currant season lasted for two to three weeks in July. Of course it was a great excitement at season's end to turn in all of our tickets and receive a little manila envelope with twenty to thirty dollars in it, and change too. There were no pennies because the pay rate was a nickel a pound. Adults and older teenagers worked one to a bush, did not waste time playing and hopefully made a lot more than we did.

In 1919, New York State produced over three million quarts of currants which made up forty-three percent of the entire national crop. Today the crop is so small that they don't even keep statistics on it. In the mid-1960s when I worked in the currant fields, there were still a large number of processing plants that accepted currants.

All of this is gone today. The currant bushes have been pulled out and put into a monoculture of vineyards, and the currant is in danger of disappearing completely from our commerce. Currant jelly has become hard to find in the stores. Fifty years ago it was a standard on every table, a condiment as common as ketchup and mustard.

There is no good reason for this traditional fruit to have fallen on such hard times. It's time to start a campaign to bring back the currant before it is completely forgotten. I consider myself very lucky to have memories of times when something of everything was grown on each farm, or so it seemed. My great uncle had cherries, peaches, pears, grapes, apples, strawberries, milk cows, pigs, chickens, geese, corn fields, hay fields and a huge vegetable garden (though no currants or gooseberries that I can remember). But today his former farm has become part of the vast monoculture of grapes, as have most farms in the "fruit belt" that runs along the Lake Erie plain.

Currants have long been popular with the British as well. In Victorian times they became one of the first fruits to be available virtually all year round. Currants grown under glass could be ripened as early as March when July is the usual season. At the other end of spectrum, bushes kept under shade cloth could ripen fruit on into November. Or remove the shade cloth in August, and get currants in September. Then expose another shaded row in September to get currants for October, and so on.

Candied currant strigs were used as tasty decorations for cakes, puddings and ice creams. To make these, tie several strigs of ripe currants together and droop them gently over a thin stick. Continue until you have currants hanging all along the stick. Prepare a wide-mouthed pan of boiling sugar syrup. Pass the stick repeatedly over the syrup until the dangling berries are sufficiently cooked and candied but not falling apart. Good luck with this part! If you do get this far, dust the candied strigs with powdered sugar, let them dry, and then store them in canisters between layers of waxed paper until you are ready to take them out to make decorations.

The farm that I'd begun at my cabin in the woods soon became too hard to run. My fruit trees died in the cold climate (zone 5) or were eaten by deer. Bears destroyed my apiary. This is when I decided to buy new land down along the Lake Erie plain at Forsyth, New York. The farm had been abandoned fifty years previously, but still I could see where they grew Concord and Niagara grapes, sweet cherries, apples and currants. Much of the land had reverted to shrub swamp, tupelo grove or oak forest, but on the two acres along the road I set up my farm again. Here the bears would not discover the bees so close to a major highway, and they did not bother them for twenty years. Here I planted my fruit trees and berry bushes.

For many years I ignored the remnants of the currant field. I bought my own currant bushes out of a catalog. I noted that the original currant bushes, which were growing in deep shade, seldom fruited. When they did, however, the berries seemed definitely larger than the currants I was growing. I erroneously assumed this was because the bush put out only a few of them. Finally, I decided to pay some attention to these old bushes and moved one out into the sunlight. Much to my amazement, the bush produced an exceptional red table currant with beautiful long strigs and huge berries. The extra sunlight made for more berries on each strig but they continued to be just as large. These beautiful old plants have a drooping growth pattern and could benefit from a trellis or espalier to keep the berries up off the ground. A strig of currants up in the air will continue to ripen and get sweeter while currants in contact with the ground will rot almost as fast as they ripen.

In cultivation, currant bushes are grown in rows five feet apart. Mildew can be a problem, as can the currant borer or the currant sawfly worm. In home cultivation, this should be less of a problem. My bushes have survived repeated defoliation by the green-blooded sawfly worm and have even managed to ripen fruit after most of the leaves have been eaten!

In the past there were many different cultivars, but most of these appear to have been lost now. In 1925, for example, there were over 125 different cultivars of currant for sale. How many could we find today? You are lucky to find a nursery with any currant plants at all, let alone a number of different cultivars.

Currants must have been known since ancient times, but perhaps only as a semi-wild fruit. *Ribes petraeum*, *Ribes rubrum* and *Ribes sativum* are the wild currant species of Europe, Asia and northern Africa, but they seem to have been late in entering the world of agriculture. They are described in the 1484 German *Mainz Herbarius*, and their first mention in English is in Gerard's *Herbal* of 1597. Currant bushes are said to have arrived at the Massachusetts Bay Colony as early as 1669. Over time the wild currant species were crossed and bred into a splendid profusion of currant cultivars, which now are dwindling in number.

The best cultivars for size and flavor today–the table currants–come from the so-called "Versailles group" of cultivars, mostly derived from *Ribes sativum*. Their names–"Laxton's Perfection," "Red Cross," "Wilder" and "Fay's Prolific"–each tell a tale from a time when unknown farmers might dream of "inventing" new cultivars. I wonder if the bush I found on my farm might not be a "Fay's Prolific"? This variety was developed just ten miles down the road in Portland, New York, by Lincoln Fay about 1868, with the currant being introduced to the public in 1880 by the Fredonia, New York, nurseryman, Geo. S. Josselyn. The currant was sold on a royalty, and the story goes that, by the early 1900s, Farmer Fay and his heirs had earned in the neighborhood of forty thousand dollars for the variety which he worked years to develop.

Though people with access to a bush can easily get enough to make jelly, "Prolific" was a misnomer. The plants were sprawling in nature with low production but excellent flavor and size. This currant had long strigs, which is good for picking, and like all currants it can tolerate partial shade and prefers cool, moist climates with heavy clay soils. The wood is brittle and "blind," which is to say it will not fruit on old wood. It must be pruned when it gets too leggy, or trained to live on a cordon or espalier along a wall.

Not long ago, my friend Mary purchased a summer cottage on the "High Rocks" of the Point Peninsula, on Lake Ontario, and has since also become involved in "currant archaeology." Currants may occasionally come from seed, but more likely the drooping bushes we found in her woods had spread by "tip layering" and are still the same old-fashioned variety which would probably have been planted there in the 1930s. They are an elegant, large-fruited red table currant. In another shady corner of her yard we found yet another surviving currant, this one large, black, and not as tart. Whether these are "lost" cultivars or just old-fashioned varieties which still survive elsewhere is a mystery yet to be solved.

Other currant cultivars still common today are "White Imperial" and "Jhonken Van Tets" (early), "Cherry Red" and "Perfection" (mid-season), and "Red Lake" and "Redstart" (late-season). The berries are self-fruitful and ripen seventy to one hundred days after pollination but will benefit from cross pollination with another variety by showing increased yields. The bushes need cool, moist weather. If the temperature gets above eighty-six degrees Fahrenheit, the bushes will begin to lose their leaves and suffer. They readily recover as soon as cool weather returns. Don't give up on a bush that is looking poorly!

Nowadays, when you say the word "currant" most people think of those little raisins used in currant scones. But are these really made with red currants? In fact, these little raisins were originally raised in the Mediterranean area and shipped to the English from the city of Corinth. "Corinthian raisins" was eventually shortened and corrupted into "currants." There is no relationship between these little raisins (from the Zante grape, *Vitis vinifera*) and the red or white berries of *Ribes sativum* or the black currant *Ribes nigrum*. I have listened to otherwise educated people maintain that the little red berries from a currant bush will dry into the little raisins in those scones. They think they are teaching me a new homophone. "That's 'currant' with an *A*."

But it's just not so! The word "currant" has been used to denote Corinthian raisins since the 1550s. The original word for the *Ribes* currants in the English language has been lost. The berries must have been known to the ancient Anglo Saxons. Perhaps they called them "wine berries" like the Swedes. For a while, they were called "red gooseberries," but this too was inaccurate because there are real red gooseberry varieties which are *not* currants. This may be due to the French who use one word, "*groseille*," for both red currants and gooseberries. Another moniker was "bastard currants" because dried red or black currants could be used as an adulterant in, or a poor substitute for, Corinthian raisins.

Here is an easy way to avoid linguistic confusion. Use the color words! Corinthian raisin currants are always brown and always dried. If you mean a *Ribes* currant, say "red currant," "black currant," or "white currant," and so on. Nowadays these will not be dried. A dried red or white currant may be light brown in color, but it's hard to believe that these could fool anyone into thinking they were raisins. The dried black currant would have done better in appearance as a counterfeit though not in taste.

One reason for the decline in currant culture was the rust scare. Rusts are fungal diseases of plants. Some rusts are relatively benign and appear as reddish-brown spots on a plant's leaves. Other rusts may be extremely damaging or even fatal to their plant hosts and have caused great losses to agriculture and to forestry. Rusts which spend their entire life cycle on one plant host are said to be "autoecious." "Heteroecious" rusts require two different plant hosts to complete their life cycle. The disease spreads by spores on the winds.

White pine blister rust (*Cronartium ribiclola*) is heteroecious. It spends half of its life on currants and gooseberries where it causes no problem. Then the fungus lives on pine trees and looks completely different. For a while it was thought to be a completely different species called *Peridermium strobi*. The rust had spread from Europe to America in 1906 and was killing white pine trees all across New York and New England. As scientists realized this was really a heteroecious rust, a solution became clear. A value judgment was made. At that time more money was being made in forestry than in currant culture. The greater harm was being done to forestry, not to agriculture. Governments began to outlaw the cultivation of currants, gooseberries and black currants in order to save the forests by interrupting the life cycle of the organism. A diseased pine could not infect another pine, but a diseased currant could. The blister rust scare is probably the single greatest factor in the ongoing decline of currant and gooseberry culture in America.

Today we take a more nuanced view. Most of these laws have been repealed and currant culture is legal once again. The vast white pine forests we sought to protect in the early 1900s have disappeared due to the timberman's saw as much as due to the blister rust. Modern horticultural white pines (and presumably many of the wild ones as well) were chosen to be resistant to the blister rust. In 1906 they had no such resistance. Resistant trees were a tiny minority back then. Today wild white pines are much less common, whereas pines planted in yards, parks and forestry plantations have been selected for blister rust resistance.

New varieties of currant and gooseberry have been developed which are not hosts to the blister rust fungus at all. The role of currant cultivation in the spread of the disease became less important after it was shown that native *Ribes* species in the local swamps are just as capable of infecting the pine trees as are the plantations of domestic currants. The native currants and gooseberries are so common that no one would imagine trying to extirpate them! They look very similar to the domesticated plants but the fruits are few, insipid-tasting and covered with bristly hairs.

For a number of years, I have sold my currants at the farmers' market with mixed success. I sell them in half-pint baskets on the strig for use as fresh fruit or as an interesting addition to pancakes and baked goods. Usually they don't sell well. Perhaps the sight of them brings back memories! "Oh those! I haven't seen those in years," a customer remarks. Another remembers, "Oh, how I hated the tedious picking in the hot sun! After I'd picked all the bunches, my grandmother made me go back through them and pick all the berries off the bunch!" The memory of hard work is the usual reason given for hating the berries, not the taste.

Even so, it shows that currants still figure in the common memory although they may be better known in my area than in other areas of the country because most of Chautauqua County is within the so-called "Swedish enclave." For example, here is what I learned from a visit to Anne Rosel Groft of Westfield whose parents had a seventeen-acre fruit farm back in the 1930s and 40s that included one acre of currants. The family did their own picking, and a truck would come by arrangement to take the baskets to farm stands all across Chautauqua County. "Currants was something the farmers did in-between," Anne explained. "Nobody raised just currants. You had a patch of a size that you could handle. By mid-July, you'd already taken off the first cutting of hay and the grapes wouldn't demand your attention for another month or two yet. You could make a little much-needed extra money by selling your currants then."

A friend from Sherman, New York, told me another interesting bit of currant lore. Currant bushes used to be fertilized with spoiled milk. Whenever a load of milk soured or took on an onion-like taste making it unsaleable, it was discarded in the currant fields. It is said the bushes benefitted from this treatment.

But currants are a "specialty crop" these days, and I am a "microproducer." The kind of people who seek out antique fruits like currants are "foodies" or "locavores" who choose to devour local foods. And then there are the people who encounter currants for the first time without knowing what they are. This describes another of my customers. After nibbling a few sample berries, he liked them very much but his untrained eye mistook the currants for the omnipresent and invasive red honeysuckle berries which look a bit similar. "Wow!" he proclaimed enthusiastically, "I didn't know those berries are edible!"

*They are not.* He would have been in for a wretched surprise if he had tried to eat honeysuckle berries, even though the fragrant flowers are redolent of honey. As children we would pick them and bite a little hole down by the green sepals and suck out the small drop of nectar there—if the bees and butterflies had not already done so. But we knew enough never to eat the flowers themselves, let alone the berries! (The *only* edible honeysuckle is the blue honeysuckle berry, called "honeyberry." It is a trans-Arctic species which lives in northern Japan, Siberia, Alaska and Canada. It has recently become a popular new crop in Canada where it is known by the Ainu and Japanese name for the berry, or "*haskap*.")

In the late 1950s, Elton Tubbs, a farmer from Westfield, New York, invented the first currant-picking machine. The machine was drawn behind the tractor and worked by agitating the branches of the currant bush until the berries fell off into chutes, which in turn let the berries fall into baskets. It was a mini-version of the automatic grape harvester which was invented a decade or so later. Tubby, as he was known, never got rich off of his invention, unfortunately. But perhaps this was because currant production was already in decline, although local packing plants would still be taking in currants for a few years yet.

A "packing plant" or "processing plant" is what local seasonal factories were called that purchased the farmers' fruit crops, packaged them and sold them in distant cities. These were the equivalent of a cannery for vegetables. Welch's Grape Juice, which began in Westfield, never processed currants as far as I know. But Rood & McClean, which was in business in Westfield from 1934 to 1952, took in sweet cherries, sour cherries, and grapes, as well as currants. The Westfield Food Products plant also took in currants. Planters Cooperative bought out Rood & McClean in 1962, but continued to take currants through the 1960s. But with local processing plants closed, local currant culture was doomed—and perhaps Tubby's currant picker, as well. It just didn't make sense for farmers to drive this minor crop greater distances for processing.

❧

The present may be bleak when compared to the noble past, but the future at last looks a bit brighter for the currant. Currants are exceedingly high in vitamins A, B and C, as well as in pectin. Currant jelly "gels" easily and a modest addition of currant juice to other fruit jellies can be of great assistance in getting them to gel. This is the so-called "currant pectin." And although currants are seedy berries, they are certainly less so than raspberries. To get around this one simply cooks and crushes the currants and strains the juice, thereby preserving the flavor. Add fresh currants to the cooked and strained ones for visual appeal and a little crunch. Currants of all colors can be dried and eaten as if they were raisins, as well, though they do not have as sweet a flavor. The legal climate has also changed, so that it is once again lawful to cultivate currants in many, though not all parts of the United States.

The currant is a time-honored fruit ready for its renaissance! It is necessary to fight the false perception that "currants are only for jelly." Jelly is the least interesting way to enjoy a currant! Although the legal climate has changed, my cousin John Beckman, of (certified organic) Pomme de Terre Farms in North Carolina, informs me that currants are still illegal in that state, so he had to decline my offer of some currant bushes. This brings us to the second reason for the decline in currant culture: lack of workers to harvest the berries and lack of a robust demand to justify the enormous expenses involved in obtaining automatic currant picker machines. In order to repopularize and bring back the currant for real, we will need to harvest tons of berries for sauces, juice and jelly. In addition to that we will need to see table currants of all colors on sale in season at supermarkets, not just quaint old farm stands. Will apple-currant pie become as popular as strawberry-rhubarb? Why not currant flavored ice cream? The present may be bleak when compared to the noble past, but the future at last looks a bit brighter for the currant.

# Currant Recipes

## Currant Serving Suggestions

- Interesting addition to fruit salads
- Apple pie with a handful or two of red currants becomes something much more special!
- Sweet breads and nut breads
- Currant pancakes! Move over, blueberry!
- Swedish oven pancake with red currants baked inside and additional berries or sauce to serve over top
- Parfait glasses with alternating stripes of graham cracker crumbs, nuts, sugared currants and yogurt or whipped cream
- Peaches with red currants
- Currant Sauce over ice cream
- Currant Jelly
- Currant Juice drinks
- Traditional pairing of currants and red raspberries for fresh fruit, sauce, juice or jelly
- Currant sauces with meats

## Currant Tart/ *Vinbärstårta*

Make three round cake layers using your recipe of choice for vanilla cake or yellow cake. Take 4 cups of red currants, crush and sugar to taste. Use one cup of whipped cream for the frosting of the top and sides. Crushing the currants will release enough juice so that the sugar will dissolve completely in them and the middle layers of "red frosting" will not be granular in texture.

## Swedish Cheesecake with Currants/ *Ostkaka med Vinbär*

For the cake:

16 ounces cottage cheese
3 eggs
2 tablespoons wheat flour

1 tablespoon barley flour
1/3 cup sugar
1/2 teaspoon vanilla
1 cup milk (or cream)

For the topping:

1/2 cup mixed currants
2 tablespoons orange marmalade
1 teaspoon water
1 tablespoon sugar

Beat the cottage cheese and eggs until well mixed, then add remaining ingredients. Pour into a well-greased 8 by 8-inch pan. Bake at 350°F for 1 hour to 1 hour and 15 minutes. As the cheesecake nears completion, assemble the topping. Cook currants briefly and stir to incorporate marmalade and sugar. Spread on top of the cheesecake and let bake with the fruit on top for the last 5 minutes. Cool. Serve with whipped cream or ice cream.

## Swedish Oven Pancake with Currants

1 cup milk
2/3 cup flour
1/4 cup melted butter
2 eggs
Pinch of salt
Pinch of baking powder
2 tablespoons sugar
1/4 cup sugared red currants
1/2 teaspoon allspice

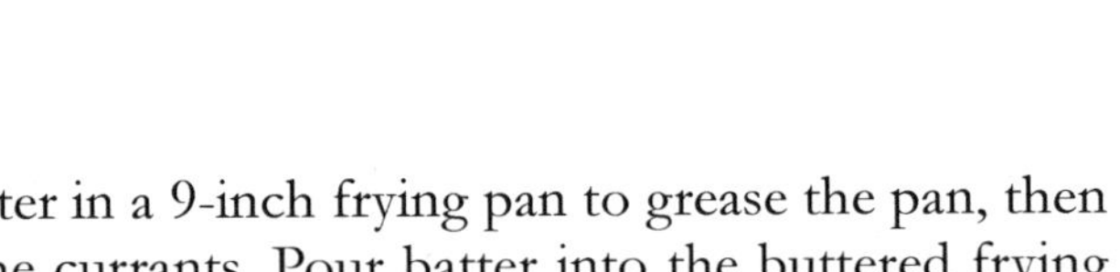

Beat together most all ingredients. Melt butter in a 9-inch frying pan to grease the pan, then pour the rest into the batter. Gently add the currants. Pour batter into the buttered frying pan and bake at 400°F for 35 minutes until golden brown and puffy. It will deflate as it cools. Cut into triangular pieces and serve on warm plates with additional currant sauce on top or dust with powdered sugar or drizzle with honey. What a luxurious breakfast!

## Rochester Jellycake

2 cups sugar
2/3 cup butter
1 cup milk
3 cups flour
1 teaspoon baking soda

Divide the dough in two. Bake in 2 separate pans. To one batch of dough also add:

1 tablespoon molasses
1 tablespoon flour
1 cup raisins, chopped fine
1 teaspoon cinnamon
1 teaspoon clove

For the "frosting" inner layer, use currant jelly. Bake at 350°F for 25 to 30 minutes. To assemble, put layer of dark cake on the bottom, then a layer of currant jelly, then the white cake. Roll up the jelly roll.

## Rolled Jellycake / *Rullad Gelekaka*

1 cup sugar
1 cup flour
3 eggs
1 teaspoon cream of tartar
1/2 teaspoon baking soda
Pinch of salt
Currant jelly as needed

Bake the cake in a thin layer on a greased and/or papered cookie sheet. Let it cool slightly then remove from the "pan" and let it sit on a flat surface. Before it hardens, spread the surface with currant jelly. Stir the jelly first to give it a silky texture. Carefully roll up the jelly roll, set it on the serving plate and let it continue to cool. Slice into pieces and serve on individual plates.

## Currant Pound Cake

1 cup dried currants
1/4 cup brandy
One pound butter
8 eggs
2 1/4 cups sugar
4 cups flour
1/2 teaspoon nutmeg

Let the dried currants soak overnight in the brandy. Cook in two loaf pans at 325°F for one hour.

This is an early American colonial recipe which could have been made with either dried red currants or with Corinthian raisin currants as available. Those ships from Corinth didn't come in often! In colonial times dried red currants were acceptable fare, but modern tastes do not find dried red currants very palatable by themselves. I mean to try this experiment.

I'll dry some of my red currants, then prepare one pound cake with them, and another pound cake with the raisin currants. I'll let my guests decide how palatable each is. In this contest I suspect that the dried red currants may have a chance.

## Currant Kuchen/*Johannesbeere Streuselkuchen*

1 package yeast
1/2 cup milk, warmed
1/2 cup sugar
3 tablespoons safflower oil
2 eggs
3 cups flour
1/4 teaspoon salt

Let this dough rise in an oiled bowl for one hour. Then beat it down, knead it and press it into a ten-inch round cake pan that has been well oiled. Sprinkle and then press this topping into it:

1/4 cup flour
1 pound red currants
3 tablespoons butter
Zest of 1/2 lemon
1/2 teaspoon cinnamon
A few more spoons of sugar

Dot the currant topping with pats of butter. Bake 30 minutes at 375°F.

## Little Currant Cakes/*Petits Gateaux aux Groseilles*

Since "groseille" means both currant and gooseberry in French and this is a French recipe, I suppose you could make these cakes with either fruit but I prefer it with the red currants. Bake these cakes in muffin tins or small cake pans about the size of a large muffin. This recipe makes 4 cakes.

5/6 cups powdered sugar
1/2 cup almond powder (if unavailable, make your own in a blender or food processor)
3/8 cup flour (pastry flour is best, sifted)
3 egg whites

1/2 cup currants
1/4 teaspoon baking powder
2 ounces of butter (one half stick)

Melt the butter and set aside. Sift together the flour and the sugar and mix in all dry ingredients. Next add the egg whites, beaten stiff, and the melted butter. Grease the little pans or muffin tins. Sprinkle the currants on top. Bake 15 to 20 minutes at 350°F.

## Linzertorte

Linz is a town in Austria and this recipe dates back to the Austro-Hungarian Empire. Originally the recipe was made with hazelnuts and red currants, but nowadays most "linzers" are a walnut/red raspberry combination. For this recipe, you will need one large or two small well-buttered torte pans with removable bottoms.

2 eggs (one of these for the egg wash while baking)
1 cup butter (2 sticks)
1 cup sugar
1 1/2 tablespoon grated orange peel
1 teaspoon grated lemon peel
2 1/2 cups flour
1 teaspoon baking powder
2 teaspoons cinnamon
1/2 teaspoon powdered clove
1/4 teaspoon salt
1 cup ground hazelnuts

Grind the hazelnuts as fine as a coarse flour, then prepare the dough. Chill the dough to make it easy to work with. Roll out the dough 1/4 to 3/8-inch thick. Use 2/3 of it for the bottom crust and reserve 1/3 of it for the lattice top. Push the dough into your well-buttered torte pans. Prick it all over with a fork. The air holes will make it cook better. Bake at 375°F with dried beans or baking weights on top of the crust in aluminum foil for 10 to 15 minutes.

Fill your linzertorte with 1/4 to 1/2 cup of red currant preserves. If they are in season (or if you have some frozen) throw in 10 or 20 whole berries. This will improve your linzertorte immensely, but don't use too much of a good thing lest it become too wet and pie-like. Spread the jam and berries carefully and evenly.

Next roll out your remaining dough to be 1/4-inch thick and slice it into strips about 1/2-inch wide. Use a metal ruler or a long flat knife to move these delicate strips onto your linzertorte. Carefully interweave them to create a latticework top layer. About half of the jam should be visible through the open areas of your lattice. Gently join your latticework to the edges of the main crust by pinching them together with your fingers. You may need to wet your fingers in water to join the dough if it's too dry.

Paint the lattice crust with an egg wash, then bake at 375°F for 20 to 30 minutes. Paint with egg wash again towards the end of the baking time.

Let the linzertorte cool to nearly room temperature before you remove it from the torte pan. Gently pry at each and every inch of the diameter so the crust won't break while you are removing it from the pan.

Let it cool completely before cutting and serving.

## Red Currant Muffins

1 1/2 cups flour
1/2 cup sugar (or less, to taste)
2 teaspoons baking powder
1/2 teaspoon salt
1 egg
1/2 cup milk
1/4 cup vegetable oil
1 cup red currants
1/2 teaspoon cinnamon

Bake in well-greased muffin tin with greased cupcake papers. 400°F for 20 to 25 minutes.

## Currant Pie/ *Vinbärspaj*

This recipe was originally printed in *Swedish-American Book of Cookery and Adviser for Swedish Servants in America,* published in New York in 1888 by Carl Grimsköld.

One cupful of ripe currants crushed fine, one cupful of sugar, one half cupful of water, the yolks of two eggs and one tablespoon of flour. Bake with an under crust. When cooked, beat the whites of the eggs with four spoonfuls of powdered sugar, spread it on top off the pie, and return to the oven to brown. (*En kopp mogna och fint pressade vinbär, en dito socker, en half dito vatten, två äggulor och en matsked mjöl. Bakas i underdeg. När den är gräddad, vispas ägghvitorna samman med fyra skeder pudersocker och bredes öfver pie'n, som ställes tillbaka i ugnen, att brungraddas.*)

This recipe is positively wonderful! I used a standard piecrust of 1 cup flour, 5 tablespoons shortening, pinch of salt and only enough water to combine the dough. Add water one spoonful at a time. The egg whites make a mini-meringue on top. You may choose to make a real meringue or to serve the pie with whipped cream or ice cream instead.

## Currant Pie

This German recipe for currant pie is a bit fancier than the previous Swedish-American one. Roll out this dough and bake for about 25 minutes at 325°F.

1 1/2 cup flour
1 teaspoon baking powder
1/2 cup butter
1/2 cup sugar
2 egg yolks
1 1/2 teaspoon lemon zest

Then add this filling and bake an additional 10 minutes or more until the top browns:

2 egg whites, beaten stiff
1/2 cup sugar
2 tablespoons cornstarch
2 1/4 cups red currants

If your crust threatens to collapse while baking, you may need to support it with foil and dried beans or some other weights.

## Red Currant Fool

2 cups red currants
4 tablespoons powdered sugar
1 tablespoon vanilla
3/4 cup whipped cream
3/4 cup Greek yogurt

Puree the first three ingredients in a blender. Add the whipped cream and Greek yogurt. Greek yogurt is particularly thick and rich tasting and can make this recipe slightly lighter on fat content. You may wish to mix until the product is a uniform pink or you can leave swirls of white and red. Pour into parfait glasses and chill.

## Fruit Pudding

Cook together the desired quantity of:

Apricots
Peaches
Red Raspberries
Red Currants

Add 2 tablespoons of water and more as needed. Cook until fruit is soft; add the berries at the end. Cook just until the juice turns red but the fruit is still intact. Let this cool. Line a baking tin with slices of bread, crusts removed, or you may prefer to use ladyfingers. Pour the pudding in over the bread. Cover the pudding with additional slices of bread. Spoon a little reserved juice over the bread on top to make sure that it will soften. Cover this and let it sit in the refrigerator all night long. Uncover and turn the pudding out onto the serving dish. You might wish to serve the pudding with a bit of whipped cream or vanilla ice cream.

## Frosted Currants

These directions, taken from the *Good Housekeeping Cookbook* of 1955, are similar to the directions previously given to produce candied strigs of currants. "Beat one egg white till frothy; dip small bunches of currants into white. Let stand until nearly dry; then sprinkle with granulated sugar. Refrigerate until dry. Nice as garnish for baked ham, pie wedges, fruit salads, steamed puddings, etc."

## Red Currant Roll

First prepare your currant sauce with:

3/4 cup sugar
1/2 cup boiling water
2 cups red currants
2 tablespoons cornstarch
1/4 cup cold water

Make a paste of the cornstarch and the cold water, blending well before you put it in the pan with the rest of the ingredients. Cook for 10 minutes. Let the sauce cool and thicken.

Prepare a batch of Swedish pancakes as follows:

1 cup flour
1 tablespoon sugar
1/2 teaspoon salt
3 eggs
3 cups milk

Let the batter set and thicken for over an hour, then cook it in a well-buttered pan. Use 2 tablespoons batter at a time to form each pancake. Use high heat. As they finish up, spread each one with currant sauce and wind it up like a little jellyroll. Keep warm on a plate in the oven. Sprinkle powdered sugar on top and serve with a side of bacon.

## Red Currant Lemon Soda

Cook together equal parts of red currants and sugar. Crush well. Pass through a sieve to separate the skins, pulp and seeds; retain the juice. Mix to taste with your favorite lemon-lime soda of choice and serve over ice. Alternately, you may wish to use a bit of fresh-squeezed lemon juice and tonic water instead of soda pop.

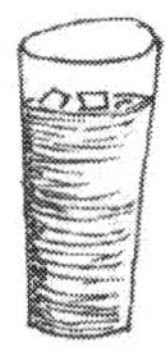

## Red Currant Eggedosis

This Norwegian recipe involves eating raw eggs mixed with currants and sugar.

3 cups currants—wash and sprinkle with 1/2 cup sugar. Let the berries set for 30 minutes until a syrup begins to form. You may want to crush some of the currants to help this along.
6 eggs, separated—beat the whites stiff with a pinch of salt.
1 1/2 teaspoon vanilla

Beat the vanilla together with the yolks, then gently unite the whites and yolks. To serve, put the currants into chilled dessert glasses, then top with the eggedosis sauce. Makes 6 servings.

## Currant Angelica Sauce

Angelica is an old-fashioned herb that looks rather like celery but has a sweet, perfumed flavor. Angelica root dug in spring of its second year and candied like this will have a lovely gumdrop-like texture but then you won't get so large a harvest of the stems, seeds and leaves if any, all of which have just as strong and distinctive a flavor as the root.

Candy your angelica stems in advance. First remove as many strings as you can from the stem as you would do with celery. Then cut the stems crosswise as thin as possible so as to minimize the remaining fibrous strings. Candy it by long, slow boiling in sugar syrup. Retain the angelica-sugar syrup for other uses. Extra angelica pieces may be put into jelly jars and processed for 15 minutes in boiling water to seal.

1/2 cup candied angelica pieces
4 cups red currants, crushed
4 cups sugar

Assemble your currant angelica sauce and let it boil slowly for 15 minutes, then put into clean jelly jars and process in a hot water bath for 15 minutes more to seal.

Use currant angelica sauce to give a unique flavor to fruit salads, cakes, puddings or pies. Try serving a spoonful of this sauce over vanilla ice cream.

## Apple-Currant Nut Syrup

3 tablespoons butter
3 tablespoons pecans, chopped
1 1/2 cup maple syrup
1/2 teaspoon cinnamon
Pinch of salt
1 cup tart apples, thinly sliced
1/4 to 1/2 cup currants

Melt the butter and toast the nuts. Add the fresh fruit and let it simmer for 10 minutes before tossing in the toasted nuts. Enjoy this syrup on pancakes and waffles. I found this combination in an old cookbook which did not specify if it was to be made with Corinthian raisin "currants" or red currants, but I know which version I prefer!

## Spiced Currants

6 cups red currants
1/4 cup water
1 teaspoon ground cloves
1 teaspoon cinnamon
1/4 cup vinegar
7 cups sugar
1 box fruit pectin

Crush and boil the currants for 10 to 15 minutes, then add the sugar, pectin and spices. Let this boil hard for 1 minute, then skim and discard the foam. Place the spiced currants in a dozen or so small jelly jars and process for 15 minutes in boiling water to seal.

## Cumberland Sauce

Simmer together:

1 quart currants or 1 cup current jelly
1 cup port wine
1 orange, both the juice and the zest
Extra sugar as needed

This is a traditional English sauce which was served with game and pork. It can be made with fresh whole currants, crushed currants or currant jelly. Why not all three? Prepare it so as to achieve the texture and sweetness which you prefer.

## Norwegian Currant Gravy

This is a gravy to be served with roast venison or reindeer, but it should work equally well with pork or wild boar. Sear the meat brown in a frying pan with a bit of butter, then roast it in the oven for over an hour in a cup or two of stock (beef, mushroom or vegetable). Baste the meat often. Use these pan juices to prepare the gravy.

When the meat is done, skim as much fat as you can out of the cooled pan juices. In a separate pan stirring continuously prepare a roux from:

1 tablespoon melted butter
1 tablespoon flour

Cook and stir this for 3 minutes, then add:

1 cup pan juices and drippings
2 tablespoons red currant jelly
*Gjetost*, a piece the size of your thumb cut into smaller pieces

*Gjetost* is a hard brown Norwegian cheese made from goat milk whey. Stir the cheese and jelly into the gravy until they dissolve, but don't let the sauce boil. To finish, stir in:

1/2 cup sour cream

Serve this sweet, rich gravy over meat and potatoes.

## Currant Mint Sauce

This sauce is good with lamb, poultry and ham.

1 cup red currant jelly
2 tablespoons candied orange peel, cut in small pieces
2 tablespoons fresh mint leaves

Chop the mint leaves very fine and add to the jelly and the candied orange peel. Stir well. Reserve some extra mint leaves to use as a garnish.

## Currant Breakfast Risotto

4 1/2 cups water
1 cup Arborio rice
1 cup half-and-half
1/2 cup sugar
2 teaspoons vanilla
2 cups red currants

Sauté the dry rice in butter or oil stirring constantly for 3 or 4 minutes, then start adding the water a half cup at a time, stirring continuously as it is absorbed. This should take about 15 minutes. Stir in the sugar and half-and-half, then the currants and vanilla last. When it starts to boil, lower the heat and let cook for another 15 minutes or until the rice is done.

## Cabbage Currant Salad

This recipe is adapted from Gerda Simonson's 1938 cookbook *Smörgåsbordet.*

1 large red cabbage
1/2 glass currant jelly
1/2 cup red wine
Juice and zest of 1 lemon
2 hard-boiled eggs, crumbled
1 teaspoon salt

Shred the cabbage very finely and refrigerate until crisp. Mix wine with currant jelly. Try half a cup or half of a "glass," presumably a large jar of jelly of a size sold in the 1930s, more to taste. Add lemon, wine, jelly salt and pepper, beaten smooth as the salad dressing. Garnish with chopped hard-boiled egg. For a richer salad, add 2 egg whites beaten stiff to your salad dressing.

## Fru Ternberger's Swedish Ham Pancake

Thanks to Fru Ternberger and to Sarvis and O'Neill's *Cooking Scandinavian* (1963) for this recipe. Supposedly "Americans always like it."

1/4 pound ham, cubed
1 tablespoon butter
1 cup flour
1 tablespoon sugar
3/4 teaspoon salt
1/2 teaspoon dry mustard powder
3 eggs
2 cups milk

Sauté the ham in butter in a skillet 9 inches in diameter. Then pour the pancake dough over the top and bake in at 375°F for 30 minutes. Cut into wedges and then drizzle the pancake with currant butter syrup. Make the currant butter syrup by melting 1 1/2 tablespoons butter with 1/3 cup of red currant jelly.

## Currant Wine

4 quarts currant juice
4 quarts water
7 pounds sugar

Let this mixture stand to ferment for two months. Skim it as necessary if any molds or scum should develop on the top. Pour into bottles. It may be "considerably improved" by adding a pint of brandy. The English called this a "summer table wine" and always made it from white currants. Currant wines were extremely popular in the past but are seldom encountered today.

## Currant Wine/Old Fashioned Recipes

Next are two very old-fashioned recipes for currant wine:

### *Vinbärsvin*

"*Four quarts of currant juice, four quarts of water, seven pounds of sugar: put in a jar and skim when necessary. Let it stand two months. Pour off and bottle. A pint of brandy added improves it very much.*" From *Svensk-Amerikansk Kokbok*, Carl Grimsköld, N.Y., 1888.

## Old Fashioned Currant Wine

"Bruise 8 gallons of currants with 1 quart of raspberries. Press out the juice and to the residum after pressure add 11 gallons of cold water. Add 2 pounds of beetroot, sliced as thin as possible to give color; and let them infuse with frequent mixture for 12 hours; then press out the liquor as before and add it to the juice. Next dissolve 20 pounds of raw sugar in the mixed liquor, add 3 oz. of red tartar in fine powder. In some hours the fermentation will commence. When the fermentation is completely over, add 1 gallon of brandy. Let the wine stand for a week, then rack off and let stand for 2 months. It may now be finally racked off; bunged up in the cask and set by in a cool cellar for as many years as may be required to ameliorate it." From *Savor and Flavor, Berries in Fact and Fancy* by Lee Maril, Coward-McCann Publishers, N.Y., 1944.

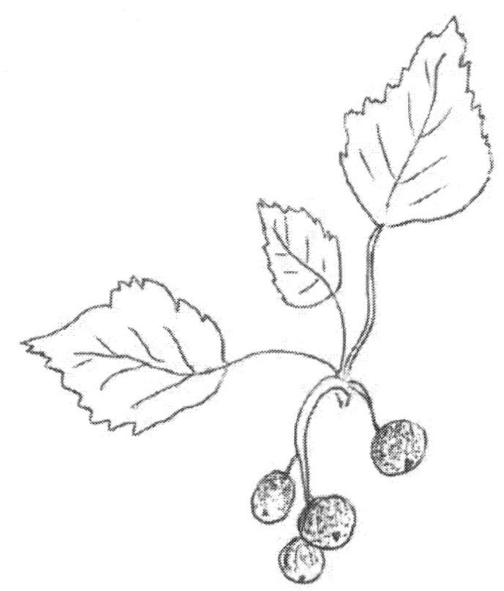

# Black Currant

*Ribes nigrum*

The black currant is another northern fruit that is relatively new to agriculture, the earliest known references being to 11th-century Russian monastery gardens. There are both European and American species of black currant, though the European species, *Ribes nigrum*, was far more common in American currant production than the native American species, *Ribes americanum*. The two other American species, *Ribes odoratum* and *Ribes aureum*, which are often called "clove currants" and "golden currants," are just as often called black currants as well. But like the red currants of the previous chapter, black currants prefer cool weather, tolerate some shade and benefit from cross pollination between bushes of the same species. Of course cavemen knew that currants were edible, but only since the Middle Ages do we know of currants grown in rows for production and improved cultivars developed. Black currant has a strong and resinous flavor. One of the earliest references to the berry outside of Russia is Gerard writing in his *Herbal* (1633) of their "stinking and somewhat loathing flavor." Others call this flavor "foxy" and although once a wildly popular berry in this country, and still in Scandinavia, Europe and the U.K., it is somewhat of an acquired taste if you are not used to it.

*Ribes nigrum* is native to northern Europe and Asia and can reach five or six feet in height. The berries occur singly or in short strigs of two or three fruits. Strig, not string, is the correct word for a bunch of currants. The botanical term is "raceme," denoting a stem with more than one flower or fruit in a row. The bush has been crossed and recrossed with closely-related species, with *Ribes bracteosum* to create longer strigs, with *Ribes dikuscha* to produce more vitamin C and with *Ribes ussuriense* so as better to resist the blister rust. Slightly underripe berries are better for jelly because they contain more pectin. Fully ripened black currants are best for making juice.

All currants either require a cross pollinator or benefit greatly from having one, those benefits being increased fruit production for you. One bush may give you a taste, but two bushes and you're making delicious pies and tarts and cider and jelly! Remember, in buying bushes for cross-pollination, that some currants are different species (and will not pollinate each other) and some are just different varieties of the same species (and will). Red, white, pink, yellow and champagne are all colors of the species *Ribes sativum*. Therefore they can all pollinate each other. Black currants, which are separate species, will not cross-pollinate with them. Neither will they reliably cross-pollinate with each other across species lines. To cross-pollinate black currants, you will want different varieties within the same species.

As for the pollinators themselves, currants bloom so early in the spring that most bugs aren't out yet, and every one that is seems to show up. I've seen strange-looking hoverflies and gnat-like insects but I'll bet that the bumblebees do a good part of the work too. Honeybees don't seem overly interested, but you may see one drop by from time to time.

Today there are many different cultivars of black currant. "Consort," "Crusader" and "Coronet" are rust-resistant varieties developed in Canada. The Russians have "Bzura," "Koksa" and "Primorskij Cempion." The Scandinavians have "Brodtorp," an early sweet table currant, "Titania" for high yields and "Narve Viking," the best for juice.

Black currant jelly and preserves have been popular in Europe much longer than in America. Black currant liqueur is known "*cassis*" in French, and this word is also sometimes used to refer to simply the fruit or its flavor. Recently, black currant juice has even made its appearance on supermarket shelves in America. It has somewhat of a niche market at present among the health-conscious crowd who drink it for its vitamins and for its plentiful antioxidants. Even in the Middle Ages the apothecary prescribed "squinancy berries" (to use an old medical word for the black currant) to soothe a throat ravaged by cold or flu. Today there are trademarked names like "Ribena," "CurrantC," and "Electric Currant." Black currant drinks are more common than drinks made from the reds nowadays, but back in the day there was a very popular home-made drink called a "shrub" made from fruit juice (red raspberry and/or red currant), shaved ice, sugar and vinegar.

Currants in general and black currants in particular are said to be "twice picked." You pick them twice, the first time to remove the strig from the bush, and the second time to remove the berries from the strig. A once-picked currant intact on its strig will keep for a good while in the refrigerator. A twice-picked currant will have its juice exposed to the air and will begin to ferment or spoil more quickly. Outside you can find, by September, currants that have even dried on the bush, but by then the birds will have made off with significantly more of your crop. If you really want dried *Ribes* currants, take them inside and use a dryer or oven on them after removing the strigs.

Black currants have stubby little strigs. Usually you cannot pick them on the strig because of uneven ripening. One berry may be perfectly ripe, but the other one or two will be overly tart or even green. "Twice-picking" for black currants means that you return to the same bush again and again during the season to pick the berries one by one. I'd even say "thrice-picked"! If you wait for all the berries on a strig to ripen, inevitably one will be overripe, fall off and be lost. If you pick each berry as it ripens you likewise end up often knocking off some of the green berries. You can't win! As tedious as black currants may be to pick, however, they are well worth the extra effort.

To make black currant juice, just cover the berries with water and boil them until they are soft. Crush them, pass them through a cloth or a fine sieve and discard the skins, seeds and pulp. You must sweeten the juice at least slightly to develop that distinctively good black currant flavor. Otherwise it is almost certain to be completely lost in the sourness.

❧

The American black currant is *Ribes odoratum* but it has many other names. It is often called the "clove currant" because its blossoms have a pleasant, spicy fragrance often compared to cloves or vanilla. Likewise, the specific name "*odoratum*" refers to the smell of the flowers, not the fruit. The fruit has none of this spicy flavor. It may also be called the "buffalo currant" because its range in nature from Minnesota to Texas is similar to that of the buffalo. Bison would be more likely to graze on the foliage than to sample the berries, I would think. The name "golden currant" likewise refers to the flowers. But whether "clove," "buffalo" or "golden," the ripe fruit of the American currant is always black in color.

European black currant bushes may grow five or six feet tall, and red currants not quite that tall, but American black currants are more petite. Mine are floppy little bushes whose branches are barely waist high. Often they are weighted down even lower with all their fruit. How can such a small bush produce such a quantity of fruit? The dangling yellow horn-like flowers in spring are two to three inches long, sometimes tinged with red in the center and very pleasantly scented. The large number of over-sized flowers on this petite bush make it attractive as an ornamental as well. You'll do a double-take, thinking it's a little forsythia bush. The other currants do not have such attractive flowers.

As for the berries of the American black currant, they are a bit larger than other currants and jet black when ripe. Some varieties have a slight "beard" which presents as a single hair and need not be removed. It is best to pick the berries in full sunlight. In shade or at twilight I find myself picking more underripe berries because I am unable to see the subtle color differences. An underripe berry will be tinged with red or purple tones, but not a ripe one. The birds never make this mistake, and you may find empty skins drying on the bush! Since they grow on the Great Plains where sunlight is the rule, I suspect that these currants are not as shade-tolerant as the other species. The flavor is sour, of course, but very fruity with less of that "foxiness" of the Europeans. *Ribes odoratum* is the last of the currants to ripen, beginning in late July and continuing on through August. Fruit production is low when compared with the copious harvests of the other currants, but the fruit quality is high.

Red currants and the European black currants grow in a more concealed manner on the larger and bushier plants with more cross branching. These berries can hang long on the bush and avoid most serious bird predation, but not so the American black currants. These berries are borne more openly at the top along the small branches. The leaves are too small to offer much concealment either. I have not yet seen the guilty parties in action, but some bird (maybe a robin or catbird) can peck the berry open, suck out the insides and leave the skin still hanging on the branch for me to pick!

  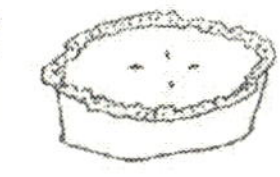

# Black Currant Recipes

## Black Currant Bomb

The "Black Currant Bomb" was a popular Victorian-era ice cream dessert named for the shape of the mold in which it was made. Back in the beginning of luxury, ice did not exist, except in the winter when it certainly doesn't count as a luxury! Then the emperor had his slaves run the ice from the mountaintop down to his villa on hot summer days to chill his fruit juice. Before long "iced creams" were being consumed by the rich and powerful. By Victorian times there was a vast ice industry. The laboring classes worked cutting block ice out of frozen lakes in the winters and hiding it in barns and caves until summer so that the aristocracy could enjoy "iced cream." There were no freezers, so this was a product made entirely at home.

Imagine the servants chopping the ice out of the lake and hoarding it in barns, packing it in hay or earth. Imagine them cultivating the bushes under glass to ripen early or prolonging the harvest with bushes under shade cloth so as to have black currants available always so that the Master could get his black currant bomb!

It was common for popular agricultural magazines into the 20th century to feature articles on how farmers could best harvest and store ice to last through August. There are still people alive today who remember their parents and grandparents working in the ice industry supplying towns and cities with ice for their "ice boxes." The special knowledge and implements for doing this are being lost to history now. In some regions farmers were relying on harvesting ice from lakes for their refrigeration needs into the late 1930s. Imagine harvesting and storing ice, and cultivating currant bushes under glass to ripen early, or prolonging the harvest with bushes under shade cloth, so that black currants were always available to satisfy the craving for a black currant bomb!

To make a "bomb," the black currants are cooked into juice, then mixed with cream and sugar and placed in the "bomb" mold and surrounded by ice. Salt is thrown on to melt the ice which freezes the bomb. The mold is then quickly dipped into hot water to loosen the ice cream. Invert the mold and let the bomb fall out on its serving dish. But you aren't done yet because the garnish is just as important. A proper black currant bomb is garnished with delicious pieces of candied angelica and candied strigs of red and white currants. And then it's "Bombs away!"

I do not personally own an ice cream maker, "bomb" or otherwise, so I leave it to others to redevelop ice cream flavors based on currants and the other fruits in this book. Back when it was popular, most people never got a taste of the black currant bomb. It may take a whole village to make a bomb, but it only takes one Master to eat it!

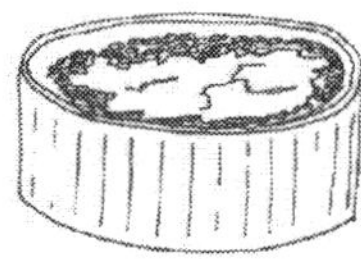

## Black Currant Cheese / *Svart Vinbärs Fromage*

3 eggs, separated
1/2 cup sugar
2 cups black currants
Gelatin, one package

Beat together the egg yolks and the sugar. Mix the berries together with the gelatin. Beat the egg whites stiff. Mix all together, pour into glasses and chill.

## Black Currant Pastry Tart

1 sheet puff pastry, thawed
1 1/2 cups black currants, fresh or frozen and thawed
3/4 cup sugar
1 teaspoon agar or 1 tablespoon other thickener (tapioca flour, corn starch, arrowroot flour)
1 teaspoon nutmeg
1/4 teaspoon powdered clove
3 ounces cream cheese, softened

Thaw one sheet of puff pastry and place it on a greased baking tray. Spread the sugared and spiced currants over the top of the pastry. The currant layer should be only one berry thick and rather sparse. Stripe with the softened whipped cream cheese. You may add a few drops of milk to make the cream cheese easier to work with. Bake at 375°F for 45 minutes to one hour.

The berries will juice themselves while cooking. The puff pastry may have a hard time cooking under the currant juice, hence the extra cooking time. Bake until golden brown. Be careful that the dough in the center doesn't stay too gooey like mine did, but it was so good I ate it anyways!

This recipe is just as good when prepared with red and white currants. Currant seeds are not overly noticeable like raspberry seeds are in jams or tarts if cooked. If raw, the currant seed seems a bit less hard than a raspberry seed. In dried form, however, the currant seed turns hard as a rock and is very noticeable. A dried currant may look exactly like a Corinthian raisin currant but the taste and this hard seed gives it away instantly.

## Pear-Black Currant Crumble

4 pears cut into cubes
3 tablespoons black currant jam and/or fresh black currants
2 tablespoons butter cut in small chunks

Topping:

3 tablespoons oats
3 tablespoons flour
3 tablespoons butter cut in small chunks
1/2 teaspoon cinnamon
3 tablespoons brown sugar
Pinch of nutmeg

Butter a 9 by 9-inch baking pan and preheat the oven to 350°F. Put the fruit-butter mixture into the pan, then top with the crumbles. Bake for 30 minutes at 350°F.

## Black Currant Cinnamon Rolls

2 ounces butter, melted
1 cup milk
1/4 teaspoon salt
1/3 cup sugar
1 teaspoon cardamom
30 grams baking yeast
3 cups white bread flour

Melt the butter and warm the milk gently but do not exceed 100°F. Add sugar, spices and yeast. When the yeast has dissolved add 1 cup of the flour and let the mixture rest for a few minutes, then add the rest of the flour. Let this rise for 1/2 hour covered with a damp towel in a warm place. Knead the dough for a few minutes then let it rise again for 1/2 hour or more until doubled in bulk.

Roll out the dough into a large rectangle about 1/4-inch thick. Spread this with:

3 ounces soft butter
1/3 cup white sugar
2 tablespoon cinnamon

Dot the dough with a handful of Corinthian raisins, a handful of fresh black currants and a handful of irregularly chopped hazelnuts. Be careful not to use too much fresh fruit. Distribute nuts and fruits evenly atop the dough.

Roll the dough up as if for a jelly roll, then cut it into pieces 3/4 of an inch thick. Place these on a greased baking sheet and let them rise again briefly.

Apply an egg wash so the rolls bake up nice and glossy. For an authentic Swedish touch, strew pearl sugar atop the rolls, but regular white sugar works too. Bake for 5 to 10 minutes in a pre-heated 450°F oven. Watch carefully so that your rolls do not burn.

## Black Currant Apple Cider

4 cups apple cider

3 tablespoons black currant syrup (Make your own if you cannot obtain Ribena syrup.)

1 teaspoon cloves

1 teaspoon allspice

2 cinnamon sticks

1 tablespoon brown sugar

1 tablespoon finely grated fresh orange peel

Let the juices steep with the spices for at least a day, then serve chilled.

## *Glögg*

This Swedish spiced fruit juice is served warm at the holiday season. There are thousands of recipes for *glögg*, most of them including wine and/or hard liquor. Here's a non-alcoholic version that includes black currant.

1 liter black currant juice (4.23 cups)

2–3 cinnamon sticks

5 cardamom seeds

2 teaspoons orange or lemon peel

4–5 whole cloves

Pinch of nutmeg

2–3 pieces peeled ginger root

1 teaspoon allspice

1 teaspoon anise seed

1 apple, chopped
1/2 cup raisins
1/2 cup sugar

Heat slowly in a kettle to give the spices time to steep, a half hour or longer. If the black currant is too strong for you, you can prepare this with half apple cider, half black currant juice.

## Black Currant Drink/*Louhisaari*

This is a fascinating recipe for a fermented ice-tea type of drink made from currant leaves and named for the manor in Finland where it was made. Let the mixture ferment for 7 days.

5 liters water (21.13 cups or 1.32 gallons)
1 liter young black currant leaves (4.23 cups)
400 grams sugar (1.66 cups)
1 lemon
1/4 teaspoon yeast

## Black Currant Compote

1 quart black currants
2 tablespoons cider vinegar
1 3/4 cups sugar
1/2 teaspoon allspice
1/2 teaspoon coriander
1/2 teaspoon ground clove

Boil the berries for 10 minutes or so. You may need to add a spoonful of water to prevent them from sticking and burning at first, or stir often until the berries are giving up their own juice for the cooking. Add the sugar, spices and vinegar. Let this cook slowly for 20 to 30 minutes, then pour it into sterile jars, process and seal, or you can let it sit in the refrigerator for a week or two so that the spices have time to mellow.

## Pickled Squash with Black Currant Leaves

2 pounds zucchini squash cut into bite-sized pieces (Young squash unpeeled or older half-peeled.)
2 dozen black currant leaves

Add these to create the marinade:

3 tablespoons salt
2 cups water

2 teaspoon sugar
2 teaspoon dill seed
2 tablespoons white wine vinegar or cider vinegar

Let these marinate for one or two weeks in the refrigerator, covered. This creates a crisp and unprocessed summer pickle. The black currant leaves create an interesting flavor but you will probably not want to eat them. Adapted from Caroline Hofberg's *Traditional Swedish Cooking.*

## Ukrainian Red Cabbage/*Kapusta*

Sauté for 10 minutes:

1/4 cup butter
2 apples, chopped (Granny Smith is best.)
1 onion, chopped

Next, add and cook for 10 minutes until wilted:

2 pounds shredded red cabbage

Now add and cook gently for 5 or 10 minutes more:

1/4 cup sugar
2 tablespoons cider vinegar
1 teaspoon salt
1/4 teaspoon allspice
1/8 teaspoon powdered clove
2 tablespoons black currant jam
1/3 cup chicken stock

# Quince

*Cydonia oblonga*

When I was a toddler in the 1950s many houses still had quince trees in their yards whether the resident family made use of the fruit or not. The quince is not a tree you can really climb like an apple tree; it's more of a large shaggy bush. Our house had one adjacent to the eastern fence with an orange trumpet vine creeper growing beneath. The trumpet vine grew rampantly and afforded me a "fort," a hidden place from which to spy on others and entertain my friends at tea parties with imaginary tea. I was the eldest of four, so this was before the era of sandbox and swing set for my siblings.

Grandpa picked up the aromatic, fuzzy fruit which fell to ground and made Grandma cook them into jelly for him. It was his influence, no doubt, that influenced us to collect the fruit. I remember gathering the fruits and watching my mother make jelly. She did not use the expensive jelly jars for canning. She "put it up" in jelly glasses and sealed them with melted paraffin. It was magical how the fruit turned into jelly and how the chipped paraffin wax came together again as it melted clear, then cooled back to a disk of opaque white. We weren't allowed to touch it as it cooled but of course we wanted to. She picked out one glass, the one that we would eat first anyway, and let us play with the hardening wax. Of course we broke the seal!

The black ants would come and try to get their fruit back again, Mother would tell us. She'd show us jellies and jams from the past year. You could easily see that the ants had been gnawing away at the wax, trying to get in. To stop them, she'd wrap the jelly jars in waxed paper and tie them up with twine. That kept the ants out!

But I was, at "Fort Quince" at the age of four, very cognizant of the fact that this was to be my last year of freedom. Next fall, I'd be in school instead of hiding here in the bushes listening to the thud of ripe quinces hitting the ground. There would be no more leisurely weekday imaginary tea parties where saucers and dolly dishes I kept in the bushes were used to serve the imaginary tea, and the real graham crackers and raisins, to my guests—the imaginary friends and the black ants that lived there. I never felt deprived or bored not having a swing set, as some suggested. When neighbor kids came to play, we'd hide inside the trumpet vine under the quince tree. This was certainly something that the other kids did not have in their toy-filled yards! I knew that the quince was pretty inedible unless cooked. I watched and laughed as boys tried to bite off a piece of this delicious-smelling fruit but managed only to break off a baby tooth or spit out a bit of fuzz. The smell of quince still takes me back to my fort under the trumpet vines when I was four.

Thirty-five years later I purchased the farmland in Forsyth, and of course I had to have some quince trees on my farm. Our quince tree in the yard had died long ago. Fewer and fewer houses now had the obligatory quince tree, berry bush and rhubarb patch which I remembered from my youth. I shopped around at various mail-order nurseries and ended up purchasing six different cultivars of quince. "Cultivar" simply means "cultivated variety" and indicates that someone selected a particular individual quince for its special agricultural traits long ago and, ever since, the same tree has been reproduced by the grafting of branches onto rootstock rather than by seed. Individual trees, in other words, get "cloned" to preserve their special traits. I am just getting to know my six cultivars, to understand the subtle differences of size, shape, productivity, color and taste which differentiate them.

"Meachem's Giant" and "Smyrna," for example, are consistently larger than other quinces, and both of these varieties set large crops. "Smyrna," named for a Greek city that is now Izmir, Turkey, is a pear-shaped quince. There are also apple-shaped quinces and a whole range of "in between" shapes. Shape seems to comprise one of the big divides in quince genetics although I'm not at all sure how it relates to the olfactory or edible side of the fruit. Another variety I have, "Portugal," is usually "shy" on production, but some people love it because it turns a brighter red color when cooked, and more quickly and readily than other quinces do.

Some quinces have been selected for their fancied resemblance in taste to other fruits. The quince cultivars "Orange" and "Pineapple," for example, were named for this reason though, personally, I can't taste much of a resemblance. A very important characteristic for would-be quince farmers is ripening time. "Ananasnovna," a square-shaped quince, is my first to ripen in mid-October. My last to ripen, a month later, is "Orange." "Orange" can develop the rich aroma of ripe quince even when the skin is still green in places while "Ananasnovna" can be ripe enough to fall off the tree before it has much of a scent at all. Quinces may also be selected for resistance to disease and insects, ability to resist drought or cold, fuzziness or lack thereof. They can be selected for horticultural reasons, like spectacular flowers or unique leaf colors. Most quinces grown in the United States come from Armenian-American farmers in California. Turkey, Armenia, Iran and Greece are the other major producers of quince, along with Australia and New Zealand.

There are of course a number of imposters, plants which used to be considered quinces but are now classified differently. Flowering quince (*Chaenomeles speciosa*) is a small Asian tree grown more for its flowers than for its fruit. The fruit is slightly smaller than that of *Cydonia oblonga* but has an even more intense "quince-like" aroma which is why they were originally mistaken to be quinces. They are only marginally edible raw, but they are cooked and made into perfumey preserves in China. Another species is so-called Chinese quince, *Pseudocydonia sinensis*, the fruit of which is more edible and commonly grown in the South of the United States. I have yet to try it myself, but my impression from reading is that the fruit is better than the flowering quince, and closer to the fruiting quince in flavor.

There were undoubtedly even more varieties of "real" quince grown in the past than today, but there are still a surprising number of genuine quince varieties out there. Some varieties of quince are best for wine and cider making. Others have medicinal or ritual uses. For those contemplating raising quinces themselves, it's probably best to jump right in, pick a range of cultivars, and get to know them as they grow.

❧

I gave some quinces to my Bosnian city neighbor Hasan once and learned in return that a commonly accepted truth about them is anything but true. Quinces can in fact be eaten fresh. "You just have to cut them into small enough pieces to chew," Hasan assured me. But of course! How could I not have remembered? "The Owl and the Pussycat" knew this too:

*The Owl and the Pussy-cat went to sea*
*In a beautiful pea-green boat:*
*They took some honey and plenty of money*
*Wrapped up in a five-pound note.*
*The Owl looked up to the stars above*
*And sang to a small guitar,*
*"O lovely Pussy, O Pussy, my love,*
*What a beautiful Pussy you are,*
*You are, you are!*
*What a beautiful Pussy you are!"*

*Pussy said to the Owl: "You elegant fowl,*
*How charmingly sweet you sing!*
*Oh let us be married; too long we have tarried -*
*But what shall we do for a ring?"*
*They sailed away for a year and a day*
*To the land where the bong-tree grows;*
*And there in a wood a Piggy-wig stood*
*With a ring at the end of his nose,*
*His nose, his nose,*
*With a ring at the end of his nose.*

*"Dear Pig, are you willing to sell for one shilling*
*Your ring?" Said the Piggy, "I will."*
*So they took it away and were married next day*
*By the turkey who lives on the hill.*
*They dined on mince and slices of quince,*
*Which they ate with a runcible spoon;*
*And hand in hand on the edge of the sand*
*They danced in the light of the moon.*

*—Edward Lear (1812–1888) (poem and illustration)*

This just goes to show that you can find culinary cues in old poems. Another nod here is to the quince's long role as a symbol of love and marriage. Quinces are still used in Greek weddings for good luck and nibbled on to make the bride's breath sweet. Opening the door to using raw quince brings you a whole new world of recipes. One of my favorites is minced raw quince served with raspberry yogurt, another dish to serve at the Owl and the Pussycat's wedding—though perhaps a difficult one to rhyme. Quince always benefits from a bit of sweetening, remember, but using it raw allows you to enjoy its wonderful perfume which largely disappears upon cooking.

❧

*Cydonia oblonga*, the species name for quince, derives from Kydonia, a town in Crete where the fruit was long grown and from which the first quince trees were exported to Rome. "*Melimelum*," from the Greek, is another Latin word for "quince." *Melimelum* in Greek means "quince" as in "honey apple." Quinces are very astringent by themselves, so they were usually served with honey. This is the word that ultimately transformed into our word "marmalade" from the Portuguese *mermalo* which means simply "quince." *Cotogna* is the word for quince in Italian (*gn* pronounced as in *lasagna*). In the south of France quinces are called *cotignac*, as in the marmalade.

The standard French word is *coing*, most likely the origin of our English word "quince." Some have suggested that *coing* is related to *coin*, the French word for "corner," since quince trees were often planted in fence corners. Others suggest *quincunx*, a Latin word for a pattern of planting in fives, four trees at the corner of a square and one at the center, rather like the fives on dice. Quince trees and other fruit trees were often planted in a quincunx pattern. Whatever the origin of our word for them, they were first brought to America by early English settlers and their cultivation was said to be thriving in Virginia by the early 1700s.

In antiquity, the fruit was associated with Venus/Aphrodite, hence its use in marriage customs to the present day. Quinces are said most likely to be the "golden apples" of Greek mythology, the prize for the beauty contest that ended up causing the Trojan War. They are identified as Hercules' golden apples and as a fruit mentioned in the Bible's racy "Song of Solomon."

It is interesting to note that in dealing with fruit names throughout history, it's not necessarily true that an "apple is an apple is an apple." At least, the name we use for "apple" today is derived from a word which once referred to fruit of any kind. Pomegranate, for example, means "apple from Grenada" in French because of its red color (*pomme de grenade*, from which we also derive the name for "hand grenade"). Mayapple, a forest wildflower, is an apple because the flower which blooms in May becomes a fruit later in the summer. In France, potatoes are "apples of the earth," *pommes de terre. Mala cydonia*, the "apple from Kydonia" in Crete, is a quince. The Romans imported particularly prized quinces from that area of Crete. So it's no stretch of the imagination to realize that references to "golden apples" in mythology could be references to quince, a far more ubiquitous and highly-prized fruit of the time and region than the ones we today call "apples."

Pomona is the Roman goddess of fruit, the "Apple Mother," and the quince is one of her special fruits. There are no Greek goddesses to equate with Pomona; she is unique to the Roman pantheon and rules over orchards and gardens. Her symbols are the pruning knife and the cornucopia basket.

Pomona might be the lesbian separatist goddess of choice if it weren't for the fact that she's married. Vertumnus, her husband, is the god of the change of the seasons. Pomona's orchard, however, was known to be an all female environment, no men allowed. She was a hard worker, ever caring for her fruit trees and gardens but considered to have a bit of an unforgiving nature. To this day, anyone who has neglected his or her orchard knows how easy it is to lose Pomona's favor.

When she was still single, Pomona was a tomboy and had all sorts of adventures. One day she went down to earth dressed as a boy, as she so often liked to do, and happened to run into Jupiter who was out cruising for boys—as he often liked to do. He thought she was a him and wanted her, but Pomona wanted nothing to do with the dirty old god, and vanished. Jupiter searched heaven and earth looking for the cute young thing but with no luck.

Various demigods also courted Pomona, but she refused both Woodpecker (Picus) and Forest (Silvanus). Vertumnus won her by dressing in drag as an old woman and singing his own praises, which will do it every time. He laid a guilt trip on her by citing the story of the mortal Iphis who loved the maiden Anaxerete. Anaxarete rejected Iphis, so he killed himself at her door. This made Venus so upset with Anaxarete for being that much of a cold bitch that she turned her into stone. The moral of the story was clear, and Pomona admitted that maybe she ought to marry Vertumnus after all. Then–poof!–Vertumnus transformed himself back into himself, and they got hitched. I still get the feeling that this was mainly a marriage of convenience, however, because Vertumnus only comes round to see her a few times a year. Pomona spends most of her days with her nymphs and numina tending the orchards of the world.

A priest or priestess of the cult of Pomona was called a *Flamen Pomonalis*. The *Pomonal* was the sacred grove at the Roman port city of Ostia which was specifically dedicated to her. November 1 was the annual feast of Pomona. August 13 was the festival of Vertumnus and Pomona.

In later years Pomona became one of the three goddess symbols used by the Grange, "The National Grange of the Order of Patrons of Husbandry," to give it its full title. This progressive American movement of farmers dating from the mid-1800s was also referred to as the "Farmers' Masonry." The Grange, as it is most commonly known, had its first lodge twenty miles down the road from my Forsyth farm, in Fredonia, New York. The goddess

Flora on its emblem (and in the nomenclature of its ranks) represents the cultivation of flowers; Ceres, the raising of cereal grains and general agriculture; with Pomona presiding over orchards and fruit, of course. Pomona was undoubtedly pleased that from its first days the Grange admitted women as equal members. Although not as important a center of social life today as it used to be, the Grange continues to play an important role in the conduct of the nation's agriculture.

Among the community of agricultural goddesses, Idunna, the Norse goddess of fruit, is often identified with Pomona. This is not accurate. Idunna has a distinct role and personality all her own. She guards the "apples," sometimes said to be "golden," which keep the Gods of Asgard eternally young. Idunna is more social, less chaste, and somewhat more of a "party girl" in comparison with Pomona. They are not the same goddess, but perhaps they are cousin goddesses. Idunna tends apples with magical health properties for the gods, while Pomona does so for everyone. Could the ancient Romans' "golden apples" have caught on with the heathen gods of the north? Quinces only grow as far north as southern Scandinavia, so I find it doubtful that the Norse gods actually ever got their hands on them—though it's easy for gods to get around, so you never know.

Quince culture began in ancient Armenia, Persia and Mesopotamia, then spread to Greece by 500 B.C.E. It was Pomona and the Romans who introduced the quince to the rest of Europe. According to Columella, the Roman writer of the first century C.E., "Quinces not only yield pleasure but health." He described the juice as "cooling and strengthening," "astringent and stomachic." Quince was believed to heal the intestinal tract of illness, to aid digestion and to restore health and beauty. Quince syrups were used as a remedy for nausea and for cough and to promote healing. Ointments made from the skins and seeds, both particularly high in pectin, helped to heal the skin and gums. Quince water was given to invalids to help them regain their strength. Dried quince was soaked in water to reconstitute it. The fruit then went on to feed the family, but the quince water was reserved as a special treat for a sick child or a weak grandparent.

This association of the quince with health continued throughout the ages and to the present day. *The London Pharmacopoeia*, a 17th-century compendium of traditional prescriptions, contains the *Syrupus Cydonarean* or "syrup of quinces." According to the treatise, to make the syrup you must set 6 pints of quince juice and one drachma cinnamon and 1/2 drachma of ginger and 1/2 drachma of cloves over warm ashes for 6 hours. Then add 1 pint of red port and 9 pounds of sugar. This syrup is taken by the spoonful and is said to be "cooling and strengthening" (the same as Columella said) as well as good against nausea. A mucilage of quince seeds may be prepared by boiling crushed quince seeds in a small amount of water. This is used for "apthous affections and excoriations of the mouth and fauces." Quince flavored wines were also seen as remedies for asthma. In Bosnia they still take tea of quince leaves and tea of dried quince as a remedy for cough, according to my neighbor Hasan.

The original marmalades always featured quince cooked with citrus fruits and perhaps other spices. Sour Seville oranges, both the peel and the juice, were used. Citrus was all the rage back in the Middle Ages. Citrus fruits had been introduced to Europe by Muslim rule in Spain and Portugal. The Crusades popularized oranges and lemons all across Europe. Since then the citrus have taken over and nudged out the quince. It's easy to find marmalade with orange, lemon, even tangerine or grapefruit nowadays. It is hard to find one with quince. The recipe section gives instructions for making a marmalade of quince and orange.

When spices enter the picture, there is a wide range of chutneys, relishes and fruit mustards based upon the quince. Mustards were originally spiced fruit preparations. The word "mustard" derives from "must," an old-fashioned word to denote grapes after the juice has been pressed from them. Fruit mustards are totally unlike the fruitless yellow preparations of today made from turmeric and ground mustard seeds. The same as the quince has disappeared from marmalade, the "must" has dropped out of mustard. Mustard seed gets its name from its use in fruit mustards, not vice versa. There is a wonderful mustard of passerina grapes and quince given in the recipe section.

Quinces were blended with grapes and apples to create special wines and ciders. Quince wine is mostly grapes but the quince offers a unique flavor. Throwing a few quince into the mash is a secret still used today by some Italian home winemakers. Columella distinguished three varieties of quince in cultivation at that time which he called the "must apple," the "sparrow apple" and the "golden apple."

Quince was used in perfumery and cosmetics and, of course, had the association with love and romance. It was used as an ingredient in wedding cake and hidden in honeymooners' chariots. Quinces not only blessed weddings, but they also deodorized closets and kept linens smelling fresh and sweet, as well as newlyweds' breath.

Too many people today see the quince as a queer and quaint thing, a useless fruit that you need to cook, an old-fashioned sort of apple that is not worth the extra trouble. They are missing so much! In the past the quince was considered a bringer of health and contentment and good luck, an air freshener and a spiritual purifier as well, and a good food and good medicine. So much of that knowledge was subsequently lost and the reputation of the quince has fallen upon hard times.

One person helping to change all that is the self-proclaimed "Queen of Quince," Armenian-American cookbook writer Barbara Ghazarian. Her book, *Simply Quince*, was published in 2009 by Mayreni Publishing and is the first book about quince written in English in over a hundred years. As a fellow missionary, I can say that she shows the true missionary zeal in promoting this wonderful fruit!

❧

Quinces need warmth and long growing seasons to ripen properly. Perhaps we are pushing things here in New York in growing quinces. Quinces grown in sunnier climates, like Turkey, are sweeter and softer. They are easier to eat fresh and can even be made into juice. I've had quince juice from Turkey that, without the addition of sugar, is almost cloyingly sweet, though it is possible that the juice was boiled to magnify this reputed sweetness which southern-grown fruit does have to a certain extent.

Quince, one of the hardest fruits most of us have encountered, is also one of the most sensitive and easily bruised. Bruises don't show up as a soft spot, as on an apple. Instead, you may notice thin brown lines where quinces were touched by mere leaves and brown patches where they bumped into other fruits on the tree. If eaten right away, there is no problem other than unsightly brown blotches on the skin. If you try to keep them for later, however, these blotches will become the first areas of the fruit to develop rot. This is why it is particularly important that quince be stored in shallow trays or boxes not touching each other and that no weight should press on them from above. Quinces at the bottom of a bushel are always the first to rot. Like other fruit, keep in a cool, dark area for best storage. If kept like this in a fruit cellar, the old agricultural manuals say that quinces should keep until April, but I have never been so lucky. My quinces don't last into the New Year. Those I have not used by then, I lose to rot. Unlike apple varieties known to have been selected for which were the best "keepers," I have never seen any observations on this matter made with regard to quinces.

Quince seeds will germinate easily if you don't let them dry out and the trees produced from them will be quite similar to the parent. My quince compost has yielded hundreds of baby trees, for example, though only two have I planted out. It will be interesting to see if I can deduce the parent tree when the seedlings begin to bear. You can also propagate quince by grafting, tip layering or cuttings. "Grafted on white thorn it escapes the borer," writes William Witler Meech in his 1888 *Quince Culture*, a publication of the American Garden Association. The borer referred to is an insect pest that kills the fruit tree by attacking the wood. If a graft didn't protect your tree, you could try a tree wrap or an alkaline wash on the bark to prevent the laying of the borer's eggs. In every age, it's always been imperative to examine your orchard regularly to avoid losing Pomona's favor! If you notice the borers' tell-tale holes and sawdust, you can always skewer the young larvae on a wire poked into the hole to save your tree.

Quince can tolerate growing in a wet soil, but the resultant fruit may be woodier and more astringent than fruit grown in drier areas. Thinning the fruits when they are as thick as your thumb will greatly improve the quality of the fifty percent you leave hanging. There will be less bruising of fruit and less strain on the branches, plus your harvest will be more attractive.

New York Quince Plantation, Cyclopedia of American Horticulture (1910)

The best fertilizers for quince are wood ashes or lime, potash or bone meal. Although the plant may respond well to nitrogen in fertilizers, the diseases will respond even better, so it may be best not to fertilize them. As one would expect with such an ancient fruit, the quince has developed a host of attendant insect problems, bacterial and fungal diseases and cultural peculiarities. You may rue the day that you fertilized your quinces. My fruit had brownish patches on the white flesh. While it didn't seem to affect the taste, I was told it would affect the salability of my fruit. I heard suggestions that the marbling might be a result of a calcium deficiency. Plants take up nutrients more efficiently if they have adequate calcium. When I saw an advertisement promoting a spray that was approved for organic production, a "foliar feed" that would be absorbed through the leaves and solve the presumed calcium deficiency, I assumed this was the solution. My trees loved it and broke out in vigorous new growth—and then fireblight struck.

Fireblight is a bacterial disease present in apples, pears, medlars, wild hawthorns and many other species—but especially those ancient quinces. It overwinters on dried leaves or in previously infected trees. Insects or wind inadvertently infect the trees at the areas of new growth. The blight kills the leaves one by one, spreading backwards down the plant, making the new leaves turn brown and dry, as if they had been burnt by fire. An apple or a hawthorn might easily keep the disease in check, but for particularly susceptible species like the quince (and many varieties of pear), it can be a death sentence. My lushly growing quince trees were transformed almost overnight into blackish-brown wilting diseased branches!

Once your quinces have fireblight there's no cure, only different ways of helping your plants live with the disease. There are chemical and antibiotic sprays that help to keep it at bay or the old-fashioned method, which requires cutting off each infected branch and burning it. This is the route I took. I gathered every leaf and fruit on the ground as well. To avoid spreading the disease from tree to tree, I disinfected my tools by using bleach diluted to ten percent. So far I've lost one tree and have had a continuing need for bonfires, but less and less as the years go by. The quince orchard is still standing. I've learned to deal with brown discolorations in some fruit rather than fertilize.

Although fireblight is the most spectacular, there are also leaf blight, quince orange rust, fruit spot, black rot and many ailments that afflict quince trees. The generic prescription to keep your orchard free of these diseases is to keep it as clear as can be. Pomona would approve! Rake and burn any leaves or twigs, trim and burn any dead wood on the trees. Don't prune the quince, as this encourages too much tender regrowth which in turn lets the diseases back in. Mow the weeds and cut the brush to ensure that there is adequate air circulation around the trees.

The insect challenges are greater yet! Borers are joined by quince scale, woolly aphids, cutworms, handmaiden moths, fall webworm, bagworm, polyphemus moth caterpillars, broadwing katydids, tarnished plantbugs, pear blisterbeetles and quince curculio beetle. Pomona's protection is very important.

Fortunately, not all of these insect pests are present in my area. Unfortunately, the worst one is, the quince curculio beetle. One reason you will never find a worm in your quince is because the larvae of the curculio beetle eat tunnels through the fruit while it is still green. By the time the quince has ripened, the bugs have eaten their fill and left to burrow into the ground to sleep until next spring. Then sometime the next May or June they emerge from the ground as adults and fly around clumsily laying their eggs on your beautiful young green quince. So although you won't find a worm, you will find tunnels through the fruit lined with insect fecal matter, or "frass."

Catching the curculio in a New York Quince Orchard, Cyclopedia of American Horticulture (1910)

In the past people would hold work bees in the quince orchards. In late May or early June, when the curculios were flying, families would converge on the orchard in the morning, spread sheets or tarps beneath the trees and hold a picnic. One person would whack at the quince limbs with a club or bat hard enough for the shock to dislodge the egg-laying curculios. As the beetles fell on the sheets they became plainly visible and were easily squashed before they could escape and resume their activities. These squashing bees would be repeated several times over a week or so until the curculios were finished with their egg laying.

Mr. Ferris supplies my food co-op with certified organic quince and has become a friend over the years. His advice on fireblight saved my orchard, so I asked him if he had any further advice on how to deal with the curculio beetles. He recounted that he cultivates the ground around the trees so as to disrupt the beetles' sleep in the ground. Then he sprays with "dormant oil" in the spring so as to coat the eggs completely and suffocate the larvae before they can hatch out and eat their ways into the fruit. Dormant oil comes in a variety of formulations and gets its name from the fact it is for use on plants when they are still in their dormant stage coming out of winter.

Do not let this horrific discussion of insects and diseases discourage you in any way from planting a quince tree. It will soon bear fruit, then more fruit than you can use. So what if half of each fruit is insect damaged? Share with the bugs. Quince must be cut into small pieces to prepare most recipes anyways, so it is easy to see which areas need to be discarded. I have been able to make nearly all of the recipes in this chapter using my "unsaleable" fruit. That is, fruit that is healthy and delicious but which is not "cover girl" fruit because insects got to it before I did. They came, they ate, and they went. What they left is still good and good for you.

Now that I have retired from my teaching career, perhaps I will have more time to devote to improving my quince orchard according to Mr. Ferris's techniques. I have never once gotten a buggy quince from Mr. Ferris, so I have always relied on his fruit to make luxury items like stuffed or baked quince for my friends and family every year. But I have not seen him this year. To my sadness, the food co-op has stopped selling his quince because of insufficient demand. The co-op's primary mission is to make a profit selling organic produce so as to stay in business. Its secondary mission, to repopularize the quince and all other foods antique and artisanal, has necessarily been put on the back burner. But if you want quince in my neck of the woods, you can still find them for two dollars each at high-end supermarkets, or sometimes cheaper at farmers' markets by the basket.

Western European traditions tend to associate the quince with sweet dishes. Quince can also feature in the main meal or be inserted into a salad. In its original homeland, the quince is just as well known for its use in main dishes such as savory soups and stews. I have included a few of these sorts of recipes from Armenia and Azerbaijan to show the quince's full culinary range. Main course uses can also include stuffings, baked or fried fish and meat dishes, and savory sauces to accompany them. Pickled and poached quinces can be side dishes and relishes or just as easily enter the realm of salads. Fresh quince chopped into perfect small cubes can form the basis of deliciously crunchy chopped salad. There are an array of desserts based on quince, of course. There are quince pudding-like desserts, sweet quince sauces for ice cream, and quince cakes and pies, and quince tarts and cookies and, as always, quince jelly.

"Consigned to jelly" has sometimes seemed to me to have been a fate worse than death for the quince. Although I have good childhood memories of quince jelly, it seems like ninety percent of the fruit has been wasted, replaced by sugar. There are dozens of ways to use the whole quince and take better advantage of its healing virtues, the fiber content, the texture and the flavor. But still, jelly can be magical. All the good essences of the fruit are boiled down into a few precious cups leading to that magic moment when your liquid finally jells. Quince possesses so much pectin that it is easy to get it to jell. This comes from someone who has failed miserably at making most other kinds of jellies! The other magic is that this beautiful yellow fruit with its whitish flesh somehow cooks up pink or deep ruby red and as clear as a jewel if properly made.

There are also Middle Eastern recipes for quince candy, and recipes for Armenian fruit leathers which are every bit as good as candy. Dried quince is a commodity seldom encountered today but easy to produce in the oven. Quinces are dried in pieces and both the fruit and the water in which the pieces have been reconstituted have their uses. More complex dry quince products are produced from quince that has already been cooked and sweetened. These may be called paste, leather or cheese. *Membrillo*, the famous Spanish quince paste, is perhaps the best known of these. A soft *membrillo* may be spread on bread or crackers like butter, whereas a firmer *membrillo* may be cut into squares and served along with pieces of dairy cheese.

My nonagenarian city neighbor Dottie even remembers a cosmetic use for quince pectin water. Gather up the seeds and put them to boil with a few tablespoons of water. (It may help to smash the seeds.) Cook until the water becomes cloudy or milky in appearance. Let it cool a bit and then use it just like setting gel to curl and set your hair with bobby pins or curlers! "That's how we did it back in the Great Depression," says Dottie, "when nobody had any money to spare for cosmetics or shampoos. Nothing was wasted."

# Quince Recipes

## Favorite Quince Recipes

An informal survey was taken to see which quince recipes were most fondly remembered from childhood. Presumably "jelly" was not permitted as an answer. Here are the top four winners:

***Quince ginger*** is a chunky jam. In the past it was more quince and less ginger, but I like to make it prickly hot with lots of crystalized ginger.

***Quince honey*** is just what it says. Barbara Ghazarian found a Greek recipe from the 1100s for quince honey. You cook quinces down to a honey-like consistency, adding honey and a bit of ginger or pepper. I found a "quince honey" recipe in an old cookbook that was nothing more than the reduced sugar-sweetened water that the quinces had cooked in! Remember that the adulteration of honey and the marketing of fake honeys was what originally prompted the government to organize the U.S.D.A.

***Baked quince with whipped cream*** is also just what it says. This would require more than an hour in the oven and perfect quince such as my own farm does not provide. It's time to get some quince from Mr. Ferris.

***Quince custard pie*** can be made with a precooked, mashed quince paste or with pieces of poached quince the more easily to incorporate the quince flavor into the egg custard and vice versa. In order to cook fresh while inside the pie, fresh quince must be minced into the tiniest of pieces. If you make quipple pie (quince-apple) be sure to cut the quince down to one third the size of the apple pieces. Quince custard pies rely on pre-cooked quince instead.

## Poached Quinces in Cream

You may prepare this with the peel but do be sure to rub off the cottony fuzz on the fruit! Peeled poached quinces taste about the same as the unpeeled but may be a bit easier to eat with a spoon. Do peel the fruit if you intend to use the poached quinces in other recipes.

Cut the quince into wedges 3/4 inch to 1 inch thick so that they'll stand up after long, slow cooking.

5 cups quince wedges
3 cups water
1/2 cup sugar

Let boil then lower the heat and simmer for 75 minutes or so. The quince will become slightly pink. If desired, you may cook them with a cinnamon stick or a few whole cloves or cardamom pods. (Discard spices.) The poached quinces will keep in their syrup for several weeks in the refrigerator or they may be processed 15 minutes in jars to can for later use.

In a fancy individual serving bowl:

3 wedges of poached quince
1 drizzle of heavy cream
1 handful of roasted butternuts

Poached quince slices are a delicacy. They can also be used to make salads, tartes, sandwiches and cakes. The pink poaching liquid is a treat in itself and should not be discarded when you finish that jar of quince. Boil and thicken it further by reduction or by the addition of a bit of arrowroot flour or cornstarch or other thickener to the consistency you prefer. You will have an exquisite and unique syrup for pancakes or ice cream. This syrup is just as interesting as the poached quinces themselves. Add more sugar if you want to but don't let the subtle quince flavor be overwhelmed by the addition of strong flavors like maple syrup.

## Quince Compote

3 quinces, cored and chopped
1 1/2 cup water
1 cup sugar
2 teaspoons lemon juice
2 whole cloves
1 stick cinnamon

Simmer gently for one hour until it forms a sauce. Discard the spices. This compote is to be served with meats or it can be used as a dessert when served mixed with whipped cream, ice cream, or yogurt.

## Simple Quince Paste

Cut 6 or 8 quinces into wedges. Let cook slowly in its own juices with a splash of water for an hour. Stir and mash as you add 1 cup of sugar and more to taste. This should be a coarse paste with some chunks of quince still visible. Use this paste in preparation of other desserts and freeze the left-overs.

## Poached Quince Cream Tarte

Prepare a crust and roll it out to set in a pie plate:

3/4 cup flour
4 tablespoons shortening
2 teaspoons sugar

Pinch of salt
Water to bind

For the filling arrange:

2 cups poached quince pieces (no syrup) and dust it with
1/2 cup sugar
1/4 teaspoon cardamom

For the custard you will need:

1 egg
1/3 cup milk
1 tablespoon smashed quince bits with syrup
3 tablespoons sour cream
1/4 teaspoon cardamom
1/8 teaspoon powdered clove

Pour the custard over the quince filling and garnish with a handful of chopped walnuts. Bake in a pre-heated 375°F oven for 55 minutes to one hour until the crust is done and the custard has set.

## Quince Cheesecake

For the crust:

5 tablespoons butter
4 tablespoons sugar
1 cup flour (half spelt flour, half whole wheat)
1/4 teaspoon salt
1/4 cup finely chopped pecans

Set oven to 350°F. Press crust out into a pie pan, use a fork to prick with small holes, cover with foil and beans or some other sort of weights. Let bake for 10 minutes while you are preparing the filling:

12 ounces cottage cheese
16 ounces cream cheese (2 small packages)
3 eggs
1 teaspoon vanilla
1 cup sour cream
1 cup yogurt
1 cup poached quince slices, no syrup

Place the quince slices on the dough, then pour the batter over top. Bake at 325°F for 50 minutes.

## Quince Cake

Dry ingredients:

2 cups pastry flour
2 teaspoons baking powder
1/2 teaspoon salt
3/4 cup sugar
1/2 teaspoon cardamom
1/4 teaspoon cinnamon
1/8 teaspoon powdered clove
1/4 cup chopped walnuts
4 tablespoons shortening, cut in

Wet ingredients:

1 cup milk
1/4 cup sour cream
2 egg yolks
1 2/3 cups poached quince pieces, chopped small. No juice.

Unite your dry and your wet ingredients. Stir to combine well but put the poached quince pieces in last, taking care not to mash them too much. Beat the 2 egg whites until stiff and foamy. Fold this into the batter with a spatula with as little stirring as possible. You want to incorporate it all together into the batter without destroying the quince pieces while maintaining the frothiness of the egg whites so your cake will be light. Butter and paper a 9 by 13-inch cake pan, then butter it again. Gently scrape the batter into the pan and bake at 350°F for 25 minutes.

## Quipple Roll

1 1/2 cup minced quince
1 cup minced apple
1/2 cup chopped golden raisins
1 cup brown sugar
1/2 teaspoon cinnamon
1/2 teaspoon allspice

Let the quince and apple steam in their own juices in a covered saucepan for a few minutes to get a head start before adding the rest of the filling's ingredients.

For the dough:

2 cups flour
2 tablespoons sugar
2 teaspoons baking powder

4 tablespoons butter, cut in
1 teaspoon salt
2/3 cup milk
(Keep another 4 tablespoons butter in reserve for the assembling of the roll.)

Roll dough out in a rectangle 1/8 inch thick, about 12 by 14 inches. Cover with fruit mixture to within 1 inch of the sides. Dot the filling with small bits of butter until all 4 tablespoons are used. Roll up like a giant jelly roll and bake on a greased baking sheet for 40 minutes at 350°F. Cool and slice to serve. Sometimes it easier to assemble if you have rolled out your dough on waxed paper or a pastry cloth. It helps also if you pierce the dough in two or three places to vent the steam as it bakes, just like a pie, so the roll will keep its shape better.

## Quince Upside-Down Cake

2 quince, sliced into wedges
4 tablespoons butter
1 teaspoon lemon juice
1/2 cup brown sugar

Steam the quince wedges slowly in a pan with the lemon juice for 15 minutes to soften. In a large cast iron skillet, melt the butter. Fry the quince wedges in the butter as you cut them a little finer. Add the sugar and let cook briefly. Turn off the fire and set the oven for 375°F.

Prepare the batter:

2 1/4 cup flour
1/2 teaspoon salt
2 teaspoons baking powder
4 tablespoons additional butter, melted
1/2 teaspoon nutmeg
1 cup white sugar
3 eggs
1 1/2 cup buttermilk

Pour the batter on top of the quince mixture. Bake at 375°F for 15 minutes. Then reduce the heat to 350°F and bake for 25 minutes more. Turn the cake out on a platter while still warm but not piping hot. Let cool. Serve with whipped cream, ice cream or yogurt.

## Swedish Quince Almond Tart/*Marsipan Kvitten Tårta*

The crust:

1 1/2 cups flour
2 tablespoons sugar
1 stick butter or margarine

1/8 teaspoon cardamom
3 tablespoons water, perhaps a bit more, just enough to join the dough.

Press dough out in a pie pan. Crease the edges decoratively with the tines of a fork. The first filling is 1/2 cup of the simple quince paste recipe (quinces and sugar).

The second filling is:

5 ounces almond paste (marzipan)
2 eggs
2 tablespoons sugar
1 tablespoon flour
1/4 teaspoon almond extract
2 tablespoons cream

Chop the almond paste into small pieces. You may need to use a food processor. Beat long and hard until almond paste is fully incorporated into the batter. Pour over the quince layer. Sprinkle the top with flaked almonds. Bake at 325°F for 45 minutes to an hour. Let cool before cutting and serving.

## German Quince Bread/ *Quittenbrot*

This traditional German food is no bread at all; it is the German version of *membrillo* and a copy of the Turkish quince paste. It is just made a little differently.

Peel, cut and core your quinces. Grind the flesh very fine before cooking, then mix with sugar and cook until light pink in color. Add more sugar to taste.

Spread the mixture out on pans or cookie tins to be 1/2 inch thick or less. Let it dry in the sun or adjacent to a warm oven for several days until you can cut it into squares.

## Quince Brown Bread

2 3/4 cups flour
1/2 cup shortening
1/2 cup white sugar
1/2 cup brown sugar
1 teaspoon salt
1 teaspoon baking soda
1/2 teaspoon baking powder
3 tablespoons cinnamon
1/2 cup walnuts
2 teaspoons nutmeg

To these dry ingredients add:

3 eggs
3 cups quince sauce

If the quince sauce preserves you use seem too dry for the batter, try adding a bit of milk. Bake at 350°F for 50 to 60 minutes in two small loaf pans.

## Quince Puffs

One sheet of puff pastry, thawed and chopped into 6 or 8 rectangles
1 cup poached quince pieces, dried
5 hazelnuts, roasted, peeled and chopped fine
1/4 teaspoon cinnamon
1/4 teaspoon cardamom
3 ounces (one small package) cream cheese
1 egg
2 tablespoons sugar

Grease your baking sheet or use parchment paper. Arrange the quince pieces atop the puff pastry rectangles. Beat together the cream cheese, egg, sugar and spices. Spread the cream cheese mixture on top of the puffs around the quince pieces. Sprinkle chopped nuts on top. Bake at 400°F for about 25 to 30 minutes until nicely browned. Cool before serving.

## Orange Quipple Pie

1/4 cup dried quince and/or apple set to reconstitute in
1/4 cup Grand Marnier liqueur
2 apples
2 quince, minced
1 cup sugar
1/2 teaspoon dried orange rind
1/2 teaspoon cardamom
1/2 teaspoon orange oil (optional)
4 tablespoons tapioca flour

Set the dried fruit to soak for several hours in the liqueur. Prepare your pie crust of choice, generally 8 tablespoons of shortening with 1 1/2 cups flour, pinch of salt and only enough water to bind the dough. Cut the quinces much smaller than the apples and be sure to avoid the fibrous core. Addition of the dried fruit helps to soak up the liqueur and the juices as the pie cooks. Bake for one hour at 375°F.

It is quite okay to cook and eat the skin of the quince. Some fine sauces call for the skins to be removed but this is not as important in fruit pies. Quince slices are easy to dry in the oven and are well worth the trouble. Their addition to this recipe gives the pie its unique and pleasing "gumdroppy" texture.

Plain "Quipple Pie" is good too, of course. Just leave out the liqueur and the orange and the dried fruit. Try not to use the standard apple pie spices. Try cardamom by itself or add ginger or nutmeg.

## Quince Custard Pie

For the open half crust:

- 4 tablespoons shortening
- 9 tablespoons wheat flour
- 1 tablespoon barley flour
- Pinch of salt

Add 2 tablespoons of water and then more by the teaspoonful until your dough binds. Roll the dough out on a pie plate and then press into the crust an additional 1 tablespoon finely crushed roasted hazelnuts

For the custard:

- 2 or 3 quince, steamed and mashed to make about 1 cup of quince puree
- 1/2 cup sugar
- 1 teaspoon lemon juice
- 1/4 teaspoon nutmeg
- 1/4 teaspoon cinnamon
- 2 tablespoon melted butter
- 1 cup milk
- 3 egg yolks, reserving the whites for a meringue, or otherwise 3 whole eggs

Set the oven to 425°F. Put in the pie but lower the heat to 350°F. Let it bake for 45 minutes. (For meringue, if desired, beat stiff 3 egg whites with pinch cream of tartar and 4 tablespoons sugar. Spoon meringue on the pie and cook at 425°F for the last 5 minutes until browned.)

## Quince Walnut Custard Pie

Prepare the custard using your previously prepared quince sauce, about 4 quinces peeled and cut into small pieces and cooked to a tart applesauce texture with 1/2 cup sugar added. This quince sauce can be used warm to accompany pork but it is also easily frozen for future baking uses, such as this pie.

Custard:

1 cup slightly sweet quince sauce
1/2 cup extra sugar
1 cup milk
3 eggs
2 tablespoons melted butter
1/4 teaspoon cardamom
1/8 teaspoon cinnamon
1/4 teaspoon powdered lemon peel

Preheat the oven to 450°F as you prepare the crust:

1 cup flour
5 tablespoons shortening
1/8 teaspoon salt
4 walnuts, ground fine
Water, just enough to bind the dough

Work the dough into a pie pan with your floured fingers. Pour custard into the pie shell. Place in the hot oven. Reduce the heat to 350°F and let bake for 50 minutes to one hour until set. Do not slice the pie until it has cooled.

## Quince Pinwheel Cookies

Dough:

1/2 cup butter or other shortening
1/2 cup brown sugar
1/2 cup white sugar
1 egg
1/2 teaspoon lemon juice
2 cups flour
1/2 teaspoon baking soda
1/2 teaspoon salt

Roll the dough out into a 12 by 14-inch rectangle.
Filling:

2 cups simple quince paste
1 cup nuts chopped fine (Pecans are great!)
1 1/2 tablespoon extra sugar

Spread the filling on top of the dough, then roll it up like a jellyroll, wrap it in plastic or waxed paper and put it in the refrigerator to rest for at least several hours. You could freeze the dough roll and bake these cookies at a later date. With a sharp knife slice the dough into cookies about 1/4 inch thick. Bake at 350°F for about 15 minutes. You may wish to keep a bit of dough in reserve so that each cookie can be made to look like the letter "Q."

Variation: Instead of simple quince paste, you can use medlar quince marmalade (cotignac) as the filling for these cookies. You may want to add additional candied orange peel as well.

## Quince Cream Pudding

2 pounds quince
1 cup brown sugar
Juice of one lemon
2 cups cream

Cook the peeled quince in lemon juice and a splash of water until soft enough to mash. Add the sugar and continue to cook. Let cool. Whip the cream. Mix together and chill in individual serving glasses. You may wish to add a bit of rum or liqueur as well.

## Armenian Quince Pudding

4 tablespoons cornstarch
2 1/2 cups milk
1/4 cup sugar
1 teaspoon vanilla
3 tablespoons quince jam
2 tablespoons toasted chopped almonds
Cinnamon to taste

Mix the cornstarch with equal parts of milk to blend, then combine it all and cook in a saucepan. Let it simmer until thick, then spoon it into individual serving bowls or parfait glasses. Dust the puddings with cinnamon and the roasted almonds. Let chill and set.

## Quince Paste / *Membrillo*

2 pounds quinces
1 pound sugar
1 lemon
Almonds

Cut the quince and boil the pieces for half an hour in a small quantity of water until the quinces are soft and can be rubbed though a sieve or passed through a food mill. Add just enough water so that the quince pieces are just floating. Reserve this poaching liquid.

Add the sugar and lemon juice to 2/3 cup of the quince poaching liquid, then the quince paste. Boil until it thickens. Turn it into a wide and shallow mold or tray. Let it dry for several days, then cut it into squares and store it wrapped in waxed paper. It should dry easily into sheets about 1/2 inch to 1/4 inch thick. Serve plain or topped with almond flakes.

To make a *Bocadillo de Membrillo,* create a sandwich with quince paste on the bottom, a layer of flaked almonds in the middle, then more quince paste on top.

## Quince Leather

3 pounds quinces
2 cups sugar
1 teaspoon lemon juice
1/4 cup water

Peel and core your quinces. Cut into small pieces to expedite cooking. If desired, you may cook the cores and peels in a cheesecloth bag for their extra pectin; discard after cooking.

Cook the quinces, lemon and sugar slowly for one and one half hours, at which point it will be easy to mash them into a fine paste. They will look brown or slightly red.

Turn out the paste onto cookie sheets lined with waxed or parchment paper. The drying process will take several days. Place the trays in a warm oven turned off. Let them be warm but not bake. In a couple of days the paste will be holding together well enough for you to dare to flip them out on the cookie sheets and peel away the paper. Let this side dry for a day.

Now you can begin to cut the leather into smaller pieces and flip them more often until dried. Do not let them mold in storage! Be sure that the pieces are small and almost the consistency of leather, not a juicy gumdrop, when you wrap them in waxed paper. If properly dried, they will easily keep for a year. If you are afraid that they may not be sufficiently dry, you can always freeze them for later.

My *piece de resistance*, or so I thought, was a quince-cornelian cherry leather. They had a beautiful red color, a delightful and unique flavor, and a wonderful gumdrop-like consistency. They would have been fine if I had eaten them right then, or frozen them for later, but I wrapped them in paper and gave them as gifts. A terrible mistake! When they were opened a few days later, they had become moldy.

## Jellied Quince

10 quinces
2 quarts water
1 1/2 cup powdered sugar
6 tablespoons gelatin softened in an additional 1/2 cup water
1 cup heavy cream

Set the quince to simmer in the water for an hour or more until it is cooked to a pulp. Strain the quince liquid off using a colander and a piece of cheesecloth. Discard the pulp. Add the sugar and continue to boil to the "thread" stage. Shut off the fire as you add the gelatin. Stir and cool. When it is lukewarm, add the cream. Stir occasionally until cool, then pour into a 2 1/2 quart mold and chill until set. Use individual serving bowls if preferred.

## Thanksgiving Quince Cranberry Chutney

1 bag cranberries
1 cup quince preserves
1 red bell pepper
1/4 cup brown sugar
3/4 teaspoon coriander seed
1 teaspoon mustard seed
3/4 teaspoon red pepper flakes
1 teaspoon salt
1/4 teaspoon black pepper
1/2 cup raisins
1/4 cup cider vinegar
1 cup sliced onion
Lemon zest

Cook slowly for one hour. Chop the onion fine and add it for the last half hour of cooking. This is to be served as a relish with meats. Add lemon zest at the end if desired.

## *Cotogna*

Here is the northern Italian way to eat quince:

Quince chunks
Pear chunks
Dried figs, cut into bite-sized pieces

Cook the fruits in purple grape juice and/or red wine. Cut the quince chunks smaller and cook a little longer than the pears or figs so that they soften up well, about one hour. Cook with nutmeg, cinnamon stick and lemon rind. Cook it long and slow but try to leave the fruits a bit chunky. When cool, top with toasted chopped hazelnuts and walnuts. Serve alongside hunks of elegant cheese.

## *Mostarda di Cotogna*

8 to 10 quinces, cored and cubed
1/2 cup dried figs
1 cup dried apricot
2/3 cup dried cherries
2/3 cup raisins
4 cups water
4 cups white wine
6 cups sugar
2 cups white wine vinegar
6 tablespoons dry yellow mustard powder

4 tablespoons mustard seed
2 tablespoons lemon zest

Let cook slowly for more than one hour. Process for 15 minutes in hot water bath to can if desired. This northern Italian fruit mustard is a condiment to eat with a spoon alongside cheese pieces, meats, antipasto trays, vegetable sticks.

## Quince Mustard with Passerina Grapes

Isabella and Livio Dalla Ragione have devoted their lives to keeping old-fashioned varieties of Italian fruit alive, the so-called heirloom varieties of the "slow food" movement. This quince recipe is from their book *Arboreal Archaeology* (Ali & No editrice, Perugia, 2008).

"To make this mustard take some black passerina grapes and only a handful of white ones. Put these with a majority of de-fuzzed quinces and a minority of mixed apples. Cook them all in a copper pot that has not been tin-plated along with an iron key. When they are done, pass them through a sieve or food mill to remove as much of the seeds and cores as possible. Place the mustard in small clay pots. Let these rest in the oven all night long after the baking of the bread so that the mustard can further reduce without boiling. When it has cooled and dried, the mustards are sprinkled with ground walnuts and topped with a leaf of the island shrub mallow, *Malva rosa.* The pots are closed with waxed papers and tied with twine, then kept in a dark place until the holidays when you eat the mustard spread on meats or spread on bread like butter."

Don't you wish you had the ingredients to try this recipe?

## Quince Jelly

6 perfect quinces (or a dozen buggy ones)
Juice of 1 lemon
1 cinnamon stick (and/or cardamom pods, cloves, citrus peel, rose petals)
2/3 cup sugar for every pound of quince juice

Once you have obtained your quinces and are ready to make jelly, be sure to rub off the fuzz. Cut into pieces, skin, core and all. Cut out and discard any insect-damaged areas. Cover the fruit pieces with water so that they are just floating and set to boil slowly for an hour. You may need to add water to ensure that the quince pieces are still floating. You should have a slurry whose pieces easily smash as you stir. Mash it a bit and cook until it turns a bit pink and looks like coarse applesauce.

Quince has a bit of a lemon taste in itself. Your jelly can profit by the addition of the juice of one lemon. Quince jelly is also traditionally spiced with cinnamon stick, cardamom pods, cloves, ginger, citrus peel or rose petals. Use these extras one or two at a time and decide which taste you prefer. Set them to cook with the quince then discard the boiled spices.

Prepare a strainer and a larger bowl to collect the juice. Line the strainer with multiple layers of cheesecloth. You can get by without the jelly bag that my mother had. Set your slurry to drain for a quarter hour or so. Resist the temptation to squeeze more juice out. If you do, you'll cloud the jelly. All the good essences of the fruit will have been boiled down into the meager cups of juice which you collect.

Measure the juice carefully. Usually jellies are one cup of sugar to one cup of juice, but quince is naturally high in pectin and easy to jell. I add for each cup of liquid, 2/3 cup of sugar (1 pound). Set this to boil and reduce very slowly for another 20 to 30 minutes until it gets thick and starts "sheeting" on a cold spoon inserted into the mixture. Instead of flowing off like water, the juice will be starting to stick on the spoon. Never let it boil too vigorously, stir slowly. If you wish to add fresher spices, now is the time.

Pour into clean jars. Process another 15 minutes to seal and preserve for later. Be sure to let some cool and set for immediate consumption as well! Quince jelly comes out pink or red, clear like a jewel, if properly made.

## Quince Pectin Water

No other fruit has as much pectin as the quince. Add a few spoonsful to other jam or jelly recipes to help them to jell. This is what people did before the stores had pectin powder. To make quince pectin water, take the clean peels and cores being discarded from other recipes. Put them in a saucepan, cover with water, let come to a boil then slowly simmer and reduce until the pectin is extracted. The longer and slower you simmer, the stronger your pectin water will be. It will look a bit milky. Pectin water will keep in the refrigerator for a few weeks. (Or to make a salve for chapped hands or lips, add 1/2 ounce of glycerin, 2 ounces of bay rum and 1/2 ounce of safe perfume).

## Quince Preserves

- 6 quinces, peeled, cored and diced
- 3 cups sugar
- 3 cups water
- 1 1/2 tablespoons lemon juice
- 1 stick cinnamon
- 3 whole cloves
- 1/2 cup slivered almonds

Cook 2 hours until thick. Lift out the spices. Stir in the nuts, then pour into jars. Process 15 minutes in a hot water bath to seal.

## Sweet Quince Pickles

Remove the fuzz from the quinces that you want to pickle and chop them into thick wedges. Cook in water to cover until tender. Prepare a good vinegar syrup, 1/3 water and 2/3 vinegar, using a pound of sugar for each pound of quince to be pickled. When the quince wedges are tender, pour off the water and reserve for another use. Spice the vinegar syrup with whole cloves, allspice, mace and stick cinnamon. One pint of vinegar should be enough to pickle 7 pounds of fruit.

Put the quince wedges in clean canning jars and pour the pickling syrup over them. Process in a hot water bath for 15 minutes to seal.

## Quince Chutney

2 cups dried quince
2 cups dried apple
1 cup raisins
1 cup chopped sweet onion
2 cups brown sugar
1 cup cider vinegar
1 cup apple juice
1 tablespoon minced ginger root
1/2 tablespoon dried hot pepper
1 tablespoon mustard seed
3-inch piece of cinnamon stick, broken into pieces

Cook slowly for one hour. This recipe makes about 1 1/2 pints. Add one cup of walnuts after cooking and you can call it "walnut quince conserve" instead.

## Quince Orange Marmalade

6 or 7 quinces, peeled, chopped and processed fine in a food processor
2 cups sugar
1 1/2 cups orange juice
1/2 cup water
1 organic orange

Add half of the orange as juice and the other half of the orange as fruit pulp with as much of the white membranes removed as possible. Bring to a boil and let simmer for one hour. Reserve the orange peel and cut it into small strips, discarding as much of the white pith as possible. Add the peel in short pieces to cook for the last 15 minutes. Ladle into clean jars and process in a boiling water bath 15 additional minutes to seal.

## Quince Ginger

(Makes five 4-ounce jelly jars)

2 pounds quince wedges, peeled and chopped small (about 5 cups total)
2 cups white sugar
1 tablespoon lemon juice
1 cup crystallized ginger, chopped fine but in irregularly sized pieces

Peel the quince and chop it fine. Reserve a few pieces to throw in later so as to preserve a bit of their shape, but put the rest of it on the stove to cook 1 1/2 hours over a low fire. Stir often, mash. If it starts to stick, add one tablespoon water but no more. When reduced to applesauce consistency, throw in 2 cups of sugar and the reserved quince pieces, a dozen or so, then let it resume a slow boil.

Chop the crystallized ginger fine or use a food processor to create a spreadable consistency. Again, reserve a few bits of larger ginger pieces for texture. Combine with the quince mixture and pack into clean jars. Process 15 minutes in a hot water bath to seal. The longer you cook or process the ginger, the less fiery the jam will be.

## Chardequynce

1 1/2 cups water
3 cups peeled, minced quince
3 cups peeled, minced pear
2 cups sugar
1/2 teaspoon cinnamon
1/2 teaspoon cardamom
1/2 teaspoon nutmeg

Mince the fruits very fine and cook at a slow boil for an hour, mashing until it takes on the consistency of applesauce. Add the spices toward the end. If you have the patience, cook it down further until it resembles apple butter. Process 15 minutes to can and seal, if desired.

Chardequynce is a "marmalade" from medieval England, a spiced quince-pear butter. This recipe does not contain orange peel but you could easily add some. A more traditional recipe would use 1 1/2 cups of honey instead of white sugar. Other spices to try, not all at once of course, are allspice, mace and the tiniest bit of clove. Feel free to be creative! No precise recipe for chardequynce has come down to us, just the name and the quaint spelling.

## Green Tomato Quince Mincemeat

This can be eaten for itself, used to accompany meats like roast pork or poultry, or added to stuffing or to apple pies.

2 quarts green tomatoes, chopped

6 quince, minced
1 apple, chopped
1 cup raisins
1 1/4 cup sugar
1 teaspoon salt
1 teaspoon of each spice: cinnamon, allspice, clove, nutmeg
1/2 teaspoon of each spice: cardamom, mace

Let boil then simmer slowly for one hour. To can, process an additional 15 minutes in a hot water bath. This is certainly a unique and old-fashioned condiment! Although at first I thought it would be unappetizing, now I'm sorry that I didn't make more of it!

## Syrian Quince-Almond Candy/*Louzina Saparzel*

2 3/4 pounds sugar
2 3/4 pounds quince
Ground almonds as desired
Ground cardamom seeds to taste

Peel and chop your quinces, then let them cook slowly in their juices with only a splash of water. Mash until very fine. Add sugar and turn out on a waxed paper-lined cookie sheet. Sprinkle the top with toasted almond flakes and ground cardamom seeds. Set it to dry for a day or two in the oven. When the sheet of candy is easier to work with, put more nuts and seeds into it and roll it out thin with a rolling pin. Cut into small squares and dust with more ground almonds or confectioner's sugar.

## Quince Recipes for Main Courses

There is no need to confine the quince to the dessert table. It is just as much at home with appetizers, salads, stews and as an accompaniment to meats and vegetables. The reality is that the quince needs to be cooked anyways, so why not do it along with the rest of the meal? Many of the chutneys, sauces, preserves and pickles also find their way to the dinner table. Eat hearty! That's English for *bon appetit.*

## Cheese-Quince Skewers

Assortment of fancy cheese cubes (Manchego, Gouda, Jarlsberg, good Cheddar. . .)
*Membrillo* (Spanish Quince Paste) cut in cubes
Fancy greens (Radiccio, arugula, watercress. . . )
Almonds

Fancy large toothpicks or skewers

On each stick skewer a piece or two of cheese, a leaf of greens and a piece of the quince paste. Stick almonds into the cheese and quince. Serve as appetizers or party fare. You can make this more substantial by adding a cube of dry sausage like *sopresata*.

## Quince Green Salad

2 quinces in slices
1 cup sugar
3 cups water

Poach your quinces for 15 or 20 minutes, until they are as soft as you like them. Then drain and cool, reserving syrup for other uses.

Prepare a green salad where lettuce is a minority using arugula, endive, radiccio, frisee, escarole, romaine lettuce, as many different greens as you can get.

Vinaigrette Dressing:

1 tablespoon balsamic vinegar
2 tablespoons white wine vinegar
1 tablespoon maple syrup
1 teaspoon Dijon mustard
1/3 cup olive oil
Pinch of salt and pepper
1 teaspoon fresh thyme leaves

Assemble the salad with the quince, dress and shave Manchego cheese on top.

## Celeriac Quince Salad

1 medium sized celeriac, boiled in water for 20 minutes until soft

Don't peel the celery root until after it is cooked. Add a few drop of lemon juice to the cooking water and retain this stock for other uses. Cut cooled root into bite-sized chunks

1 cup poached quince chunks
2 tablespoons olive oil
2 tablespoons lemon juice
2 dozen black olives
1 dozen capers
2 stalks celery, strings removed and cut
1/2 yellow carrot, cut to half coins and matchsticks
2 tablespoons purple onion, sliced fine
4 leaves radicchio, torn into small bits
Lots of fresh ground black pepper

Serve this salad cold on top of a romaine lettuce leaf. It is a riot of colors, red, pink, yellow, white, purple, and a collection of contrasting textures and flavors.

## Bean Bacon Quince Salad

For the salad:

2 cups cooked cannellini (white kidney beans)
1/2 red pepper, diced
2 1/2 tablespoons chopped sweet onion
3 or 4 leaves radicchio, finely shredded, about 1/4 cup
1 cup poached quince in bite-sized pieces
Salt and pepper

For the dressing:

1/2 cup olive oil
1/2 cup lemon juice

For the garnish:

Fry 5 slices bacon until crispy, discarding fat
Cut the bacon into bite-sized hunks
1/4 cup chopped parsley

## Pork Tenderloin with Quince

Set your pork tenderloin to roast in the oven spiced with garlic, mustard, cider vinegar, ginger and a small bit of red pepper. While it is roasting prepare your quince sauce.

1/2 lemon, juiced
6 cups water
6 quince, peeled and cubed
2 parsnips, peeled
4 tablespoons sugar
1/2 teaspoon salt
Pinch of allspice and cinnamon

Set this in a saucepan covered to boil for 30 minutes. Mash repeatedly, then add:

4 tablespoons heavy cream
2 tablespoons butter

Serve your tenderloin with roasted or boiled potatoes surrounded by this quince sauce.

## Sautéed Quince

2 quinces, sliced thin
2 tablespoons butter

Sauté the quince in butter until soft. Sprinkle with a little sugar and cinnamon and continue to sauté, adding more butter if necessary. Fry until golden brown. Serve with turkey, chicken or pork.

## Glazed Quince

2 quinces, cut in half and core removed

Place quince halves in saucepan with the cut side upwards. Put 1/2 tablespoon butter in each. Sprinkle quinces with sugar. Cook in 1/2 cup water and 2 tablespoons butter for 45 minutes at a slow boil. Baste the quinces often so the tops do not dry out. Serve with meats.

## Baked Quince

4 quinces, peeled, core removed and lids carved as for a jack-o'-lantern
5 tablespoons melted butter
1/3 cup brown sugar
Cinnamon to taste

Peel and core your quinces, taking care to carve lids. Brush the fruit with butter. Fit them tightly into a buttered baking pan or casserole, then sprinkle with the sugar and replace the lids. Bake at 350°F for 75 minutes. Brush with more melted butter.

These can be served hot with poultry, meats and rice. They can be served cold as a dessert with whipped cream or pomegranate syrup, "*narsharab*." To approximate your own pomegranate syrup in case there are no Armenian stores nearby, add 1/3 cup of white sugar to a cup of pomegranate juice and let it boil and reduce on the stove. Any consultation with Caucasian cookbooks will give you dozens of other things to do with your quince!

## Azeri Lamb Soup with Chestnuts, Prunes and Quince/*Parcha Bozbash*

1 pound lamb in cubes
3 tablespoons butter
1 onion, chopped
4 cups broth
1 potato, cubed
1 quince, cored and cubed
1/2 cup prunes
1/4 pound chestnuts, peeled
2/3 cup cooked chick peas
Salt and pepper

Brown 1 pound of cubed lamb and the onion in the butter. To this add the 2 quinces, cut into bite sized cubes, and 4 cups of water enhanced by one or two vegetable bouillon cubes or use a prepared broth. Add the prunes and the chestnuts, peeled and cut in half. Let simmer at a slow boil for 30 minutes, then add the potato cubes. I used fingerling potatoes instead! Continue to simmer. Add more water if needed. Add the chick peas for the last 15 minutes of cooking, along with a bit of ginger root or saffron.

Simmer for at least one hour. The quince pieces will still be recognizable but the prunes will have cooked into the broth. Remove any chestnut skin papers that may decorate the broth. Add salt and pepper to taste. For a richer soup, add a bit more butter. Garnish with parsley and mint leaves, plus sumakh if you have any.

## Armenian Stuffed Vegetables / *Echmiadzin Dolma*

Prepare this stuffing:

1 pound ground lamb
1/2 cup uncooked long grain white rice
1 onion, diced small
1/4 cup tomato juice
Salt and pepper
1/4 cup mixed fresh herbs (mint, parsley, basil, marjoram, tarragon . . . )

Use this stuffing to fill:

4 small eggplants
4 green peppers
4 tomatoes

Cut lids on the vegetables and remove as much of the innards as you can. Reserve for other uses. Arrange stuffed vegetables in a large fry pan with a lid. Add 3 tablespoons butter, 1 1/2 cups water or broth and 1 chopped quince. Let boil slowly for 45 minutes covered until the rice is done. Drizzle with quince poaching broth and serve.

# Blackberry

*Rubus laciniatus*

Our family always got blackberries from the wilds, not from stores or farm stands. Grandpa carefully watched the abandoned hayfields, railroad rights-of-way and other prime blackberry habitats. He took into account that berries up on top of the lake escarpment ripen a week later than berries down on the lake plain just a few miles away. He knew when it was time to load up the car with baskets and grandkids and head out on a country ride. He would even scout out the sites in advance to make sure to find his favorite sort of berries, the warty-looking ones, would predominate.

We loved our country rides! We might get to see a deer, blue heron or bluebird. These were our omens of good luck, but even cows or horses were cause for excitement. The biggest excitement of all was when we got to see the stump! Grandpa had shot off half of his left arm when he was a teenager in a "hunting" accident when his gun went off while he was climbing over a fence. Usually he kept the stump neatly hidden under his shirtsleeve, but whenever we went around a corner the stump would come out and hold the wheel for a second while his good hand grabbed the wheel again and completed the turn. This was long before seatbelts or child seats, so Grandpa might have four or five of us crammed in the backseat, all eagerly awaiting our glimpse of the stump.

Eventually we would arrive at whatever remote site Grandpa had scouted out, pile out of the car and scamper off to pick berries and fill the baskets in no time. Younger children were to pick close to the car. Older ones were sent off into the deeper brambles. Since Grandpa only had one hand, he didn't pick much except to sample the crop and decide if they were decent or "those soft, sickly sweet dewberries fit only for a child's taste." With some luck we'd get a popsicle on the ride back into town, or a slice of Grandma's pie that evening.

Blackberry pie was a staple at family reunions. Grandma also put up jam and jelly for the winter. "Blackberry shortcake" meant a warm biscuit cut in half, spread with butter and topped with blackberries in their own sugar syrup, and perhaps a bit of whipped cream or ice cream. If you put the blackberries underneath the biscuits and baked them together, then you'd have a "blackberry cobbler." Another sort of "cobbler" used oatmeal batter instead of biscuit dough. Sometimes these are also called "buckles." Just plain berries atop vanilla ice cream was fine. Peach-blackberry shortcake or cobbler were other popular combinations since these fruits are in season around the same time. The berries also went into pancakes and muffins. Few people in my area of western New York bother to grow blackberries still because there are so many growing wild. The abundance of wild berries may actually hinder the entrance of the blackberry into local commerce. Why grow or purchase, people reason, something which is so overly abundant in every abandoned field?

Blackberries are a "bramblefruit" which, along with raspberries, are a species of the genus *Rubus* in the rose family of plants. Most of our common fruits are members of the "rose family" which includes apple trees as well as blackberries, or *Rubus laciniatus*. There are a number of other "berry-bearing" species that are commonly considered to be blackberries in our area. I have at least four in my wild blackberry field. There is an upright cane that bears large berries. There is a tall upright cane with smaller berries. There is a vine-like cane that snakes along the ground and bears huge berries. There is a petite "running blackberry" only a foot or two high that spreads by underground runners but seldom gives fruit. When it does they just seem like small dark blue blackberries, pretty to look at but insignificant in flavor. You do not want this one invading your flower garden.

According to my grandfather, however, most of these are not "true" blackberries. They are nothing but second-rate imposters such as "dewberries," for which my grandfather had nothing but scorn. To him, the *only* blackberry worthy of the name is one that is borne on medium-sized canes of reddish color and is about waist to chest high. The berry it produces is raspberry-sized with a protrusion on one side, a "drupelet" which is bigger than the others and sticks out. Not every berry on the bush will have this wort-like condition, but many will. This and this alone was the true blackberry, according to his judgment, the best for pies or jellies. Grandpa knew no Latin, but he was even fussier about his blackberries than the botanists.

It is said that people come in two sorts, "lumpers" and "splitters." As far as blackberries go, botanists tend to be "splitters," whereas ordinary folks are more likely to be "lumpers." The practical result of this is that botanists have identified over three hundred separate species of blackberries in the world whereas ordinary folks lump them together and just see one. If the berry is small, black and composed of little round balls (the drupes) joined together by a pithy center, they declare it a blackberry and into the mouth it goes. My grandfather must have been a "splitter."

The botanist studies a plant's structures, even the genes, and then assigns Latin binomial names. They declare what species of plant it is and isn't, determine its range in nature and what other species it may interbreed with. After much study the scientist can declare which species it is and how many species there are, and they have declared that blackberry and blackberry-like fruits are just about everywhere.

If the interior of the berry is an open depression, then it isn't any kind of blackberry. It's some sort of raspberry, whether the fruit is black, red, yellow or purple. Then there is the "Japanese wineberry," long canes with many prickles and not-so-painful thorns whose fruit is a translucent reddish-orange berry. There is also the "thimbleberry," a native American plant whose red fruits will rest on your fingertip just like a thimble. The botany books call it "purple flowering raspberry," *Rubus odoratus*. Both of these fruits fall on the raspberry side of things, but they are far too fragile and crops are far too sparse for this berry to enter into commerce. The Japanese use wineberry to flavor wine, hence the name, but I have fancied a wineberry pie on those rare occasions when I have gathered enough of this fruit to bake with. Look for it in late July.

Besides the wild blackberries and the berries which pass as blackberries but aren't, there are many improved, cultivated varieties ("cultivars") of blackberry. They are not so popular in my area for the reason that we fancy the ones we happen to find on our own, or the ones we've grown especially attached to. Folks complain that "catalog blackberries" are too bitter or too plain or too big. Why not use the wild ones? Some may be inferior to the cultivated varieties, but others will certainly be better. Each one will be unique and different. It's true that with a cultivated blackberry patch, you have convenience. You don't have to wander all over to get enough of the fruit for a recipe, but I find that this is exactly what I enjoy most about berrying.

I have a friend who bakes and sells blackberry pies. She has a few rows of the "catalog berries," but most of her berries come from the wilds. "Those catalog berries are so bitter!" she complains. "The wild berries are so much more flavorful!"

She is probably gathering a half dozen different species, all of them unselected cultivars. They are different sizes with subtly different flavors and degrees of sweetness or bitterness. Wild berries make for a more interesting combination of flavors.

A demanding customer once asked her, "You don't use those nasty little wild berries, do you?" "Oh no!" said my friend innocently. But after that, she kept separate containers of blackberries in her freezer, one for the "wild ones" and one for the larger garden variety. One day she used the wrong berries in this customer's pie by accident. When the customer returned again, it was not to complain, but to comment on how unusually good the last pie had been. "You see now how it pays to use those selected garden varieties? They're just so much larger and sweeter!" the happy customer exclaimed. "Oh yes!" said my friend again, which just goes to prove that old saying "the customer is always right," especially when they are wrong.

The marionberry is an improved cultivar which grows in the Pacific Northwest. It can be easily harvested by machine and is converted to jams and jellies, pies and berry juices, syrups and ice creams, on a grand scale. It has a complicated family tree that includes dewberry and raspberry as well as Himalayan and Pacific blackberries. Over half of the berries grown in Oregon are marionberries. It was first tested in Marion County, Oregon, and can yield up to six tons per acre. The marionberry has become the dominant blackberry of commerce and is said to have a more powerful flavor than your average blackberry of lesser lineage.

The loganberry is an accidental hybrid cross between a red raspberry and a blackberry which appeared in California around 1881 on the lands of plantsman James Harvey Logan (1841–1928). Loganberry canes are thorny and have an "undisciplined" growth habit that resists the trellis and machine-harvesting. The berries are not easy to pick because they are hidden under the leaves. They were found to be particularly high in vitamin C and used in anti-scurvy tonics by the British Navy in the early 1900s, however, as well as in a popular juice drink of the time marketed under the name of "Loju." Manufacturing the juice was a perfect use for unemployed breweries in Oregon when the state went "dry," as well as providing an outlet for the increasing number of loganberry farmers. Today, every restaurant in Canada seems to feature "loganberry" soft drinks right next to the lemonade, I've noticed, whereas in the States we have "wildberry."

"Tayberry" is another hybrid between red raspberries and blackberries produced in 1979 near the River Tay in Scotland. These berries are purplish red when ripe and even larger and sweeter than the loganberry with which tayberry lovers compare their favorite berry at every turn. The berries are not easy to pick, and since there is no machine harvesting, tayberries are not grown on a commercial scale. They are a real delicacy and rare to find, so if you do you should quickly buy them!

The cloudberry is a sort of yellow-orange raspberry which grows on low bushes in the far north. In Sweden they are called "*hjortron*" from "*hjort*" meaning "hart" or male deer. They are not grown on farms but are foraged from the wilds (just like the more common lingonberries), then sold to the preserve producers for a premium price. What I would like to know is why we have the word "cloudberry" in English? In Nova Scotia this same berry is called "bakeapple." My guess is that Britain may have a few mountains whose summits are arctic enough to keep these plants happy up there closer to the clouds. Cloudberry prefers the tundra or the boreal forest but it still grows on some mountain tops as a relic of the Ice Age. It can survive dry conditions, acid conditions and is also salt tolerant. It is also known as "averin" in Scotland and "knotberry" in England.

Hatho, the spirit of the Frost, Jesse Cornplanter (1889–1957)
(Courtesy of the New York State Museum, Albany, NY)

The Seneca have an interesting legend that tells how the blackberry saved summer. According to this legend, Hatho the frost spirit snuck south early one year in hopes of making some mischief. As he entered the lodge of O'swinoda', the "spirit of summer," a small boy noticed this strange and unfriendly spirit in the house of his father even though no one else could see him. Now there happened to be a huge pot of blackberry sauce bubbling away on the fire, and the boy splashed it all over Hatho's frosty face which caused him to flee north again as fast as he could.

Ever since Hatho had this painful experience, he has taken pains to avoid all contact with blackberries, whether as flower or fruit. It doesn't ever frost while the blackberry is in bloom, nor does it frost until after the blackberry has ripened its fruit. The Seneca may be better known for revering the strawberry, the first fruit of summer, which has its own thanksgiving ceremony, but the blackberry is a sacred fruit to them too. Blackberries were dried on the cane and saved as a special food for the sick. Blackberry syrup kept them summery warm and healthy throughout the frosty months of winter.

I love the weather wisdom coupled to berry lore in this traditional story, and how it is a child whose quick action scares away the frost spirit. Why did the adults not notice the danger? Overturning the pot of bubbling blackberry syrup made the boy a hero by saving the day, instead of earning him a spanking as would have happened to us if *we* had done anything similar! But here it is all just part of the scheme of things.

This brings us to the last berry on our list, thimbleberry. It is here by virtue of its name, which is the only thing about it that my mother liked. The thimbleberry is also known as the "purple flowering raspberry," *Rubus odoratus*. It has huge, vaguely maple-shaped leaves and bristly hairs instead of thorns. The red berry is thin and weak. Mother showed us how it can sit perfectly over the end of your thumb, just like a thimble. (The hole in other raspberries is too small to permit this.) The berry will probably break apart on the way to your mouth if you try to pick it up again with two fingers. Don't bother to pick enough for pies or jam because this berry is seedy and a bit insipid in flavor.

"Red but too red" is what Mother used to say. She preferred red raspberries to all the other berries, but not if it was a thimbleberry.

# Blackberry Recipes

## Blackberry Buttermilk Pancakes

Prepare a batter with:

1 cup flour
3 tablespoons cornmeal
1 cup buttermilk
1 cup maple yogurt
1 egg
2 tablespoons melted butter
1/2 teaspoon salt
1 teaspoon baking powder
2 dozen blackberries

Cook these pancakes with plenty of butter or margarine. Two tablespoons of batter will make a good-sized pancake. Keep a few extra berries around to add to those pancakes which may happen not to get any. You want each pancake to have 2 or 3 berries. Flip with caution, as these are very delicate. Serve with plenty of maple syrup.

If you are using over-sized selected varieties of berries, you may want to cut each one of these in half. The wild berries come in many different (and smaller) sizes.

## Blackberry Sour Cream Muffins

2 cups flour, sifted
1 teaspoon baking powder
1/2 teaspoon soda
1 cup sour cream
2 eggs
4 tablespoons melted butter
3/4 cup milk
1/3 cup sugar
1 cup small blackberries (You may vary this recipe by adding part red and/or black currants.)

Before you bake these muffins in buttered paper "cups," drop a bit of crumble into each one:

1 1/2 tablespoons marzipan mixed with 1 1/2 tablespoons bread crumbs

Bake at 400°F for 20 to 25 minutes.

## Blackberry Cake

2 eggs
2/3 cup sugar
1 cup flour
2 teaspoons baking powder
grated rind of one lemon
5 tablespoons milk
3/4 cup blackberries
1 1/2 tablespoons brown sugar
1 1/2 tablespoons white sugar

Sugar the berries in advance and let stand. Butter a round cake pan (9 inch diameter), preferably one with a removable bottom. Bake for 40 to 45 minutes at 400°F.

## Blackberry Squares

1 1/2 stick butter
2 1/2 cups sugar
4 eggs
2 1/2 cups flour
1/2 teaspoon vanilla
2 cups blackberries
1 tablespoon flaked almonds

Line a pan with parchment paper. Pour in the batter and spread the berries and almond flakes on top. Bake at 325°F for 30 to 35 minutes. Let cool somewhat, then lift the paper to remove the cake from the pan. Let it cook on a rack. Cut into squares.

## Blackberry Cobbler

2 cups blackberries spread into a buttered baking dish
4 tablespoons sugar or more to taste
Dot with 1 tablespoon extra butter.

Prepare the batter:

1 beaten egg
1/2 cup milk
1/2 cup melted butter

1 1/2 cups flour
2 teaspoon baking powder
1/4 teaspoon salt
1/2 cup sugar

Mix the wet and the dry ingredients well, then pour the batter over the sugared blackberries and bake at 400°F for 25 to 30 minutes until the berries are bubbling and the cobbler is starting to brown. Serve spoonsful of cobbler topped with ice cream or whipped cream.

## Blackberry Shortcake

1 quart blackberries
4 tablespoons sugar

Crush a few of the berries to encourage them to juice with the sugar. Set aside to let a syrup develop. Don't add water. Prepare a sweet biscuit dough:

2 cups flour
2 tablespoons sugar
4 tablespoons butter
2 teaspoons baking soda
1/4 teaspoon salt
3/4 cup milk
Additional fresh butter for serving

Work the butter into the dough with a fork, then add the milk. Fashion the dough into individual biscuits about 3/4 inch thick. Bake on a buttered baking sheet at 400°F for 15 to 20 minutes until they are beginning to brown on the underside. While still warm, cut the biscuit in half, spread it with butter and top it with the blackberry sauce. We were raised on simple buttered biscuits with blackberries, but some people may want whipped cream as well.

## Blackberry Bread Pudding

3 tablespoons butter
1 pound stale bread, torn into crumbs
4 eggs
6 cups milk
2 1/2 tablespoon vanilla
2 1/2 teaspoon cinnamon
2 cups blackberries

Let the bread soak in the liquids and spices, then cast your berries on top. Bake in a buttered baking dish at 375°F until set, probably about half an hour. Prepare the following hot sauce to pour over the bread pudding as you serve it still warm:

1/2 cup butter, melted

1 cup brown sugar
1/8 teaspoon salt
1 egg
1/3 cup water

## Blackberry Roll

1 cup butter.

Melt half of this to make a syrup with:

1 cup sugar
1 cup water

Work the rest of the butter into the dough along with:

1 1/2 cups flour
1/4 teaspoon salt
2 1/4 teaspoons baking powder
1/3 cup milk
1/2 teaspoons cinnamon

Cut the butter into the flour and form the dough. Knead it, then roll it out into a large rectangle perhaps a foot long and 8 inches wide, 1/4 inch thick. Spread the berries on top of the dough and roll it up like a jelly roll. Rolling it out on waxed paper may help with this step. Cut the roll into pieces that are also about 1/4 to 1/2 inch thick. Spread these out in the buttered 10 inch round baking dish. Preheat the oven to 350°F. Now pour the sugar-water-butter syrup over top and bake for 30 minutes. Remove from the oven briefly and sprinkle with an additional 2 tablespoons sugar, then return it to the oven to bake for 15 minutes more.

## Spiced Blackberry Juice

2 quarts blackberries
8 cloves
1 stick cinnamon
1 whole nutmeg or a few allspice berries
1/2 cup sugar
1/2 cup water

Mash the berries and let them cook with the spices and water at a gentle simmer for half an hour. Strain using a strainer and cheesecloth. Add the sugar and bring to a boil again. Pour into clean jars, seal and process for 15 minutes in a boiling water bath.

This juice is too dear to drink as is. Let more people enjoy it by using your spiced blackberry juice to flavor a whole gallon of apple juice or cider. It is also good in hot mulled cider. Save it until winter, for it makes a good tonic for coughs and flu even though it does not have the same anti-viral effect as elderberry. Administer by the spoonful. Don't wash away the juice by drinking water or other liquids but let it linger in your throat.

## Blackberry Vinegar

Prepare your vinegar. In a heavy bowl, cover your berries with vinegar and then crush them to release the juices. Let the crushed berries stand in the vinegar for 24 hours, then strain off the liquid. Add a nearly equal volume of sugar and simmer for about 15 minutes to reduce slightly. Pour off into clean bottles.

## Blackberry Vinaigrette Salad Dressing

Mix 2 tablespoons blackberry vinegar with 1 tablespoon oil, and salt and pepper to taste. You can vary the dressing by using your finest olive oils or by using walnut oil or grapeseed oil.

## Blackberry Spinach Salad

3 cups spinach
1/4 cup shredded radiccio
1/2 cup romaine lettuce
1 green onion, cut in slices
1 pint blackberries
1/4 cup walnuts
1 pint cherry tomatoes
6 ounces feta cheese

Of course you can serve this salad with blackberry vinaigrette dressing.

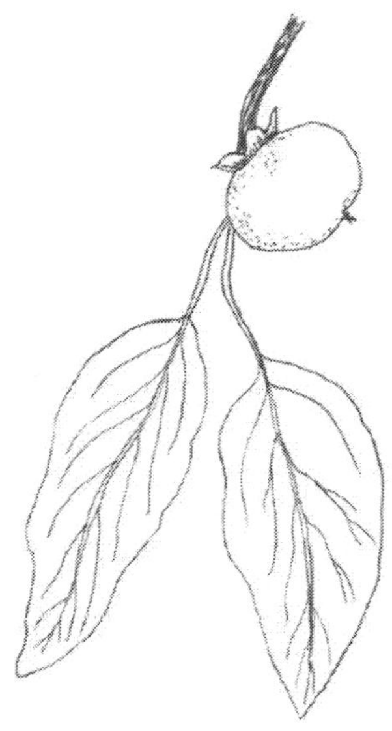

# Persimmon

*Diospyros kaki*

The persimmon is an ancient and venerable fruit whose scientific name, *Diospyros*, means "food of the gods." Indeed, few fruits are sweeter to eat when ripe or more horrible to eat when unripe. The fruit can be a pleasing yellow or orange-red color and still taste bitter and astringent. For their medicinal properties, these qualities may be valuable. In culinary uses, however, they are anything but! So it's important to remember that until the entire persimmon has softened to a jelly-like texture, it is not ripe no matter how ripe it looks. Then, however, it becomes as sweet as honey with a luscious gum-droppy quality and the subtlest hint of apricot flavor, as divine-tasting as its name indicates. Persimmon season is late in the year, November and December. There are both Asian and American species of *Diospyros*, the main difference between them being the durability, and therefore the transportability, of the fruit crop. The Asian persimmons beat out the American species on this point and thus have been more of a factor in commerce. In folklore, however, the American species quite holds its own.

*Diospyros kaki*, the Asian persimmon, has been in commercial cultivation for thousands of years. It originated in China and eventually spread to Japan, Korea and throughout all of Southeast Asia. Marco Polo encountered it during his travels in the 13th century. Six hundred years later, Commodore Perry introduced it to America from Japan. The large, long-lived trees can produce up to four hundred pounds of fruit per tree. There are over two thousand varieties. Asian varieties are usually self-fruitful. The plants are male and female but they can also produce bisexual flowers and may even be a different sex in different years. Pollination is not generally a problem.

In Japan the fruit of the persimmon was dried and used as sugar prior to the introduction of cane sugar. It is said that drying removes the bitter taste and that the cultivar "Hachiya" is the best one to dry. The fruit was picked from the tree while still firm, peeled and allowed to dry for several weeks. Some skin was left at the top and at the bottom of the fruit. During the drying process, the fruits were "massaged" weekly to encourage the inner juices to come out and dry. It is necessary to avoid contact with iron pots or cookware during the drying (or cooking) process, as this can cause the fruit to blacken.

In China the persimmon was used to produce vinegar and brandy, as well as sugar. Asian persimmons tend to cling to the tree even after they are ripe and so they must be picked individually. A ripe persimmon is so soft that it cannot be picked or tossed into baskets without causing damage to the fruit. The fruits are therefore picked slightly "green," not green in color but "green" as in unripe. A persimmon picked while green in color will probably never ripen. You wait for the fruit to turn yellow in some varieties, or more usually bright orange. It is still not ripe, but at least it is no longer green! You pick it while still firm and then you wait.

Many are the tricks to get a persimmon to ripen off the tree. Time seems to work always, unless the fruit was picked too early. To speed up the process the Japanese stored the fruit in *sake* casks where the alcoholic vapors enabled the ripening to proceed more quickly. A more modern technique is to spray the fruit with whiskey and store them in plastic bags for several weeks. You can also try storing them in paper bags with an overly ripe apple (the ethylene gas method). The Chinese soaked the fruits in ten percent lime water or an infusion of *hon laat liu* (a *Polygonum* species) or stored them in jars along with crushed banyan leaves (*Ficus benghalensis*) to induce earlier ripening.

This horrible astringent flavor is caused by the presence of a tannin-like chemical called "leucodelphinidin" which bonds to proteins in your mouth. You can spit and spit and still not get rid of that unpleasant but relatively harmless flavor. Be advised that even one area of unnoticed unripened fruit can ruin your enjoyment completely. When cooking with persimmons it is said that the addition of one half teaspoon baking soda to one cup pulp will remove any lingering astringency.

Drying removes this astringent flavor, but there are also non-astringent cultivars of persimmon. These were not popular in the past because the fruit cannot be dried for sugar. It becomes tough and hard. These fruits tend to be smaller and flatter than the astringent varieties. They are better in today's economy in that they can be picked earlier, then boxed and shipped long distances. It doesn't matter as much if they are not completely ripe. The *fuyu* is one of these, as is the "Sharon fruit," as persimmons are called in Israel. These fruits you can eat while still slightly crisp, but the flavor is so much better if you wait until they ripen to goosh. Don't be goosh-phobic! Pears or apples may be disgusting when they have ripened to goosh, but this is when a persimmon is at its best.

Persimmon trees are somewhat cold tolerant and can grow in zones 7 through 10. The trees are hardy even to 0°F if they have gone dormant for winter, but they can be killed by the cold. Although I have not tried any on my zone-6 farm, these cultivars of Asian persimmon are said to be especially cold-hardy: "Eureka," "Giambo," "Great Wall," "Peiping," and "Saijo."

The American persimmon *Diospyros virginiana* grows from Connecticut to Florida and as far west as Kansas. It is relatively rare and unknown in my area of western New York, however, so I have no warm, childhood memories of persimmon pudding smothered in cream. My first memories of the persimmon are quite different indeed. When I was a teenager our family moved south to North Carolina so Daddy could further his career with the race cars. Here, American persimmon trees are more common. There was no need to have persimmons in the stores because everyone knew them from their yards and forests. Why would you pay for fruit which dropped by the ton and was mostly wasted? It accumulated in disgusting goosh piles on the sidewalks faster than the raccoons could eat it. We Carpetbaggers didn't even know that the fruits were edible! I picked them up to throw at neighborhood "enemies." They splattered nicely on contact. Even if you did know how sweet they were, you would be unlikely to eat a smashed fallen fruit mixed with dirt, leaves and cigarette butts.

By my early twenties we had returned to rural New York. I cherished my childhood memories of gathering wild raspberries, strawberries and blackberries, my first jobs picking grapes and currants, my mother's home canning of cherries, prunes, pears and peaches. But it was when I moved away to college in the big city that I first encountered persimmons for sale in the supermarket. They were Asian persimmons and looked like large, orange tomatoes. I was sure that they would be delicious as well as exotic, so I bought one without any prior experience. I was salivating already as I cut it into attractive wedges with the serrated knife.

At the first bite the astringency spread throughout my mouth and would not go away despite profuse spitting and rinsing with water. I contemplated the hospital emergency room in case I'd been poisoned by some chemical spray used on the orchard, but after an hour or so the wretched taste faded. Needless to say, the persimmon ended up in the garbage and it was years before I finally dared to try them again and fell in love with them.

❧

Captain John Smith was the first Englishman on record to encounter the American persimmon in colonial Virginia. He wrote "The fruit is like a medlar, it is first green, then yellow and red when it is ripe. If it is not ripe, it will draw a man's mouth awrie with much torment." It is unfortunate that I did not read Captain John Smith until long after my first experience with the persimmon.

Food historians lament the nearly complete lack of information about food in the past. Cooking was considered women's work and therefore not important enough to merit mention in a book or treatise. Certainly our ancestors averted starvation by consuming a great variety of foods—meats, vegetables, roots and fruits many of which are not even considered to be foods today. Our word for "persimmon" is derived from the Algonquian word "*pasiminan*," meaning simply "dried fruit." This suggests that Native Americans were drying persimmons and the English knew about it long before they learned that some of the "date sugar" from the Orient was really dried persimmons as well as dried dates. *Diospyros lotus*, the so-called "date plum," is another related species whose sweet yellow-brown to black-blue fruits have a sweet taste similar to dates. This species is no longer produced commercially because it is susceptible to so many diseases.

The ancients did not have the specificity required in their languages to discuss these things. The Linnaean system of scientific nomenclature was devised by a Swedish botanist in the 1700s. Even today, only a quirky amateur botanist like myself might ask "Do you find the *Diospyros virginiana* tastes as good as the *Diospyros kaki*?" It does. If I asked a non-botanist whether he or she would like a taste of the *kaki* or the *virginiana*, I imagine most people would go for the *virginiana*. There are, however, a few differences, as I will explain, although these are not differences in flavor or sweetness.

# Persimmon

It is often unclear in the scant food writings from the past which food item is being discussed. Is that apple really an apple? Is that corn really Indian corn as in the American usage of the word, or does it just mean the grain most commonly grown in that land, in which case it could be wheat, rye, barley, oats or something else? A text might call something a "medlar," for instance, when what it really means is a "fruit that only becomes edible when it is so ripe and soft as to seem damaged, like a bletted medlar." Avocado, persimmon, cornel, rose hips, rowanberry, medlar and other fruits are in this category.

Although widely known in American folk culture, the American persimmon is generally not available in commerce, as mentioned. The fruit is so sensitive, it doesn't travel or store well. Native Americans sieved the seeds and flower pieces out of the pulp, then dried it into finger-shaped loaves which could be added to flavor gruel, grits, cornbread and puddings. Persimmon was also an important sweetener when the maple sugar was not available. Dried fruit pieces or persimmon jam can sometimes be found in the stores but as fresh fruit, only the Asian varieties are available. References to persimmon beer go back to the early 1700s where in one version the persimmon pulp is paired with a cornmeal mash and honey locust pods, then fermented. Recently one of the early recipes was recreated and persimmon beer is being marketed commercially.

American and Asian persimmons are no different in flavor, but there are differences in size, the "sensitivity of the fruit," and cultural practices associated with it. The fruits of *Diospyros virginiana* are smaller than the Asians, about the size of a large marble, and there are no non-astringent varieties. They are "dioecious," that is to say each individual plant is either male or female. This can lead to pollination problems that are not encountered with the Asian persimmon. The issue is further complicated by the fact that trees from the southern part of the trees' range will not pollinate those from the north.

The Asian fruits must be picked from the tree whereas the Americans tend to drop by themselves. The trees are fifty to seventy-five feet tall and can produce fifty to one hundred pounds of fruit. That's quite a distance to fall for a very delicate fruit, so much of the harvest ends up being ruined. The American persimmons are still fine to cook with but impossible to market as fresh fruit. It helps if you spread a sheet or tarpaulin on the ground to keep them out of the dirt.

I purchased a dozen seedlings so as to be sure to get both males and females but only four of them survived and three of those have turned out to be male. The female is now too tall and robust for me to shake down any of the harvest, so I must patrol beneath the tree by day to beat the animals to the fruit. Diseases and insect pests do not appear to be a problem.

Persimmon trees prefer sandy soils and full sun. They will tolerate dappled shade of an open forest but they do not tolerate wet feet. The deep tap roots make it difficult to transplant specimens of any great size. Give your trees ten to fifteen feet of room on all sides.

"Early Golden" is a cultivated variety of American persimmon selected for its yellowish fruit. "Wabash" was selected for its red fall foliage. Generally persimmon leaves turn yellow in autumn. The flower appears in June and is not particularly noticeable. Some cultivars do not drop their fruit so readily and you can let the harvest freeze on the tree for some interesting winter "popsicles." Good luck getting them down! At least they won't smash so easily if they are frozen solid.

The "Meader" persimmon is the one to go for if you have limited space; it is the only American persimmon to be self-fruitful. It accomplishes this by the occasional production of male flowers which can fertilize the females on the same plant.

The cultivars "Morris Burton," "John Rick" and "Lena" are said to be the best varieties for cooking. These kinds are also the best to freeze on the tree. Most American persimmons will tend to drop off the tree around ripening time.

I'll mention one other cultivar of interest and that is the "*Rosseyanka*." This is a cross between the Asian and the American persimmon accomplished by the botanists in the Ukraine. The fruit is slightly larger than that of the American, about three ounces each, the size of a golf ball. The trees are tall and attractive, like the Americans, but they hold on to their fruits longer, like the Asians. "*Rosseyanka*" suckers profusely from the roots, but I have not yet had any success in transplanting these suckers elsewhere.

Crops can be prolific. At last, I thought, a fruit that will make me rich without any spraying or pruning! I was wrong. I picked the fruit in early November at the time that I noticed that the first ones were ripening. By the time they were ripe in December they weren't so pretty looking. The skin had wrinkled a bit and developed some brownish splotches. They were fine but urban consumers, besides being size queens, demand cosmetic perfection. A fruit worthy of the gods and of special notice by Marco Polo and Commodore Perry was not good enough for them! The market where I had them for sale "on consignment" threw them out just as they finished ripening.

"Oh, they spoiled" was the explanation I received. When I begged to differ they explained "No one would buy something so small and ugly." If only they had returned the fruit to me, I could have eaten persimmon pudding all winter!

# Persimmon Recipes

## About Using Persimmon

Make sure that your fruit has ripened through and through so there is none of that astringent flavor remaining in any areas. If there are any hard areas, give it your tongue test, or just cut it out and discard it. Don't be afraid of goosh! If the skin has stayed intact, your fruit will probably not be spoiled. If it has molded, you will probably be able to smell it. The skin is perfectly edible, perhaps even better that the rest of the fruit. Just mash it well or cut it into smaller pieces so that you don't end up with a large quantity of skin in your mouth at any one time.

For fresh use, pair the fruit with tart apples or berries or yogurt. It also pairs well with bananas. Try it as a "sauce" on ice cream.

## Persimmon Corn Muffins

1/4 cup persimmon pulp
2 tablespoons melted butter
1 cup milk
2 eggs
1/4 cup sugar
1/2 cup walnuts or pecans, chopped fine
1 teaspoon salt
3 teaspoon baking powder
1 cup yellow corn meal
1 cup wheat flour

Bake in well-buttered muffin tins, or line the tins with paper baking cups slightly buttered. Bake at 400°F for 20 minutes.

## Persimmon Swirl Cookies

Prepare a dough consisting of:

1/2 cup butter
1/2 cup brown sugar
1/2 cup white sugar
1 egg

1 teaspoon lemon juice
2 cups flour
1/2 teaspoon baking powder
1/2 teaspoon baking soda
1/2 teaspoon salt

Roll the dough out on waxed paper into a rectangle about one foot wide and only slightly longer, perhaps 15 inches. Cover this with the following filling:

2 cups persimmon pulp
1 cup walnuts in small pieces
1/2 cup white sugar

Roll the dough up the long way and let it chill in the refrigerator for several hours. Preheat the oven to 350°F. Slice the dough into 1/4 inch rounds and place on well-greased cookie sheets with a spatula. Bake for 15 minutes at 350°F. Makes in excess of 50 cookies.

## Persimmon Butter Frosting

2 cups confectioners (powdered) sugar
1/2 cup butter (one stick)
Pinch of salt
1/3 cup persimmon pulp
2 teaspoons lemon juice

This makes an interesting, slightly orange-colored frosting that is good for vanilla cakes, carrot cakes (add some cream cheese too) and cookies.

## Persimmon Oatmeal Cookies

1 cup shortening
3/4 cup brown sugar
1 egg
1 cup persimmon pulp
1 cup flour
1 cup oatmeal
1 teaspoon baking soda
1 teaspoon baking powder
1/2 teaspoon cinnamon
1/2 teaspoon nutmeg
1 cup chopped walnuts
1/2 cup raisins

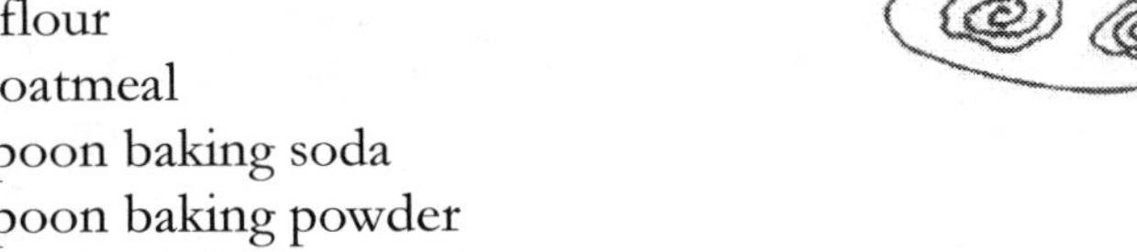

Drop the batter by the spoonful on a greased cookie sheet and bake at 350°F for 12 to 15

minutes. If the batter seems too wet, add a small additional amount of flour. To make the cookies more regular in shape, press down on the top slightly with a butter knife to flatten them before baking.

## Persimmon Banana Bread

2 ripe bananas, mashed
1/2 cup persimmon pulp
2 cups flour
1/2 cup sugar
1/2 teaspoon salt
1 teaspoon baking soda
1/2 cup chopped nutmeats (pecans or walnuts)

Place in a small buttered loaf pan (9 by 5-inch pan) and bake for 1 hour at 350°F. Serve with butter or cream cheese at room temperature.

## Orange Persimmon Pie

Prepare a crust from:

5 tablespoons shortening
1/2 teaspoon salt
1 cup flour
5 tablespoons cold water

Set the crust in a pie plate and preheat the oven to 400°F.

Prepare the filling:

2 large persimmons, completely ripe, or 2 cups of pulp
2 small eggs
1 cup milk
1/2 cup brown sugar
1 tablespoon arrowroot flour (or cornstarch or tapioca flour)
1/4 teaspoon dried orange peel
1/4 teaspoon orange oil

You may choose to use fresh orange zest or to replace part of the liquid with orange juice or to add a few drops of orange oil to make the flavor more prominent.

Pour the filling into the pie shell. Bake at 400°F for 10 minutes, then lower the heat to 350°F and continue to bake for 50 minutes more. Serve with ice cream or whipped cream. It looks like pumpkin pie but it isn't!

## Persimmon Meringue

5 egg whites, beaten to stiff peaks with a bit of the sugar
1 cup persimmon pulp
1/2 cup sugar
2 tablespoons lemon juice
1/4 teaspoon salt

Thoroughly mix the persimmon batter before folding it into the egg whites. Stir only enough to combine the mixtures. The goal is to leave as many bubbles in the egg whites as possible. Butter a 9-inch baking dish and place it in a boiling water bath that reaches half-way up the baking dish. Bake for 1 hour at 350°F.

## Indiana Persimmon Pudding

2 cups persimmon pulp
2 eggs
2 cups flour
1 cup white sugar
1 cup brown sugar
1/2 teaspoon salt
1 teaspoon baking powder
1 teaspoon baking soda
1 teaspoon cinnamon
1 teaspoon allspice

Pour the batter into 2 greased 9-inch round cake pans and bake for 50 minutes at 350°F. Serve the pudding with whipped cream while it is still warm. This recipe is based on the one in Billy Joe Tatum's 1976 classic, *Wild Foods Cookbook and Field Guide*.

Persimmon puddings may also be cooked on top of the stove in boiling water baths. Cover the pudding bowl with aluminum foil or waxed paper tied in place with string. When cooked in this fashion the pudding is lighter than the oven versions. Steam gently for 1 to 2 hours.

All persimmon puddings are basically the same things. A Native American version may use cornmeal instead of wheat flour. You can change the recipe with nuts and spices, the presence or absence of dairy products or liqueurs. A fancy New York Times recipe even included 20 threads of saffron.

Don't use too much or too many spices. Vanilla, cinnamon, nutmeg, allspice, cardamom or ginger are all possibilities. Just don't let them overwhelm the subtle flavor of the persimmons.

## Persimmon Pudding

1 cup persimmon pulp
2 tablespoons cream
1 egg
1 cup flour
2/3 cup sugar
1 teaspoon baking powder
1/4 teaspoon salt
1/4 teaspoon nutmeg
6 walnuts or butternuts

Crack the nuts and add the nutmeats, chopped fine, or position larger pieces on top of the puddings. Bake at 350°F for 45 minutes in individual service-sized bowls placed in a water bath. You can cat this pudding hot with whipped cream or cool with ice cream or yogurt. This makes 4 to 6 servings, depending on the size of your serving bowls and how full you fill them. If baked without the water bath, the puddings will brown more and come out with a more gooey and chewy (but totally acceptable!) texture.

## Persimmon Fruit Pudding

1 large Hachiya persimmon
4 dried figs
4 dried apricots
2 tablespoons golden raisins
Grand Marnier liqueur

Soak the dried fruit in 3 tablespoons Grand Marnier liqueur and 1 tablespoon water. Cut the fruits into smaller pieces and mash the persimmon. You should have about 1 cup of fruit pulp.

1 egg
1 cup flour
3/4 cup sugar
1/2 teaspoon baking powder
1/2 teaspoon baking soda
Pinch of salt
Pinch of allspice

Combine the fruit and the other ingredients. Cook in a greased baking dish at 350°F for 45 minutes until the pudding has browned and set. For a lighter and fluffier pudding, bake in a water bath. If you use individual serving-sized oven-proof bowls you can reduce the baking time slightly.

## Persimmon Jam

2 quarts persimmon pulp
1 cup white sugar
1 cup orange juice
Zest of one orange, grated fine

Cook the jam for about 20 minutes, stirring continuously. Pour into sterile jars and process in a boiling water bath for another 20 minutes. You may enjoy this jam on toast or serve a dollop of it to accompany pork or poultry instead of the usual applesauce or cranberry.

## Persimmon Nut Candy

1 cup persimmon pulp
1 cup brown sugar
1 cup walnut pieces
1 tablespoon butter
2 egg yolks

Cook this slowly in a double boiler for half an hour, then let it cool for one hour. When the candy is cool enough to touch, roll it with your greased fingers into balls about the size of a walnut. Roll these in a dry mixture of:

1/4 cup confectioners sugar
1/4 cup very finely ground walnuts

Let these cool and harden on a plate in the refrigerator. Serve cold.

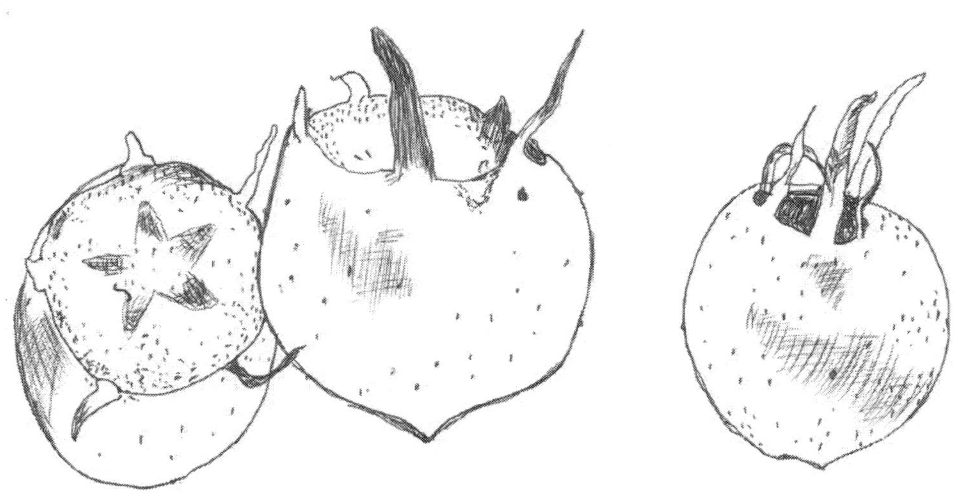

# Medlar

*Mespilus germanica*

The medlar has been in cultivation for over three thousand years. *Mespilus germanica* is not native to Germany despite its name, but it is naturalized there and all across Europe. Originally the medlar grew in the eastern Mediterranean region from Turkey to Persia. It arrived in Greece around 700 B.C.E. The Romans were growing it by 200 B.C.E. Pliny the Elder mentions three cultivars. Medlars are depicted on the mosaics at Pompeii. They were probably originally domesticated in Azerbaijan as this country has the most biodiversity in its wild medlar populations. Oddly enough, fossilized medlar leaves from the interglacial period have been found in Germany. It appears that the medlar is recolonizing areas where it lived before the last Ice Age.

Charlemagne paid tribute to the importance of the medlar to the Holy Roman Empire in his decree *Capitulare de villis* ("Decree Concerning Towns"), in 800 C.E., stating that all royal estates and monasteries should grow medlar trees. If you have ever seen the Unicorn Tapestry at the Cloisters in New York City, you might have noticed that there's a medlar woven into the tapestry to the left of the fountain, near the two dogs. That's the sort of thing antique fruit missionaries tend to notice.

As well known as the medlar was in the ancient world and even up to early modern times for classically informed poets and writers, it has fallen into near obscurity today. It is much more likely now for people to encounter medlars in literature than in real life. When they do, they aren't likely to find much useful material for a modern-day marketing campaign! That is because the medlar's association with the primal aspects of life and death, or sex and decay, was intertwined with its importance as food and medicine. To make the medlar into a "respectable" fruit, you'd have to wipe out much of its long past. For example, D.H. Lawrence, in his poem "Medlars and Sorb Apples," writes,

*I love you, rotten*
*Delicious rottenness.*
*I love to suck you out from your skins*
*So brown and soft and coming suave,*
*So morbid, as the Italians say.*
*What a rare, powerful, reminiscent flavor*
*Comes out of your falling through the stages*
*of decay;*

The poem goes on to call the medlar "wineskins of brown morbidity" and "autumnal excrementa." Lawrence is drawing from an already long tradition involving the medlar to play on Christian associations of death, rottenness and sexuality. Similar associations are found in earlier literature. Chaucer, in "The Reeve's Tale," compares his old age to a medlar as in,

*We olde men, I drede, so fare we;*
*Til we be roten, kan we nat be rype.*

Two hundred years later, the "rotten/ripe" theme is still going strong, as in the Elizabethan playwright, Thomas Dekker, who writes in *The Honest Whore*, "Women are like medlars. No sooner ripe but rotten." Shakespeare's use of medlar imagery in *Romeo and Juliet* is downright graphic:

*Now will he sit under a medlar tree*
*And wish his mistress were the kind of fruit*
*As maids call medlars when they laugh alone.*
*O Romeo, that she were, O that she were*
*An open etcetera, and thou a pop'rin pear!*

It took until the 1960s for the euphemism "open etcetera" to be replaced on stage by the words long understood to be meant by it, which were none other than "open arse." Don't blame Shakespeare for that. The Old English name for "medlar" was, quite simply, "openaers," as attested by Aelfric of Eynsham's eleventh-century *Grammatica latino-saxonica.* A French term was even more specific, *cul de chien* ("ass of dog").

References like these hardly encourage us to view the medlar as the luxury taste that it is. But in ancient times the fruit held more positive associations with women and fertility. It was also very important as the last fruit harvest of the year to ripen. Known to cultivation for over thirty centuries, the medlar was undoubtedly being enjoyed by cavemen long before that. One evening as I was pondering the meaning of the medlar and its lore after a long and monotonous toiling to produce a medlar sauce, I fell into a dream-like state in which I saw two cave girls playing a game. The object of the game was to see who would grow up to have more children. It reminded me of the modern-day children's game "he loves me, he loves me not" played while plucking a flower's petals. In my dream state, I watched as the girls carefully used a flint-stone cutting edge to slice the fruit's skin, then placed the fruit between them at the mouth and gleefully tore the medlar apart and chewed to see which one of them had gotten more seeds. The medlar is a powerful fruit!

In heathen times the temples had their vestal virgins but also their temple prostitutes, both male and female. Sex could even be a part of the ritual devotions, another way to gain the gods' favor and to bless and ensure the continued fertility of the earth. Such an attitude is far removed from the sexual customs of the Middle Ages when the medlar became so reviled in literature. Is it rotten or is it ripe? It is clear that the medlar is a sacred pagan fruit of long ago which has gotten a "bum" rap in the sex-negative Christian era. Its associations with women and fertility have been perverted into a fixation upon the evils of all sexuality. The "open arse" jokes denigrate the fruit further and create a sort of scatology around the medlar. "To meddle with someone" has meant "to have sex with" since Elizabethan times and this expression is related to the medlar, the fruit and its lore, whether as a pun or as a direct derivation.

The Italians have an odd proverb: "*Se vedete la nespola piangete perch'e' l'ultimo frutto dell'estate; se vedete una donna con un prete, che dica il pater noster non ci pensate.*" "If you see medlar, you have reason to cry, as it's the last fruit of the summer; if you see a woman with a priest, don't think she might be reciting the *pater noster.*"

The biggest clue to the ultimate sacred nature of the medlar is the plethora of denunciations and jokes against it. Medlars are not any kind of "stud fruit." There are no aphrodisiac claims in the herbal lore. As a medicinal herb, medlar is more associated with fertility, menstruation, avoiding miscarriage and maintaining intestinal health. Still the fruit has somehow become associated with licentiousness, sex, whoredom, anal intercourse, vaginal intercourse and the putrefaction of the body because of sex. How could this be? This sounds like a lesson in "original sin." The medlar might just as well be the forbidden fruit itself! Although usually depicted as an apple, the *Old Testament* does not identify the fruit specifically. Some scholars think that it might be the fig tree instead, as there were some wild rites of yore to honor the Goddess and her figs. Whatever the case, it seems that not the apple, not the fig, but the medlar has inherited most of that "bad" reputation.

It is time to look at the medlar's long heritage and give this fruit more of the respect to which it is due. The fag and whore jokes go back a mere six or seven centuries, but the medlar was in cultivation for over two thousand years before that. Before the Christmas stocking had an orange in it, people looked forward to medlar sauce to serve at Yuletide along with that roast boar. The medlar ripening season begins around Hallowe'en and continues on past the winter solstice. Certainly our ancestors were most grateful for a fruit that made its appearance at this most special time of the year.

Medlars are often described as tasting like applesauce, but this is more what they look like when prepared for eating than what they really taste like. Why would anyone go to so much trouble in order to produce a small quantity of "applesauce"? They wouldn't. This is just like saying that a quince is an apple which you have to cook and is therefore not worth the trouble. To me, the medlar tastes more like the tamarind (*Tamarindus indica*). It is tamarind that gives the tangy flavor to Worcestershire sauce. Medlars are also a "sub-acid" fruit, quite sweet in themselves but with a little bit of tang. The tamarind is tangy enough to stand up to most foods and spices it is paired with, but medlars are more subtle and their flavor is more easily overwhelmed by other flavors. The method of preparation is similar, however, in that you scoop out the pulp and seeds, discard the skin or seed pod, add a small amount of water and cook gently until the seeds separate easily from the pulp.

*Quenepa* (*Melicoccus bijugatus*) is another fruit that reminds me of the medlar although its taste is sweeter, with vague hints of citrus or melon. It is a tropical American fruit that looks like an oversized bunch of grapes hanging on a tree. You discard the skin and eat the fruit layer which is barely one-sixteenth of an inch thick and adheres tightly to the large spherical seed. Children never tire of trying to chew every last bit of goodness off of the seeds. Medlar seeds are smaller and oddly ridged—but in the same way, children carefully chew every bit of fruit off of the seeds, one by one. Some *quenepas* have two fruit-coated seeds in one skin. It is considered good luck to find a double-seeded fruit like this one, rather like finding a four-leafed clover for us. To guarantee good luck, you proclaim "*Guaril!*" when you find one, which is the Taino Indian word for "twin."

The most interesting aspect of a fruit for me is not the taste, or the vitamins, and not the commercial potential—but the fruit lore. I am fascinated by the words used to name the fruits, the words we use to describe them, their associations with mythology, their medicinal uses—the complete ethnobotany. It is fascinating how the *quenepa* can make Spanish speakers cry out in a language that has been gone for three hundred years.

The medlar is particularly rich in lore after being in cultivation for so long, and yet I feel that, as with the lost language of the Tainos, even more may be lost than what we know. The medlar was so thoroughly woven into the tapestry of life, with both its usefulness and its lore, that we have much non-verbal evidence of its importance. Wood of the medlar tree is particularly good for making spear points, cudgels, clubs and walking sticks because it is so hard and durable, for example. The Dutch used medlar wood for windmill parts. The Germans traditionally used medlar wood to make cudgels for "thrashing wicked women." The Basques perfected the use of medlar wood in the making of their traditional *makila*, a walking stick and a weapon and a personal icon all rolled into one. The staff is first carved into a living medlar tree, decoratively scarred and left to grow for another year or two. After that the wood is cut, the bark is peeled and the staff is fitted out with a steel point and bands of brass, silver and even gold. Spells, proverbs or verses are carved into the stick. It must first be hardened with fire and seasoned in pork fat. Don't "meddle" with anyone armed with a *makila*! Some of the fancier models even contained a hidden sword. *Cotignac*, the traditional marmalade from Orleans, France, prepared from medlar, quince and orange, was given to Joan of Arc when she first triumphantly entered that city, and to the French kings thereafter.

With a history and reputation like this, of course I had to try my hand at raising medlars. Fortunately, there are many cultivars of *Mespilus germanica* still available in the nursery trade today. The oldest and supposedly best-flavored variety of these is Nottingham from England, also known as Neapolitan, probably because it came from Naples, Italy before that. The fruit is about an inch and a half in diameter, yellow-brown with some russeting. I have not had luck with this variety, however. My Nottingham medlar died, as did its replacements the following year.

"Breda Giant" is a Dutch cultivar that did grow for me. Medlars were especially important in the Netherlands as evidenced by the fact that the cities of Lochem, Beek en Donk and Geldern feature the medlar on their traditional city emblems. Breda is the medlar to get for production; it is far more productive than my other varieties. The flesh is dry and brownish-orange dulling to brown as it cooks.

"Russian Giant" is an attractive medlar easily two inches across with more pulp than the other varieties, but I've only managed to get three or four on my tree at best while "Breda Giant" gives me dozens more fruits each year as it increases in size.

My favorite cultivar so far is the Italian "*Pucimol*." The fruits are not overly large but there is a sizeable harvest. The flesh is more liquid-like than the other medlars I grow and a bit grayish-brown in color. The taste is excellent, especially when eaten as fresh fruit.

There are many other varieties which I have not yet grown—the Dutch, the English Royal, French Seedless, Italian "*Castel Raniero*" and "*Supermol*," the Spanish "*Nadal*." There must be many additional varieties of medlar in Turkey, as well, where medlars are eaten fresh, pickled, boiled, made into vinegar and pressed and dried into paste.

Medlars have beautiful leaves in the fall that turn yellow with splotches of orange, red and brown. There are also "*argento-variegata*" medlars which have white-flecked leaves whereas "*aureo-variegata*" turn more golden yellow in the fall. With medlars, you can plant one variety and still get a fruit crop because medlars set their fruit parthenocarpically, a fancy way of saying they do not need to cross-pollinate with other varieties in order to set fruit.

It's a little ironic that this fruit so associated with sex can produce its crop asexually! They say a medlar can live for three hundred years. Now that my medlars are over ten years old they give me hundreds of fruits each year. There are also special landscaping varieties of medlar which are not grown for their fruit particularly, but for their usefulness in hedges and for the fantastic shapes they sometimes achieve.

Wild medlars still have thorns and my trees occasionally develop one at the end of a branch, rather like the buckthorn tree does, to which medlars are related. Like any other fruit tree, medlars have various pests and diseases. The trees are somewhat susceptible to fireblight, a bacterial infection which also bothers quince and pear. New leaves at the tips of branches may turn brown or black and die; these should be cut off and burned to stop the spread of the disease. Medlars are subject to insect damage the same as apple and quince. Some medlars have a black discoloration around the seeds. Is this a fungal problem or has some insect been feeding on the seeds? Because medlar is no longer a crop of any economic importance to us, there is a corresponding lack of modern scientific information on these subjects.

The one other medlar species in existence has the honor, or perhaps the misfortune, of being one of the rarest plants in the world. Stern's medlar, or *Mespilus canescens*, was discovered in 1990 in Arkansas in a grove of about twenty-five individuals. It has blue-green leaves and white flowers and is considered endangered. It has not been observed to set viable seed in the wild although the Center for Plant Conservation is attempting to propagate this rare plant at the Missouri Botanical Garden in St. Louis. I am sad to say that I have not found any commentary on the quality of the fruit. Perhaps this is because no one has yet been allowed to eat it.

# Medlar

ıs friends in December by approaching a medlar tree, ing the skin with my canine tooth and then greedily ges under pressure from my fingers. I always let a few ter eating. A more elegant approach would be a medlar on.

ut they really come into their own when briefly cooked l bit of sweetening. You can get a little more pulp off mes less fibrous and takes on the silky texture of freeze or to can for later use. Medlar pies, puddings, y duckling of a fruit begin to shine! Medlar is certainly prefer to emphasize its specialness with allspice, mace e and unique flavor of medlar be overwhelmed by too

products for sale myself, but in 2008 an item in the *New* made of medlars, available for sale from a fancy Park Avenue chocolatier for the mere cost of seventeen dollars for seven ounces! It was suggested that this rarity be used to complement roast pork, a traditional food usage of the medlar. At this price my five young trees are putting out over five hundred dollars of crop each year! In my recipe section, I have tried to focus on other uses of the medlar than for accompanying pork, but for anyone interested in researching medlar products for sale themselves, perhaps less dear than "*confiture de nèfle*," try Italian, Turkish or Iranian stores. A medlar jelly is still available from Wilkin & Sons, Ltd. of Tip Tree, England, as well.

I had never even met anyone else who had eaten a medlar until I took some over to my nonagenarian city neighbor, Dottie, next door. "Oh those," she said. "I haven't seen those in a long time. My aunt used to have a tree of them. They are very good, of course, but the little bit that you get makes you wonder if it was worth all the work you did to get it." Dottie remembered playing under the table as a toddler in the 1920s while the ladies of the household tediously scooped the medlars, spoonful by spoonful, to prepare a sauce for the evening meal. Dottie got her own bowl and one medlar to eat with a spoon under the table.

A few years later, I took some medlars to another neighbor, Hasan. "*Mušmula!*" he cried, "I haven't seen those since we lived in Bosnia!" He grabbed a medlar out of the basket, yanked off the skin by peeling strips from the flower end, ate the pulp and spit out the seeds just like that. The second medlar had some frass on one side. "Bugs got that one," he said, throwing it into the bushes and going on to happily eat the rest. According to Hasan, medlars are sometimes available in the market in Bosnia but more usually they are grown in people's yards. Sometimes people make preserves, he reported, but usually medlars are eaten fresh.

❧

I took my first sizeable medlar crop to the produce manager at my food co-op. In the past she had tried to sell some of my other rare fruits with mixed success. This time she put her foot down and refused, saying that she didn't want to sell things that were "rotten." I decided to donate my crop to the co-op instead and arranged to have an in-service for staff to teach them about medlars. The teach-in was not a success. The staff was horrified when I ate a medlar in front of them, expecting me to keel over any second. Not many dared to taste the free samples I provided.

I tried them on my family next. My niece replied haughtily "I don't eat things that are brown." I reminded her of brownies, chocolate cake, gravy and a number of other familiar comfort foods to no avail. But on another occasion she did try some pear-medlar salad just to please me. Sadly for my mission of promoting a medlar renaissance, she hurled her first bite back up while her sister filmed the whole drama on her cellphone and posted it on the internet. "Girl Hurls Medlar-Pear Salad" is probably still going around out there in cyberspace somewhere.

So, you may need to use trickery to get people to give medlar a chance. Don't let them see the ripe fruit; just present the finished bread, pie or sauce. Let them believe it's "pumpkin pie." When they ask why it tastes so different, say "Maybe because I spiced it with allspice?" Only when they are hooked and begging for more will you reveal the shocking truth: they partook of the dreaded medlar!

In order to experience medlars as our ancestors did you will need to have hundreds. Keep them in flat boxes or trays as they ripen. Traditionally they were kept on the floor cushioned with straw or hay. You can't keep them in baskets because a medlar that ripens at the bottom of the pile will be crushed by the weight of those above it. You need to run your fingers across them every few days to determine by touch which ones are starting to ripen. You will need fifty ripe at the same time to make that sauce for the wild boar. A dozen would suffice to prepare a luxury like medlar sauce swirled in cream. You'll need over a hundred to make a medlar cheese. (Medlar cheese is really just another presentation of medlar sauce, cooked and dried and sweetened. It was cut into chunks and eaten as an accompaniment to dairy cheese.) Our ancestors also knew medlar juice drinks. Medlars were cooked and mashed in boiling water, then filtered. The juice could be added to cider, mead or wines. This juice may be boiled down yet again to produce fine medlar preserves as is still done in France and Italy today.

❧

The first medlars will begin to ripen around Hallowe'en when the stark white interior softens or liquefies, turns shades of brown and tan and falls to the ground. Be careful not to step on them! Clean any medlars gathered from off of the ground and inspect them for any damage from mice, earthworms or raccoons. By mid-November you can pick whatever fruits remain on the tree with a good chance of their eventually ripening. It is not true that medlars require a frost to ripen, as we commonly hear, but the longer they remain on the tree the sweeter they will be when they finally do ripen.

When it comes to ripeness, medlar has to look rotten. It even smells a bit vinaigrous, rather like an old, empty wine bottle. The papery skin breaks easily. This can open up the fruit to insect and fungal damage. The instructions for keeping your medlars after you have harvested them can never be repeated too often! Lay your medlars out flat and not touching each other. They must be kept in single layers in a cool environment as you wait for them to ripen. Left in a basket, the lower ones might ripen first and smash under the weight of those above it. If kept in a warm kitchen on display, your curiosities will quickly dehydrate and turn into rocks that never ripen at all. Check them every few days so you'll know which ones are starting to ripen. Sort them on trays according to degrees of ripeness—those that are hard as rocks, those beginning to soften, and those all ready for eating. Unripe medlars can last for months if treated properly. Even a fully ripe medlar can last for a week or two if its skin remains unbroken.

"To blet" is an ugly word coined by the botanist John Lindley in 1839 specifically for medlar and medlar-like fruits. It means "to undergo that kind of change which results in the formation of a brown color, without putrefaction, as in the fruit of the medlar." It comes from the French word "*blesser*" meaning "to wound" because a medlar isn't ripe until it has softened and the skin has taken on a puffy and bruised appearance. The tannins change into sugars and the fruit becomes so soft that it is easily damaged by the slightest rough treatment. As the hard fruit of the medlar undergoes this process, the inner white flesh changes to yellow and then to brown. In other words, as it ripens it begins to look rotten, which is why the medlar has been forced to stand in for so many jokes on this point. In any case, I prefer the Italian word *ammezzire*, "to be left to soften."

In the more remote past the words for "medlar" in various languages may have denoted not just this one fruit but a whole class of fruits which share this same way of ripening. The etymology of *mespilus*/medlar is still being debated. In some old texts it seems to refer to the hawthorn or to the cornelian cherry or *Sorbus* fruits, all of which are small fruits with a peculiar way of softening dramatically as they ripen. In a similar vein the ancients used the word "apple" to refer to a whole class of desirable, large fruits, not just what we think of as an apple today. "Corn" used to mean whatever kind of grain was grown in that land whereas today we just think of maize. It seems that we demand a greater degree of specificity in our botanical words today than did our ancestors.

❧

I first heard of medlars not as food or as medicine, but as a traditional element in the design of the herb garden. If you look at a large medlar fruit on a tree from below, the flower end of the fruit often forms a perfect five-pointed star—a pentagram. I have attended rituals of the Reclaiming tradition of paganism where the high priest at a magical moment cuts an apple in half and displays two perfect five-pointed stars. Who knew? Nobody cuts an apple in half that way! The high priestess could just as well open her hands suddenly to reveal two medlars with their natural external pentagrams for equal dramatic effect. This will set some minds to wondering: What are those old-timey magical fruits and how can I use them?

In addition to utilitarian objects made from its wood, there is no shortage of herbal medicinal and magical uses for the medlar according to its lore. A cross made from the wood was thought to scare away evil spirits and protect babies from harm. According to the herbal "doctrine of signatures," the medlar could be of benefit to any of those body parts which it most resembled. The fruit is considered to resemble the vagina and the anus and so would have been considered beneficial to those important human organs, and the oddly shaped seeds or "stones" were seen as reminiscent of kidney stones.

Medlar with honey was taken to calm morning sickness. Leaves and unripened fruit might be put in bath water to protect against miscarriage, to ease hemorrhoids and to regulate excess menstrual flow. Powdered leaf and seeds were sprinkled on wounds to stop bleeding and to promote healing. Mix wine with parsley root and powdered medlar seeds to create a traditional remedy for those kidney stones medlar seeds were so reminiscent of.

Mouth-puckering unripened medlar fruit mixed with water can produce an astringent mouthwash. Unripened fruit if eaten can cause constipation, which is a *de facto* remedy for diarrhea. Culpeper, the famous herbalist, notes that "the fruit eaten by Women with Child stayeth their Longing after unusual Meats." Medlar's astringent action can also protect the lining of the intestine. Unripened fruits and leaves were dried to use in these medical pastes and decoctions dating back to the days of the Roman Empire and earlier.

❧

My favorite appearance of the medlar in more recent literature is in a short story by Saki entitled "The Boar Pig." A couple of social climbers in Edwardian England are trying to crash the garden party event of the season to which they have not been invited by going in the back way. They end up spending the afternoon in an inner walled gooseberry garden because a mischievous tomboy named Matilda has let loose "Tarquin Superbus," a large and unfriendly boar. Finally, Matilda consents to help the trapped ladies to escape for a considerable sum of money. She climbs down out of her perch in a medlar tree and lures the boar back to its pen by throwing him a trail of overripe medlars.

"Come, Tarquin, dear old boy; you know you can't resist medlars when they're rotten and squashy."

The ladies realize that they have been bilked when a mere schoolgirl so easily brings about their rescue without running off to summon the field hands.

"Well, I never! The little minx!"

Matilda donates her perhaps ill-gotten gain to the Fresh Air Fund which was the charitable excuse for holding the garden party in the first place. This story completely rehabilitates the medlar's dubious image in literature, making it an instrument of salvation and charity rather than corruption and downfall!

# Medlar Recipes

## About Using Medlars

There are many presentations for the medlar. First of all it is a fresh fruit available in the late fall or early winter. It could be eaten out of hand by the peasants or placed on fine china with a little silver spoon for the nobility. When cooked or mashed into sauces, medlars were eaten with cream or used to accompany meats, especially wild game or roast pork. Medlar sauces can be used to create pies and puddings as well. Medlar juice or medlar water is a drink in its own right; it was also added to wines, mead or cider to create subtle differences in flavor. When cooked, sweetened and slightly dried, medlar can become a paste, "leather" or "cheese." In this form it could be sliced and served with sausages or dairy cheeses. (Guava paste is still served in similar ways in South American cuisine or *membrillo,* quince paste, in Spain.) Medlar is also processed into a variety of jellies, preserves, jams and marmalades. *Cotignac* was a special honorific marmalade mixing medlar, quince and orange. Another traditional marmalade mixed medlar with sloe berries. Medlars were roasted whole with butter and cloves or mixed with beaten egg whites to produce meringues.

## Medlar Pulp

15 minutes of your time
One dozen ripe medlars
1 bowl
1 pan
1 compost receptacle
1 knife
1 spoon
Reading glasses (if you use them)

Here is how to pulp a medlar most easily. Cut each medlar in half lengthwise from the stem to the leafy calyx end. You are after the middle 1/8 inch of soft pulp that rests between the seedy core and the papery skin. Insert your spoon, resting it on the seedy core. Scoop inwards and upwards, using your finger to press the skin downwards onto the spoon and aid in removal of the pulp. Let the good pulp or paste accumulate in the bowl one teaspoonful at a time

Some areas of your medlars may have blue, black or white molds. Avoid scooping from these areas and discard them immediately into the compost. Smell the pulp from these fruits to make sure it smells good to you. You don't want to spoil the whole batch! Luckily the molds, like the frass, seem to inhabit the seed core areas more readily than the fruit pulp.

Frass is sawdust-like in appearance. It is from the German word *fressen*, to devour, and can refer to piles of fecal matter left by termites in wood or to insect damage inside of fruits. It is dry, brown and granular. It doesn't smell bad but its bitter taste and gritty texture can ruin your final product. Hold your medlar so that the frass falls into the compost as you scoop, not into the good stuff. With practice it becomes easy to avoid frass and fungus and to harvest high quality pulp from imperfect fruit.

Medlar pulp ranges from dry to wet, from dark brown to tan, orange or even dull yellow. The marbled tan and white areas of pulp that look most inviting to us are actually the least ripe but still acceptable, as long as it has softened. Patrol your pulp with extreme diligence so as to notice any stray white maggots. This is why reading glasses may be needed! If you are processing 50 medlars or more, there *will* be some. These are not the insects that produced the frass earlier in the year inside the fruit but interlopers who have come for the tasty juices that bleed through the papery skins.

Take care to dispose of all moldy and insect-damaged areas immediately. Reserve the good seeds and skin residues in the pan for the "second pressing," if you will, to produce the juice.

## Medlar Sauce

3 tablespoons medlar pulp
3 tablespoons water
1/2 tablespoon honey or other sweetener to taste

Take your medlar pulp and set it to cook on the stove with equal parts of water and a bit of honey or other sweetener. Let the pulp boil briefly, then simmer. Stir in more water if needed and cook to the consistency that you prefer. The motley spoonfuls of pulp quickly cook together to make a fine sauce. The warm sauce can be served with roast pork and wild game. The cooled sauce can be served with cream, ice cream or yogurt. Larger amounts of sauce can easily be canned or frozen and used later to prepare other recipes in this book.

My medlar season begins around Hallowe'en and lasts until New Year's, but with canning the sauce and freezing the pulp this season can be extended to all year round!

## Medlar Juice

Begin your "second pressing" with the unsightly pulped seeds and skins. Check once more to exclude mold and frass, then run water to cover the medlar pieces so that they are just floating. Bring to a boil and let simmer for 15 minutes. Stir and crush with a spoon or masher.

Set up a colander in a bowl and line it with cheesecloth. Some people may prefer to use a food mill or sieve or other filtering method. Pour off the juice and let the fruit residues drain. Discard residues to compost. Let your juice settle, then carefully pour it off leaving behind the last thick half inch or so of liquid. This liquid is a luscious deep-brown color and undoubtedly contains some of the best flavor but it also harbors a bitter slurry of the frass that you may have missed. Discard it or refilter it later at your own risk.

Medlar juice is just fine as it is, slightly sweet and very refreshing. You can upgrade it by adding a touch of sweetener. Return it to the stove and add a bit of pulp more, freshly scooped, for another upgrade. Stir until the pulp has been worked in and your juice has a pleasing consistency.

If you have a crop surplus, you can make a higher quality juice yet—a first pressing! Take as many perfectly ripe medlars as you can spare for the project. Put them in a kettle and run water until they are just floating. Bring to a boil and let simmer for about an hour, accompanied by some smashing and mashing as the fruit cooks enough to begin to come apart. Drain and filter. Add more water if it seems too pulpy but do be sure to discard the bottom inch of sludge after the juice has settled.

Medlar juice is pale brown and looks like cider but has its own unique flavor. Presumably it could ferment just like cider does, but I haven't tried this yet. Enjoy the juice plain or mix it with wine, mead, cider, ice tea, seltzer or other fruit juice of choice. I have left medlar juice in my refrigerator for months at a time without its even fermenting. The pulp does separate from the juice and sink to the bottom of the bottle. Just shake the juice before serving.

## Traditional Medlar Serving Suggestions

- Eaten out of hand (or spoon)
- Pulp or sauce with cream
- Baked whole
- Stewed with butter
- Roasted with butter and clove
- Eaten with wine or brandy or other liquor
- Eaten with game
- Jam, marmalade or jelly
- Meringue
- Mousse or pudding
- Medlar juice drinks
- Medlar "cheese"
- Traditional Christmas fruit (before oranges)
- Medlar pie

## Medlar Pie Recipe from 1653

*To make a Tart of Medlars.*

*Take Medlers that be rotten, and stamp them, and set them upon a chafin dish with coales, and beat in two Yolks of Eggs, boiling till it be somewhat thick, then season it with sugar, cinamon and ginger, and lay it in a paste.* (And then put it into a crust)

## Medlar Custard Pie

2 cups medlar sauce (about 100 ripe medlars)
1/2 cup sugar
3 eggs, separated if you want to make meringue
1 cup milk
1 teaspoon lemon juice
1/4 teaspoon cardamom or mace
2 tablespoons melted butter

Make an open pie shell from 4 tablespoons shortening and 3/4 cup flour, a pinch of salt and as little water as possible. Reserve egg whites for meringue if desired. Pour the custard into the pie shell and bake at 425°F for 10 minutes, then at 350°F for 30 minutes longer or until custard sets. For the meringue, beat egg whites stiff with 1/3 cup sugar and a pinch of salt and a pinch of cream of tartar. Set the oven back up to 425°F. Top the pie with the meringue and bake 5 minutes more until nicely browned.

## Medlar Pie

Prepare an open pie crust from 1 cup flour, 5 tablespoons shortening, a pinch of salt and only enough water so that your dough can hold together.

1 1/2 cups medlar sauce (More is better!)
2/3 cup brown sugar
2 eggs
1 cup milk
1/4 cup cream
Pinch of salt
1/4 teaspoon mace
2 1/2 tablespoons tapioca flour or arrowroot flour

Bake pie at 450°F for 10 minutes, then 375°F for 50 minutes until nicely browned and set.

## Medlar Nut Pie

Here is a nut pie without that cloying sweetness of which most pecan pies are so guilty.

Prepare the preceding recipe for medlar pie. Before baking, sprinkle the pie surface (or artfully decorate) with 1/4 cup of chopped walnuts, butternuts or pecans. Go all out and use all three kinds of nuts if you can. Add a pinch or two of sugar around the nuts to caramelize during baking.

## Medlar Almond Pie

Prepare a crust from:

1/2 cup wheat flour
1/2 cup spelt or barley flour
1/4 cup almond meal
5 tablespoons shortening
1/2 teaspoon cardamom

Add only enough water or milk for the dough to stay together.

Filling:

1 1/2 cup medlar sauce
2/3 cup brown sugar
2 eggs
1 cup milk
1/4 cup cream
1/2 teaspoon salt
1/2 teaspoon allspice
2 1/2 tablespoons arrowroot powder
Pinch of almond meal

If you don't have almond meal, you can create it by running almonds in the food processor until they are the consistency of cornmeal. Bake 10 minutes at 450°F, then 50 minutes at 375°F.

## Medlar Apple Stripe Pie

Here you follow a medlar pie recipe (no top crust) but also insert a stripe of chopped apples. Peel one apple and chop fine. Cook briefly by frying the apple pieces in butter until they start to soften. Sugar it lightly, then put it into your crust of choice. Make sure that the apple is partly cooked and chopped into small pieces so that the texture will not contrast too much with the overlying stripe of medlar.

Prepare a custard of:

1 cup sweetened medlar sauce

2 eggs
1 cup milk
1/4 cup cream or half-and-half
Pinch of allspice

Pour the custard over the layer of chopped apples and bake at 375°F until set, about an hour. Medlar is often said to be similar to applesauce but I am of the opinion that this is primarily due to the similarities in color and texture, not the tastes. This pie contrasts the flavors of the two fruits in a very nice way. Don't use cinnamon or the usual apple pie spices, as these are too strong for the subtle taste of the medlars.

## Medlar Almond Tarte

Prepare a slightly sweet open face pie crust by adding a spoonful of sugar to your pie crust recipe of choice. Fill it with:

1 cup medlar sauce
3 eggs
1 teaspoon almond extract
1 cup cream
1 tablespoon tapioca flour
1/4 cup almond flakes, chopped fine
1/8 teaspoon mace
1/8 teaspoon cardamom
1/3 cup brown sugar

Bake 10 minutes at 450°F, then 50 minutes at 375°F.

## Medlar Cheesecake

This will cook in a deep pie pan. Grease your pan with the solid butter, then use the rest of it in the recipe.

4 ounces sour cream
8 ounces Neufchatel cheese or cream cheese at room temperature
3 eggs
2/3 cup medlar pulp (about 2 quarts ripe fruit)
2/3 cup sugar
2 tablespoons pastry flour
1/4 teaspoon allspice
1 teaspoon vanilla
1 teaspoon lemon juice
4 tablespoons (half a stick) of melted butter

Sprinkle 2 tablespoons ground walnuts on the pie pan. Pour on your batter and bake at 325°F for one hour.

## Medlar Cheesecake II

Prepare an ordinary pie crust. Use 2/3 of the dough in the pie plate and reserve 1/3 of the dough to create the lattice top.

2 cups flour
1 teaspoon baking soda
1/4 teaspoon salt
1 stick butter
8 tablespoons water to bind, more if needed.

Cut the flour and the butter together with the other ingredients. If the dough is too wet and sticky to work, dust it with additional flour until it behaves. Divide the dough into two balls, one containing 2/3 of the dough and a smaller ball for the remaining 1/3. Chill. Roll out and place in a pie plate. Roll out the smaller ball and reserve it to cut into strips for an interwoven lattice top. Prepare the filling:

5 tablespoons chopped hazelnuts
1 tablespoon flour or other thickener
15 ounce ricotta cheese
4 eggs
7/8 cup sugar
1/2 teaspoon vanilla
1 1/4 cups medlar paste
1/2 teaspoon allspice

Pour the filling into the pie shell, and weave the lattice top with strips of dough about 1/2 inch-wide. Use water and your fingers to glue the lattice strips to the crust. Medlar is surprisingly sweet on its own; the extra sugar here is to sweeten the cheese. Bake at 375°F for 45 minutes or until set. For another interesting variation on this cheesecake, try using 1 cup white (wheat) flour, 1/2 cup rye flour and 1/2 cup walnuts. Run it through your food processor to grind the nuts into a fine powder. Omit the hazelnut bits in the filling.

## Medlar Walnut Cheesecake

This cheesecake will cook in a pie pan. To prepare the crust, grind the first three ingredients in a food processor until fine.

1 cup white flour
1/2 cup rye flour
1/2 cup walnuts
1/4 teaspoon salt
6 tablespoons shortening
1 teaspoon baking powder
1/8 teaspoon allspice
1 teaspoon white sugar

Chill the dough before rolling it out. (Reserve 1/3 of it to form the lattice top later.) Prepare the filling:

1 cup ricotta cheese
1 cup medlar pulp
2 eggs
1/4 teaspoon allspice
1/4 cup half-and-half
1/2 cup sugar

Pour the filling into the pie shell and complete your lattice top. Bake at 350°F for 45 minutes to one hour.

## Medlar Cake

1 cup medlar sauce
2 eggs
2/3 cup sugar
4 tablespoons cream
1/2 cup butter (Grease your pans first, then add remaining butter)
1 cup white flour
1 cup barley and spelt flour, mixed
1/4 teaspoon mace
1/4 teaspoon ginger
1/4 teaspoon salt
1/8 teaspoon powdered cloves

Bake in a 9 by 12-inch baking pan, well greased, or in two cake round pans for layer cake 350°F for 40 minutes. Note that the cake round pans will cook more quickly.

## Medlar Almond Pancake

1/2 cup medlar sauce
1 cup buttermilk
1 cup wheat flour
1 egg
2 teaspoons baking soda
1 teaspoon allspice
2 tablespoons oil
2 tablespoons almond flakes

Pour this batter into a buttered cast-iron fry pan and cook in the oven at 375°F for 45 minutes or until set. Serve with butter and syrup.

## Medlar Nut Bread

1 cup medlar sauce
1/2 cup sugar
1/4 cup butter
1/2 cup milk
1 teaspoon baking soda
1 3/4 cups flour
Pinch of salt
1/2 cup nuts
1/8 teaspoon spice of choice: cardamom, mace, nutmeg, cinnamon, allspice, ginger or clove

Pour batter into a small greased loaf pan. Bake at 350°F for about 50 minutes.

Medlar is a subtle flavor, so don't overpower it with spices. Chop the nuts fine (hazelnuts, walnuts or pecans) but leave a few pieces whole to decorate the top of the loaf.

## Medlar Nut Bread II

3/4 cup medlar sauce
1 cup buttermilk
1 egg
2 tablespoons oil
1 cup wheat flour
1 cup mixed flours (spelt, barley, buckwheat, whatever)
Pinch of salt
1/2 tablespoon baking powder
1/2 tablespoon baking powder
1/2 cup brown sugar
1 teaspoon allspice
1/4 cup flaked almonds
1 teaspoon vanilla
1 dozen raisins

Bake at 375°F in a greased loaf pan for one hour.

## Medlar Pudding Custard

1/2 cup medlar sauce
2 eggs
1 1/2 cup milk
Pinch allspice

Pour into buttered ramekins or individual pudding cups. Bake in a "bain-marie" water bath for 30 minutes at 375°F, perhaps longer, until set. Serve chilled.

## Medlar Pudding

3 tablespoons Medlar paste
4 tablespoons cornstarch
2 1/2 cup milk
4 tablespoons sugar
1/8 teaspoon allspice
1 1/2 tablespoons hazelnuts
Pinch of salt

Roast 1 1/2 tablespoons hazelnuts in a frying pan over a low flame for 10 minutes, stirring so as not to burn. Let cool. Pick off the bitter papery skins and grind into small bits with a pinch of salt. Add 3 tablespoons medlar paste to 1/2 cup milk and beat until smooth. Mix 4 tablespoons sugar and 4 tablespoons cornstarch, then mix into the milk/medlar blend. Beat smooth. Add remaining milk and allspice. Heat slowly, stirring often so as not to boil too hard, until the mixture has thickened, about 10 minutes. Pour into pudding cups to let harden. Sprinkle the tops with chopped nuts and an additional dusting of allspice. Chill. (Use a bit less sugar if your medlar paste was pre-sweetened.)

## Medlar Jelly

12 to 16 fully ripe perfect medlars, enough to cover the bottom of your pan
Water to cover medlars so that they are just floating

Bring this to a boil and let simmer for one hour until the fruit is starting to come apart. Add more water if necessary. Add quince cores or seeds for their extra pectin if desired, and half of a lemon, peel and all, crushed. Mash into a coarse slurry and continue to cook.

Line a sieve or colander or drainer with several layers of cheesecloth. Let the hot slurry drain for a few minutes. Don't press on the cheesecloth in any attempt to get more juices, as this could cloud the jelly. Just let gravity do its thing.

For each cup of medlar juice, add one cup of sugar. Add pectin powder at this point if using. Return the jelly mixture to the fire at a slow boil for another 15 or 20 minutes until it reduces and thickens enough to "sheet" on a cold spoon. Makes 2 small (4 ounce) jelly jars. Pour into jars and process in a boiling water bath for 15 minutes to seal.

Of course you can just let the jelly set and consume it immediately.

For a richer Medlar Jam, pulp 2 or 3 more medlars and add the new pulp at the same time as you add the sugar.

## Quince-Medlar Marmalade

Here is my attempt to recreate the secret recipe for *cotignac*, the famous French marmalade that dates back to Joan of Arc:

4 cups peeled quince, minced fine

Set the quince on the stove to cook for about an hour while you cut up and pulp the medlars. Set the fire on low and add the juice of one orange. Reserve the peel.

1 cup medlar pulp
2 cups sugar

Add the orange peel last. Use the zest with a few larger bits. You want orange flavor throughout, but also some texture too. Let the ingredients cook together for about ten minutes more, then put in jelly jars and process to seal. Makes about 3 1/2 cups marmalade.

## Modern Medlar Serving Suggestions

- Yogurt medlar swirl
- Yogurt medlar pecan swirl
- Medlarsauce cake (use any applesauce cake recipe)
- Medlar sweetbreads (variations on medlar nut breads)
- Medlar butter (cook sauce long and slow until smooth and dry)
- Medlar pie (similar to pumpkin but distinctively different)
- *Mispel mandelformar* (medlar sauce Swedish thumbprint cookies)
- Medlar honey (spread on toast)
- Medlar mincemeat (with raisin and orange peel)
- Pancakes with medlar maple syrup
- Vanilla layer cake with a medlar sauce stripe in the middle
- Medlar ice cream

# Gooseberry

*Ribes uva-crispa*

The gooseberry odyssey began for me when my sister got her first house and moved back to town. The bush had grown in the backyard there since forever. We called it "Roy's Goose" to honor the previous resident of the house. All kinds of special plants grew in Roy's yard because he had made his entire living there on a quarter-acre lot, complete with a homemade greenhouse on the back of the house. Roy was a queer bird. He'd cared for his ailing mother, now long gone, by growing African violets and cacti and impatiens to sell to the five-and-dime stores. On the back of his lot grew the gooseberry bush. Our mother maintained that it had been his mother's "goose," as it would have been "just like her" to have such an old-fashioned fruit. We always called it "Roy's Goose" anyways.

We didn't have gooseberries growing up, ourselves. Our great-uncle grew just about every other fruit on his farm, but not the gooseberry. Little did we realize at the time, however, that gooseberries were in the government surplus fruit cocktail that they fed to us in the schools in the 1950s! I'm not sure if that really counts but those green globes tasted better than anything in the whole cocktail because of their crisp texture. I remember calling them "grapes," but in fact they were bearded gooseberries. Some of the smaller ones would even have their little stems left intact.

"Come here, little fox! Come pick your grapes," I'd mockingly say as I dangled that berry out in the open while my other fist was clenched and hidden, ready to attack anyone who stole my "grapes" in second grade. This was a game we played inside our desks when the teacher wasn't looking.

For years I continued to think of them as "grapes" until my friend Mark reminded me that gooseberries had indeed gone to the government for the fruit-cocktail program. By reminding me of the stems he made me realize that in fact I'd been eating gooseberries as a child all along without knowing it! That gooseberry epiphany made the berries all the more interesting to me and helped launch me down the road of old-fashioned fruit rediscovery.

The "beard" of a gooseberry is the calyx, the remains of the flower all dried and shriveled at one end of the berry. A small berry will have an insignificant "beard" but a larger berry may have a much more pronounced one. There's nothing wrong with eating the beard; it's just a little extra fiber in your diet. Purists insist on removing it with a small scissors or serrated knife before making gooseberry recipes for fear that the final product will have unsightly blackish-brown specks in it. After bearding the gooseberries for a pie I baked once, however, the work was so tedious that it was the last bearded gooseberry pie that I ever baked. Just go for the extra fiber! Of course, it may be more proper to say "I removed the beard" or "I de-bearded" the berries, but in common parlance you will hear things like "Don't bother to beard every berry, just the big ones." Gooseberries are most likely named for the fact that their leaves look like the footprint of a goose, not because this berry was especially popular with geese.

The European gooseberry *Ribes uva-crispa* has a five hundred-year long domestic history. There were once hundreds of named cultivars whereas today there remain only a few dozen. The British in particular made breeding a better gooseberry an obsession but now many of these favorite cultivars of old have been lost. This problem is compounded in America where *Ribes hirtellum*, the American gooseberry, is resistant to most of the American fungal diseases whereas *Ribes uva-crispa* is not. The named European cultivars had to be re-hybridized to incorporate American disease resistance. There are also a number of wild American gooseberries, some of which even have spines coming out of the berry, making them look similar to a miniature mace.

The original British gooseberry societies selected berries for size, but larger berries don't always mean better flavor. The American variety "Pixwell" was selected for its lack of thorns and consequent ease of picking, but the flavor is said to be mediocre. I don't know for sure, because mine never produced a single one!

Presumably there would also be sour gooseberry varieties selected for cooking and canning as well as sweeter varieties for desserts and fresh eating. Most of the gooseberry cultivars described in the old books are not available at the nursery nowadays and may no longer be in existence.

Gooseberry bushes are two to four feet high and thorned. Their leaves appear very early in the spring. The plants grow best in cooler weather and may look poorly in the heat of summer. They flower early but the flower is not particularly attractive. The sweetest gooseberry is said to be the yellow variety called "Early Sulfur." The bushes are slow-growing, finicky and very subject to mildews. Output is severely reduced. "Early Sulfur" and its cousins are deemed "dessert berries" because they may be presented uncooked, perhaps even unsugared, as a dessert. I haven't yet tried to grow any "dessert gooseberries," but I will.

Gooseberries ripen during the middle weeks of July here in western New York. They may be pink, red, yellow, green, purple, or any combination thereof. Most taste crisp and pleasingly sour, and even when described as "sweeter" or even "sweetest" are only slightly sweet. As a flavor, gooseberry takes sour to new heights. My friend Rosco, a British chef, assures me than an overly ripe gooseberry is past its prime. It may not be rotten yet but it's still no good for cooking. The best gooseberry flavor, says he, comes from a slightly unripe berry.

Berries may be harvested at the green stage a week or more early for use in game sauces, ketchups, preserves and conserves. Or at the fully ripe stage for fresh eating or for use in pies and other desserts. A gooseberry will be slightly translucent when it's sweet-ripe but as a fresh fruit it will always be for the connoisseurs of sour. My mother claimed gooseberries never ripened at all!

There are two ways to make copies of a gooseberry or currant. One way is to dig up the entire bush, hack it into pieces and replant. Water regularly and probably all pieces will live, if each piece had roots and if you do your hacking early enough in the spring. Tip layering is far easier, however, and leaves your original full-grown bush in place, relatively unmolested. Bend several longer, lower branches down to the ground and bury them in contact with the earth, weighted down with a large stone. Make sure that some leaves or buds are showing on the stem above where you buried it. Leave these unmolested over winter. By spring they should have rooted. Snip the back of the stem off at the ground level, dig the new roots and carefully pot them up. Water them frequently. After you have noted strong new growth on the potted bushes, they should be strong enough to set in the ground and grow on their own.

I opted for the tip-layering method and before long had myself a patch of my own "Roy's Goose." The bushes have long, painful thorns but the reward is a harvest of huge green berries and an equal number of smaller berries growing toward the branch tips. These berries seem to ripen late, that is to say mid-July on the Lake Erie plain. They keep well on the bush. Being green even when ripe, they don't attract as many bird pecks as do the pink and red berries.

In my youth, I picked wild berries for my mother as I played on the abandoned farms in our neighborhood and had received approval for my many quarts of raspberries, strawberries, blackberries and currants. After my sister moved to Roy's old house, I began to bring my mother quarts of "Roy's Goose" gooseberries. Out of loyalty to old-fashioned fruits and local lore she tried to like them, but it was a losing battle. "They're not even fit for a pie!" she claimed. "You put in a whole cup of extra sugar and they're still sour!"

Yes, gooseberries are just fun to hate! Mention the Christmas goose and my mother would roll her eyes and remember a tough and greasy bird that never seemed to get done and was not a child-pleaser. Mention a berry named for a goose and she'd make the same expression for a tough, unjuicy berry that never seemed to get sweet and was not a child-pleaser either. I began to collect gooseberry bushes and gooseberry recipes, determined to overcome the gooseberry prejudice.

First I bought "Pixwell," which grew fine for me but never produced a berry. Next I bought "Finnish Red" whose thorny petite bushes produce more than their weight in small, red berries. While a pie of Roy's Goose bakes up yellowish-green, the Finnish gooseberry bakes up an attractive deep red color.

Next I tried "Captivator" whose bushes are very large but not so thorny and whose berries have pleasing stripes of pink with green. My latest trial is "Sabine"; she is purplish pink with some green.

Bearing in mind that gooseberries are never sweet, only sour and less sour, I'd say that "Captivator" and "Sabine" are sweeter than "Finnish Red" by a bit, and sweeter than "Roy's Goose" by a mile. On the few occasions when I've been able to purchase gooseberries at market, the cultivar names were not known to me. I wasn't really able to reliably compare degrees of less-sourness in tasting them, but I have found that color is no guide to flavor. Since when is pink-green or purple-green sweeter than pure red? How can a green berry be ripe? It can if it's a gooseberry!

The bottom limbs of the bush can drag the berries on the ground. Normally the gooseberry is a good berry that can "hold." That is, it can hang a long time on the bush, avoid bird predation somewhat and not fall off. It gradually becomes translucent and as ripe as ever it can be. Berries on these bottom limbs, however, will quickly reach the ripe-rotten stage from humid conditions and contact with the ground. A good trick is to line the ground with newspaper. The berries won't touch the ground and neither will you as you sit or kneel to pick them. A ripe gooseberry should be somewhat soft but still crispy bouncy. If it is soft and soggy without bounce, it has gone ripe-rotten.

Of course the gooseberries would be happier if they grew in a cultivated row, complete with fertilizer and protective bird-netting, but I keep mine in vague rows or stashed here and there. I mow around them and mulch them with newspapers. They do fine with a minimum of attention. In shade they continue to grow and that fruit ripens a bit later than berries in full sun, effectively extending the season. In deep shade the bushes will grow but not fruit at all. In my gardens the "Finnish Reds" ripen first by July 10 or so, whereas "Sabine" and "Captivator" are ready by about July 20 and "Roy's Goose" ripens last. By comparison, currants ripen a day or two before gooseberries and jostaberries begin a day or two after.

There is even a gooseberry impostor, *Physalis peruviana*, commonly known as the "Cape of Good Hope" gooseberry due to the fact it was heavily cultivated in the Cape of Good Hope region of South Africa, coming there from its native South America via England in the 18th and 19th centuries. It's actually a relative of the tomatillo (*Physalis ixocarpa*), a small, yellow "husk tomato" or "ground cherry" that is sweeter than a genuine gooseberry could ever be. You can treat it as a "dessert berry." It also makes a delightful golden jelly. If you really want to grow this impostor, you'll need to start the seed inside as you would tomato plants. You will also need to have lots of room and lots of sun. The plants are enormous and somewhat rampant, but by September they'll pump out a regular supply of fruits hidden in a paper husk, like the berries of the perennial Japanese lantern plant, *Physalis alkekengi*, which have a similar but not so fine flavor.

I raised *Physalis* for a few years but let it lapse. My garden is small and I never could grow enough of a supply to try making jam or syrup. So, instead of pies or other lavish recipes, my guests only get one or two alongside their yogurt or pudding or ice cream. There are a number of other impostors (Ceylon Gooseberry, Otaheite Gooseberry and Barbados Gooseberry to name a few), but only the Cape of Good Hope gooseberry has developed much of a following. It is marketed in the United States under the names "goldenberry" or "Pichuberry," a reference to its South American origin.

Traditionally the gooseberry has been an accompaniment for meats, especially game. There are gooseberry game sauces, mustards, relishes and other not-so-sweet recipes that emphasize this potential of the berry. I have even seen green gooseberries on the market as hard as rocks (and just as hard to eat). I assume that these green, early-ripe gooseberries were to be cooked into recipes like these. It is true that not so long ago people enjoyed a whole variety of pickles and relishes made from green fruits. Green tomato relishes come to mind, and my great-grandfather particularly enjoyed pickled green Seckel pears.

When eaten fresh the gooseberry will need a sweet foil, whether nuts and raisins in your granola or banana and papaya in a fruit salad. Try pairing them with cheese, or put them into a mango salsa.

Because the berries can be so many different colors, gooseberry pies can be yellow or red or even green. Green is my favorite color pie. It's especially alluring when I throw a dozen frozen blackberries or black currants into it as well. The resulting pie is green with pale pink stripes or polka dots. I have tricked many a gooseberry-hater into giving the berry a second chance by changing the colors in this way. Sometimes it works. Extra sugar also helps to recruit new believers.

❧

One of my neighbors, Martin, had a dream once about the back of our lots next to our barns. In his dream there are currant bushes growing along my barn covered with gleaming red berries, and he sneaks his hands through the hedge to steal some. So I decided in honor of my neighbor's dream to interplant a few real-life currant bushes with my pretty "Sabine" gooseberry last year. After the currant bushes began to set fruit this year, I reminded Martin of his dream and suggested he'd better sneak his hand through the hedge to steal them first, or I might pick all the berries for myself!

Sure enough, the next day Martin approached my barn-side "wilderness garden" of borage, angelica and sweet cecily. He reached his hand through the shady tangle and before his wife could stop him, had popped several gooseberries into his mouth. "Those weren't currants!" she cried out in genuine alarm. And indeed, they weren't. No one knew what Martin had eaten. The children worried whether poison nightshade might be growing between our barns. Martin wondered if perhaps he should call poison control. What he had eaten had tasted pretty good, though, so he didn't. I was away on a camping trip and did not return to calm apprehensions until the following day by which time it was already clear Martin was going to live. This amusing anecdote shows how far we have come from our European ancestors who held the gooseberry in much higher esteem!

In the end, however, I'd made a gooseberry convert. The currants did not go to waste, either, for I split the remaining crop with Martin.

  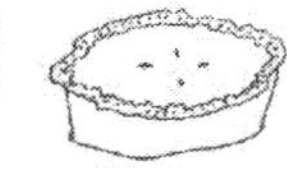

# Gooseberry Recipes

## Gooseberry Fool

1 quart gooseberries
1 cup sugar
3 cups heavy cream

This is the most well-known gooseberry dessert. Cook the berries over low heat for 30 minutes, then mash them with the sugar. Set aside and let cool. Beat the whipped cream until it has stiff peaks. Fold in the fruit purée, but do not overmix so that it keeps that marbled look. Serve chilled in individual bowls or parfait glasses or aside a vanilla cake.

You can produce a lower-fat version by trying Greek yogurt instead of cream.

Some may expect the gooseberry skins to be discarded from the fool. In this case you have the extra step of forcing the stewed berries through a sieve or colander. It is also possible to purée the skins and berries in a food processor until smooth.

## Gooseberry Bread Pudding

1 quart gooseberries, stewed and mashed
2 cups sugar
1 cup bread crumbs
4 egg yolks
2 egg whites, beaten
1 tablespoon butter

Butter your baking dish, then strew the top of your pudding with pats of butter before baking. Beat the egg whites stiff and add gently to the pudding. Bake for 20 minutes at 375°F.

Use your own large bread crumbs from real stale bread, not the processed, fine bread crumbs out of the supermarket container.

You may also choose to mix your whipped egg whites with 2 tablespoons of powdered sugar and let it brown on top of your pudding during its last 5 minutes of baking.

(Thanks to NAFEX and to *Good Housekeeping magazine*, July 1903, for this recipe and many others in this chapter.)

## Gooseberry Pie

Prepare a pie crust using:

1 3/4 cups flour
8 tablespoons shortening
Pinch of salt
Water to bind

For the filling use:

1 quart gooseberries
1 1/4 cup sugar
1 tablespoon tapioca flour
1/2 teaspoon cinnamon
1/8 teaspoon nutmeg

Some recipes advise cooking the berries in a little water and the sugar before assembling the pie, but I find that one hour at 375°F is enough to cook the berries sufficiently.

Gooseberries come in many colors—red, pink, green, green with purple stripes... Usually your pie will have a pleasing pink color, darker if you have added a few jostaberries or black currants. A pie baked with only green gooseberries, however, comes out a very pleasing yellow-green color. If you throw in a dozen or so frozen, darker-colored berries you might get a totally unique polka-dot pie. The berries thaw in time to cook but not in time to color all areas of the filling, hence the "polka-dot pie."

Gooseberry pie is very tart and not to everyone's taste. You'll notice that I've added a bit more sugar than is used in most pies. If your pie is still too sour, you can easily sprinkle a bit more sugar on top of the piecrust or serve it à la mode with ice cream.

## Gooseberry Catsup

1 1/2 pounds gooseberries
1 pound brown sugar
1/2 cup cider vinegar
1/2 inch of cinnamon stick (or 1 teaspoon powdered)
1 teaspoon allspice

Cook the berries gently until they have broken down, then process for 10 to 15 minutes in clean jelly jars. This is not your familiar tomato-based catsup but it is very interesting to try in familiar catsup roles such as over that hotdog or slice of meatloaf. You can also prepare this recipe with currants.

## Gooseberry Relish

2 quarts gooseberries (remove stem and beard)
1 cup cider vinegar
4 1/2 cups sugar
1 orange, both the juice and the zest
1/2 teaspoon cinnamon
1/2 teaspoon clove

Let this relish boil gently for 2 hours until thick. It should yield 3 to 4 pints when canned.

## Spicy Gooseberry Relish

5 cups gooseberries
1 1/2 cups raisins
1 onion, chopped
1 cup brown sugar
3 tablespoons dry mustard
3 tablespoons ginger
1 teaspoon turmeric
1/4 teaspoon cayenne
1 cup vinegar
Salt to taste

You can speed up the process by smooshing your gooseberries in a food processor before you begin the boiling. Pack into jars and process to seal.

The original version of this relish used 1 quart of vinegar and 3 tablespoons salt but I find that this is far too much for modern tastes.

## Gooseberry Jam

4 pounds gooseberries
3 pounds sugar
2 cups red or white currant juice

Beard the gooseberries if it isn't too tedious. Some varieties have very little beard and it is quite ok to include them in your jam, but some berries with a bushy beard may leave brown specks in the jam.

Boil until your jam reaches the desired consistency. Add extra pectin if desired. Pack the berries into the jars, pour all the juice-syrup over the top and process to seal.

## Gooseberry Almond Tarte

2 cups gooseberries
1 1/4 cups sugar
1/4 teaspoon cardamom
1/4 tablespoon flaked almonds for topping
In a pie pan set a crust made from:
1 1/2 cups flour (Try interesting combinations like wheat-barley-spelt, or other)
1/8 teaspoon salt
1 teaspoon sugar
5 tablespoons shortening

Preheat the oven to 375°F. Roll out your crust and place it in the pie plate. Prick the empty crust with the tines of a fork all over to help it to bake under the berries. Bake it for 5 minutes, then put in the berries, sugar and spices gently. Bake for 55 minutes. This dessert is (like gooseberries) very tart, so serve it with ice cream or whipped cream to provide additional sweetness.

## Gooseberry Fruit Soup

2 cups gooseberries
1 cup sugar
1/2 cup raisins
1 1/2 cup water
4 teaspoons cornstarch

Cook your soup for 5 to 10 minutes until the berries are breaking apart and the raisins have plumped. Add 1/2 cup of cream, but only cook for a short time more and do not let it boil. This soup is good served with meats during the main meal, or you can serve it as a cold soup dessert with whipped cream on top.

## Bohuslän Gooseberry Sauce

Bohuslän is the Swedish province bordering on southern Norway. Serve this refreshingly different sauce over fish that has been boiled in salted water with 1 tablespoon of vinegar.

2 1/2 cups boiled gooseberries (boil until easy to moosh)
1 1/2 cups water

Drain and pass the berries through the sieve to crush, if you are a Swedish maid in the last century, or use the blender. Add 1 tablespoon melted butter, 2 teaspoons sugar, and pinches of salt, nutmeg and white pepper.

## Gooseberry-Rhubarb Conserve

1 1/2 pounds gooseberries
1 pound rhubarb, sliced
2 cups honey
3/4 cup chopped walnuts

Boil this together for 15 minutes, then add the nuts and boil for 5 minutes more. Pack it into clean jars and process for 10 minutes to seal.

## Freezing Gooseberries

Gooseberries freeze well and need no more preparation than cutting off the beard with small scissors, if you deem it necessary. Take care not to puncture or crush the berries because, unlike so many berries, gooseberries retain a bit of their crunchy celery-like qualities even after freezing. Of course they retain all of their sourness!

This makes the gooseberry especially amenable to inclusions in fresh fruit salads. Whereas raspberries would turn into an uninspiring red or purple smudge, gooseberries retain their shape and can be a central attraction of your salad. Pair them with sweeter fruits like bananas, peaches, melons, pineapples and pawpaws.

Whether fresh or frozen, gooseberries make an interesting addition to molded gelatine salads as well.

# Jostaberry

*Ribes nidigrolaria*

The modern-day jostaberry, *Ribes nidigrolaria*, is a new-fangled fruit based on two old friends, the gooseberry and the black currant. It combines the thornlessness and high vitamin C content of black currant with the larger size and sweet, tart flavor of the gooseberry. The bushes are robust and easily grow six to eight feet tall. The fruits occur singly and also in strigs of two, and occasionally three berries.

In the 1950s, after many sterile attempts, Dr. Rudolf Bauer of the Max Planck Institute in Germany, treated the plants with colchicine, a derivative of the autumn crocus. This is where the new-fangled part comes in. The chemical caused the plants' chromosomes to double and the resultant plants flowered and ripened fruit. Seeds from these plants sprouted and grew into the jostaberries we have today. The jostaberry is a complex, three-way cross between species of the *Ribes* family—the black currant and the gooseberry, with a touch of Worcesterberry thrown in for good measure.

The plants first became available in the United States in the late 1970s. The name Jostaberry is a combination of "*Johannesbeere*," German for "currant," and "*Stachelbeere*," German for "gooseberry." Give it the German pronunciation, as in "Yostaberry."

"Jostaberry berries" begin ripening here in western New York the third week of July and continue for three weeks. Green fades to a dull red, but don't pick them yet. Jostaberries are not ripe until they reach a purplish-black color. Then the berries are so juicy that sometimes they break open during harvest. This makes for a sticky mess that can attract fruit flies, so use these berries first. The fruit hangs long on the bush and does not ripen all at the same time, so you will be returning to your bushes to pick again and again. Jostaberries freeze very well for winter use in fruit salads and baked goods.

I do lose some of my crop to bird damage. So far I have chosen not to indulge in propane cannons or netting but to share my crop with the birds. They usually get ninety percent of my cherries and juneberries. They'll take my red currants quickly if I don't pick them in a timely fashion. Being red seems to attract more attention in July than being purplish black because I always get most of my jostaberries. Some fruit up top may be bird-pecked but most of the crop is safely inside the bush.

You won't find many old-fashioned recipes for jostaberries, so treat them as you would currants or gooseberries. I am particularly fond of a jostaberry pie spiced with a touch of clove and mace or nutmeg, for example. The berries may look purplish black when they are ripe, but they bake up a beautiful, dark purplish red.

Applejack and shrub are old-fashioned vinegar-based drinks. Applejack can be as simple as a tablespoon of sugar and a tablespoon of cider vinegar mixed with water, or a richer version using some apple cider as well. Shrub is a vinegar-sugar drink too, but here we have the added luxury of shaved ice, or ice in irregularly-shaped pieces. The usual flavors are raspberry or red currant or a mixture of both. So why not a jostaberry shrub?

There is no drink more elegant and refreshing on a hot summer's day. The name alone sparks interest and so, too, the beautiful pale pink color that jostaberries yield when used this way. Avoid the chemical additives and high fructose corn syrup of most soda pops by making your own healthful shrubs. Children will love this old-timey drink that hearkens back to a day when ice itself was a rare luxury. Just don't mention that the secret ingredient is vinegar!

In the future when I get around to tweaking this recipe more, I'll try changing sweeteners to honey or agave syrup. I'm afraid that maple syrup might overwhelm the delicate fruit flavor of the berries. I'll also try infusing the vinegar with herbs for a few weeks before making the shrub syrup. Imagine a jostaberry shrub with hints of lavender flowers or basil or mint or lemon verbena! Or instead of infusing your vinegar, you could make your shrub with iced mint tea. A bubblier variation would be with carbonated soda water. The possibilities are endless. So, don't ask them if they want a soft drink. Just tell them you're fixing them a shrub!

❧

Jostaberries are the largest of all the *Ribes*, eventually reaching six to eight feet in height. They can be planted close to each other to create a thornless hedge that serves very nicely as a privacy screen. As with all *Ribes*, jostaberries are mostly self-pollinating, but the crop set will increase if the planting is a mix of cultivars. Fruit plantings can remain productive for up to twenty years. They benefit from pruning because the canes become woody and unproductive after three or four years.

My jostaberry hedge has lasted for nearly twenty-five years now. Production dropped off as the bushes became old and woody, but by then they were tip-layering themselves as well as coming up from the roots. I got rid of the old wood and the new replacement stock is already in place. Jostaberry has that "hybrid vigor" and grows quickly. It has competed well with weeds, even mugwort, and has resisted the road salt.

# Jostaberry recipes

## Jostaberry Shrub Syrup

Mix together:

1 quart jostaberries
1 cup water
1 cup white vinegar

Let this stand for 24 hours. Stir and mash the berries several times. Squeeze the mash through a cheesecloth to extract all the juices. Discard pulp. Measure juice in a measuring cup. Mix it with a equal volume of sugar and concentrate by letting it boil slowly 20 minutes.

You can put this syrup in clean jars and process it 15 minutes more to reserve for winter use, or use the syrup fresh.

To use, add irregularly smashed or shaved ice to a tall water glass, 3 tablespoons of jostaberry shrub syrup, then fill with water, sparkling water, iced tea or other desired liquid. Stir and enjoy.

## Jostaberry Syrup

1 quart jostaberries
1 cup plus 2 tablespoons sugar

Cook the berries in a sauce pan until soft and boiling. Pass them through a food mill or applesauce spinner, add sugar and a small amount of water if needed to make the sauce the desired consistency. Another method is to boil the sugar and berries until soft, then squeeze them through a cheesecloth.

## Jostaberry Fruit Salad

Any decent fruit salad should have at least 4 kinds of ingredients, most of them fresh fruit. Jostaberry freezes well and offers a very satisfying tart foil for sweet fruits like banana, melon, pineapple or papaya. Try this combination:

2 bananas, sliced

1 apple, peeled, cored and diced

1 cup pineapple pieces

1 cup watermelon pieces

1 cup green grapes, cut in half

3 dozen jostaberries

Handful of crumbled walnuts

Use plain yogurt for the dressing.

## Jostaberry Serving Suggestions

- In pancakes
- On granola or breakfast cereal
- In muffins
- Jostaberry pie—just add extra sugar!
- Apple-jostaberry pie
- Jostaberry syrup on ice cream
- Jostaberry shrub
- Jostaberry iced tea

# Saskatoon

## *Amelanchier*

Berries of the various species of the genus *Amelanchier* have been called juneberries, serviceberries, shad, shadblow and saskatoon. How can one berry have so many different names? As I go through the chapter, I'll use each of the names and give a little history. Bear in mind as you read, however, that a saskatoon is a saskatoon by any other name—including juneberry, serviceberry, shadblow and shadberry!

The Indians of the Yukon in Canada called the berries of *Amelanchier alnifolia*, "*mis-sask-quah-too-min*," hence the name "saskatoon." This shrubby species is the origin of the Canadian-selected cultivars such as "Regent," "Pembina" and others. Other shrubby species of this berry are *Amelanchier stolonifera*, *Amelanchier laevis* and *Amelanchier alleghenienensis*. There is a tree form as well, called *Amelanchier canadensis*, which grows wild in the forest understory and is also available through the nursery trade. The Indians added these berries to dried buffalo or deer or elk meat to create pemmican. (Other berries could be used as well, like blueberry or wild plum, blackberry or chokecherry, perhaps persimmon.)

I first came to know this berry as a "serviceberry" at those first gatherings at Blue Heron Farm in DeKalb, which is in the northern park of New York State east of Lake Ontario. Bryan Thompson, the owner, had a tree at the side of the sheep pasture which was always filled with delicious berries by the 4th of July. Bryan called them "serviceberries," which he explained as follows: "The ground is frozen all winter long and in the past you could not bury the dead. Then the ground thaws up and the trees bloom right at the time when there are lots of funeral services, hence 'serviceberries.'" Serviceberry is the name for the fruit which is perhaps most widely used.

Later on I bought my mother a bush for Mother's Day. The berries ripen at the end of June and are "gone to the birds" by early July, hence they are also often called "juneberry," the name my mother always preferred. Juneberries are good as a fresh berry though perhaps not spectacular. After I had the jam, however, I got hooked on it. When cooked into jams and jellies and syrups, the flavor intensifies and really becomes something special. Cooked long and slow the berry has enough pectin to gel by itself; just add sugar. The late Mabel Harkness of the Rock Garden Society and the Bergen Swamp Preservation Society maintained that the best berry for jam was that of *Amelanchier laevis*, a particular specimen that she had dug up in Oil City, Pennsylvania, although she always secretly wondered if it wasn't really an *Amelanchier allegheniensis* instead. At any rate, what is absolutely certain is that the purple jam she made from it was out of this world!

When baked, the seeds of this very seedy berry add an almond-like flavor to pies and cobblers. (This flavor can be intensified by addition of a half teaspoon of almond extract to a recipe.) Straight juneberry pie is wonderful for its almond flavor, but can sometimes be mealy and have too much of a laxative affect. So for baking, I prefer to use these berries in combination with other berries and fruit. I've become fond of triple-berry pies—juneberry, black currant and blackberry or raspberry. And juneberry-apple pie is also especially good! The berry freezes well and a handful of them can make any fruit recipe into something very special.

There are question to consider when purchasing *Amelanchier*. Do you want the tree form or the bush form? Do you want a plant selected for its early and showy bloom, or do you want one selected for its fruit? Berries from the tree may not be as fine for fresh eating as those from the bushes, and certainly more difficult to pick. Some of the bushes get as big as small trees and will sucker from the roots. Maybe we had better be like Mabel Harkness and dig a "sport" from an *Amelanchier* that we know and like already.

Early on after being introduced to them, I discovered a village street that was planted in tree-form *Amelanchier* and another tree adjacent to my woodland cabin. Serviceberries of the tree form give lots of fruit out there in the woods, but that fruit will be very difficult to harvest. You are more likely to procure a harvest in more horticultural settings. But you need as many sources as you can get. The picking of saskatoon is extremely tedious and must be done from a chair, if not a ladder–and the birds always make off with most of the crop! They don't care *what* name you're calling it. Between the wild, the orchard and the village sources, it's still difficult to pick enough juneberries for a big batch of jam. I purchased bird netting to protect my crops, but it was soon shredded to worthlessness by my letting wild blackberries and roses grow up through it.

The berries are borne in such profusion that the birds go wild. The bird feeding frenzy leads to a purple pooping frenzy as well. Nobody appreciates the purple stains on the walkways and sidewalks which can easily be brought indoors, and few people will want to go to the effort of picking the berries unless they know how delicious they are. That neighbor who enjoys the first flowers of spring on a bush will probably not enjoy the "berry problem" of late June. He or she will probably be delighted to have you take the berries instead of the birds. Just ask. But when I am about town seeking juneberries this way I often encounter "concerned citizens" who are convinced that I am a madman about to poison myself. I'll munch a few berries in front of them to see if they flinch, and then offer a taste. This usually confirms them in the first part of their suspicion, but relieves them on the second.

There *is* poison out there to be picked but it's not in the berries; it's on them. Fortunately juneberries (by any name) are easy to wash clean. Raspberries and blackberries are too fragile to wash. But currants, gooseberries, jostaberries, elderberries and serviceberries are all strong enough to rinse in cold water, though berries that have been cleaned do not keep for long. For this reason, clean them just prior to use or freezing. Berries which have been picked after a rainstorm are cleaner, of course, but also in greater danger from mold. So any of these should be eaten or processed quickly as well.

Come winter I'm not content unless I have several jars of saskatoon jelly or syrup (the jelly that didn't gel) waiting to be enjoyed, plus several containers of frozen berries for baking. I'll add canned berry juice to maple syrup to serve over pancakes or to use to sweeten yogurt. Serviceberry syrup can make pancakes into something really special.

Pick as much as you can during the short season, late June to July 4 or thereabouts. To make jelly, cook the berries long and slow adding only a splash of water at the beginning so that they don't burn. Usually the residual water left on the berry surface after washing will be enough. Stir and mash continuously. After an hour or so when they are liquefied, squeeze them through a cheesecloth if you mean to discard the seeds and skins. These might be fine in jam or syrup but are not so desired in jelly.

By now your many hours of picking and kitchen work have been distilled down to a few cups of juice. For each one cup of juice, add a cup of sugar. You may can and process this for use as syrup but I prefer to cook it down thicker and thicker over a low flame until it gels on its own. Jams which include the skins and seeds are good but perhaps not so fine a product as a juneberry jelly.

At the farmers' market in town it's easy to sell all of my red raspberries, which I have in short supply, but much more difficult to sell my "special" berries. So I came up with the idea of the "breakfast blend," a mixed-berry basket at a premium price. On the bottom I put gooseberries and currants of different colors, followed by three colors of raspberries. Then I top it all off with saskatoon I've kept fresh in the refrigerator and a few strigs of golden currants. These last are so alluring that customers usually eat them on the spot. When presented on their own, my juneberries do not tend to sell well, so I usually only make a couple of baskets for sale this way. But this year my berry missionary efforts were rewarded when I had one returning customer who exclaimed, "I'm so glad you have serviceberries! I remember you from last year with the berry mix, and serviceberries are my favorite berry of all!" So I know I've made another convert.

Finally, "Shad" and "shadbush" are yet other names for this berry, referring to the runs of fish at *Amelanchier* blooming time, but as there are no shad around here so far from the ocean, I've decided I prefer to use the names saskatoon–or serviceberry, or juneberry–depending entirely on what seems right at the moment. I have also heard "sarvis" or "sarvisberry" based on an archaic American English pronunciation for serviceberry.

  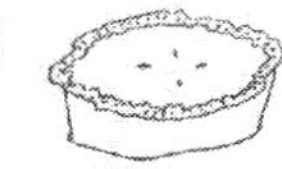

# Saskatoon Recipes

## Saskatoon Syrup

Jellies, syrups and jams made from these berries are very tedious to produce but in my view they are the most delicious things that you can make with these fruits. Long, slow cooking rounds out the flavor and accents the almond flavors in the seeds. Undercooking may leave bits of visible, slightly leathery skins. Any saskatoon syrup or jam or jelly can easily be processed in boiling water for 15 minutes and sealed into jars for winter use. You'll be happy you went to all this work!

## Juneberry-Apple Pie

2 to 3 apples
1/2 quart juneberries
4 tablespoons tapioca flour
1 cup sugar
1/2 teaspoon almond extract
1/2 teaspoon cinnamon
1/4 teaspoon mace

Prepare a pie crust with:

1 stick of butter or 8 tablespoons shortening of your choice
1 1/2 cups flour
Pinch of salt
4 tablespoons cold water (add more by the teaspoonful until your dough will hold together the way that you want it to)

Roll out the crust, put in the filling, pinch down the top crust using a fork. Puncture the center with a knife 4 to 8 times to create steam slits and to suggest future pieces. Bake at 350°F for one hour.

Experiment with your flours. Add 1 cup of white flour, then try 1/2 cup of something else. Try barley or spelt flour for a nutty, soft crust. Amaranth flour makes for a harder, nuttier crust. Almond flour is going all the way. Millet flour makes it hard and yellow; quinoa flour, hard and grayish. Even the addition of part bread flour or whole wheat flour will make your crust much more interesting. Rye flour is an excellent addition to crusts for savory sorts of meat and vegetable pies but I don't favor it with fruit pies. Powdered walnuts are also good but in the case of juneberry pies, almond flour or powdered almonds are the best.

## Serviceberry Cream Muffins

4 eggs
2 cups sour cream
2 cups sugar
1 cup oil or melted butter
4 cups flour
1 teaspoon baking powder
1 teaspoon baking soda
1/2 teaspoon almond extract
1 1/2 cups serviceberries

Mix the baking powder into the flour. Beat your eggs until light, then add the remaining wet ingredients and mix well before adding your dry ingredients. Stir in the serviceberries at the end. Bake 20 minutes in at 400°F in greased muffin tins or cupcake papers. Those who are fond of blueberry muffins may just find a new favorite.

# Pawpaw

*Asimina triloba*

*Picking up pawpaws*
*Put'em in a basket*
*Way down yonder*
*In the pawpaw patch.*

—Appalachian Folk Song

We sang this song in music class at school even though nobody knew what a pawpaw was. Although it is one of the most important North American fruits and is native to this part of western New York, it was years and years before I ever found a wild tree. This area marks the northernmost limit of the pawpaw, *Asimina triloba*, a member of the otherwise tropical Custard-Apple family (*Annonaceae*). Pawpaw is a northern cousin to *cherimoya* and *guanábana* (soursop). "Michigan banana" is another name you will hear for it because the pawpaw does grow in southern Michigan and it has a soft, aromatic flesh whose texture is reminiscent of bananas. Pawpaw fruit, however, has its own unique sweet taste which is quite distinct from either banana or papaya.

As a tree or large bush, pawpaw is part of the forest understory. It prefers to grow in partial shade and can reach heights of twenty to thirty feet. A well-established tree will soon start to sucker and form a pawpaw patch but cross-pollination is required to set fruit. Make sure there's more than one individual in your pawpaw patch! A pawpaw growing in full sun will fruit more than a pawpaw grown in partial shade but a seedling in the sun may get fried to death during a dry spell.

Pawpaw leaves are enormous and smooth-margined, reminiscent of the leaves of the cucumber magnolia tree but longer. The longest cucumber magnolia leaf will just be equal in length to the shorter pawpaw leaves. How can such a small tree have such a huge leaf?

The brownish-purple flowers appear in early June in my area and aren't very noticeable on the tree. It's a good thing that the flower's scent is likewise nearly unnoticeable! The flowers are pollinated by carrion flies which *do* notice the faintly unpleasant scent. Just as growers of peaches and cherries try to boost their yields by hiring pollination hives in the spring, you could do the same thing for your pawpaw patch by leaving roadkill around in June to attract more flies!

My hired hand, Jim Turner, started his own organic farm in Nova Scotia and raised chickens among many other things. It was our joke that he would market "pawpaw pollinator kits" that were certified organic. He'd keep the heads of his butchered chickens until they were rotten and pungent, then affix them to coat hanger hooks and freeze them in a fancy box with instructions. It's too bad pawpaws don't grow as far north as Nova Scotia!

Pawpaw trees are a little finicky about being transplanted. I've tried bare-root and potted plants and have had about fifty-percent mortality with each, but after the pawpaw is well established, the plants need little care. Pawpaw shows its tropical heritage by being one of the last trees to leaf out in the spring. Frequently the leaves will die back and the plant resprouts from the roots, so don't give up hope on your feeble transplants until well into their second year.

Sun-grown adult pawpaws give more fruit, but shaded saplings survive better. I compromised and planted a row of pawpaw at the back of my orchard in the dappled shade of the locust grove. Then I waited ten years. One tree grew much more quickly than the others and began to set fruit before the others had even begun to flower. That means it must have been pollinated by other pawpaw trees in the area which I've never seen! Now I've begun to naturalize pawpaw in the woods. Heavy clay soil doesn't seem to bother them, but the fruits of my tree in poor, sandy soil are about the size of a lemon. My friend Richard's pawpaws in pampered garden soil produce huge pawpaws the size of a mango.

The pawpaw is better known in Southern cuisine. Its fruit is high in vitamins, proteins, minerals and calories. It fed the starving men of the Lewis and Clark expedition in 1810 and is of high nutritional value. Pawpaws are fragile and ephemeral. Fruits the most blemished and least cosmetic are really the best. The flavors in the pawpaw are very volatile, so it is best used with as little cooking as possible, if not raw.

In western New York, the fruits begin to ripen around the time of the fall equinox. Be sure to beat the raccoons to the tree! You can smell when the fruit is ripe. The green skin will develop brown stripes and patches. Let it ripen as you would an avocado. Cut the fruit length-wise and eat it with a spoon. The large and woody seeds are easy to separate from the gooshy pulp when the fruit is ripe. It has a low water content (seventy-five percent) like bananas. The ripe pulp may be frozen or dried for later use, but it is best consumed fresh. The fruit doesn't travel, stores poorly and so is generally only available in late September and early October. For these and other reasons, the pawpaw has not yet found its place in modern American commercial agriculture, but efforts are underway to breed improved cultivars. Traits being followed are orange versus yellow flesh, large versus small fruit, and the presence or absence of metallic undertones in the flavor. Sweetness is not an issue. Any ripe pawpaw is incredibly sweet, almost cloyingly so. A few ripe pawpaws can perfume an entire room. The other improvement being made is in the seed-to-pulp ratio. My unimproved pawpaw gives about three-quarters cup of flesh to one-quarter cup of seeds.

Ripe pawpaws are easily shaken from the tree but may be damaged in their fall. I prefer to pick mine a bit green and let them ripen safely on the table at home. They may not be as sweet those ripened on the tree, but the fruit is so sweet in general that you will scarcely notice the difference. You may speed up the ripening process of selected fruit by putting them in a paper bag closed up with an overripe banana or apple.

Each fruit will contain numerous dark-brown seeds with a woody texture. Plant the seeds in the fall but don't expect them to germinate until July of the next year. Even then, germination may be sparse. The seedlings are small and feeble. Some sources suggest not letting your seed freeze, so I let mine overwinter in the cheese compartment of my refrigerator. The good news is that the deer do not especially like pawpaws and will probably leave your seedlings alone after the first bite.

Remember the hippy health food co-ops of the 1970s? Papaya juice was then a new discovery for mainstream American cuisine, *de rigeur* for anyone who wanted to show his or her mettle. The juice was always sold in large wide-neck bottles of sludge which you then diluted with water. Three tablespoons of the sludge was stirred with a spoon into a glass of ice water accompanied by a lecture on the good effects of "pulp" and "enzymes."

It turns out that pawpaw, also known as "green papaya" in this context, just happens to share many biochemical properties with papaya itself, and then some. In fact, the pawpaw is a fount of bioactive compounds. A group of chemicals known as acetogenins present in all parts of the pawpaw plant are known to poison insects and show promise as anti-carcinogens. The other chemical of interest is the enzyme papain, same as in regular papaya, which functions as a very special digestive aide. These therapeutic chemicals are present in the bark, seeds, leaves, roots, latex and green fruit of the pawpaw, but as it softens and sweetens, these compounds diminish in concentration to practically nothing in the ripe fruit, but the other parts of the plant can be used. The woody seeds may be ground fine and used as a kind of "pepper." The leaves can be dried to make a tea which in turn is especially good to make fermented kombucha tea. You can make a "sauerkraut" from mature green pawpaws (for example, a large pawpaw in early September before the fruit softens) which will be better from a medicinal standpoint, but bitter if you leave the skins on and probably not as nice as the green papaya salad that they serve in Thai restaurants. These pawpaws may be insipid to wretched in flavor but they contain more vitamin A than carrots and more vitamin C than oranges, as well as vitamins B and E and enzymes which can digest proteins, carbohydrates and fats. Papain is the miracle enzyme which is superior to the pepsin and pancreatin produced in our bodies. Your pancreas can take a little break with some papain around! Papain works under both acidic and basic conditions. It promotes colon health by cleansing the intestine, doing the work that other enzymes miss. It is known as a mucus and puss solvent. It gets rid of mucoprotein, undigested residues in the intestine, which could worsen problems with constipation, high blood pressure, arthritis, epilepsy and diabetes. Such are the claims anyway.

Arginine is an essential amino acid that is not produced in humans. We get ours from eating eggs or brewer's yeast. When papain digests proteins, it changes a part of those proteins into arginine. This in turn can influence our production of human growth hormone. Arginine has also been shown to inhibit breast cancers.

Pregnant women are supposed to avoid these medicinal uses of the green pawpaw. Unripe fruit, leaves, skins, seeds and latex have also been used as a "traditional contraceptive" or abortifacient to bring on an early miscarriage.

Besides being an antique fruit geek, I am an also a word geek and here the pawpaw is a very rich vein of ore. The word "pawpaw" has its origins in a mistaken pronunciation of the Spanish word "*papaya*." Papaya and pawpaw are very different fruits. Pawpaw is more closely related to *cherimoya* and soursop (*guanábana*). Papaya is an indigenous fruit first introduced to the Spanish by the Taino Indians of Puerto Rico. "Papaya" is one of the few words in the

Taino language to have entered the English language. "Canoe," "hammock" and "tobacco" are other examples.

Jamestown colonist William Strachey used the word "*assessemin*" in 1612 in English to mean the pawpaw. "*Assimin*" was the Powhatan word for pawpaw. Pocahontas ate the fruit and called it by this name, but for some reason the corruption "pawpaw" came to predominate in English. By the 1700s the French were using the Powhatan word for pawpaw. They'd first encountered the fruit among Native Americans of Algonquian extraction living in what is now Illinois and called it by the name they used, which would be anglicized as "asimine." French speakers in France and Québec, however, don't use the word often because pawpaws do not grow in these places. Louisiana, which is within the pawpaw's range, is where you can still hear it. Sometimes it is also called "jasmine" there. The tropical flower known as jasmine has an intoxicatingly sweet odor, just like the pawpaw—though it imparts a bitter flavor to tea in which it is sometimes blended. This makes the word "*jasminier*" ambiguous in Louisiana French. Is that a flowering jasmine bush or a pawpaw tree?

The past importance of the pawpaw is attested to by the fact that it appears in so many place names across the country. Pawpaw, Illinois, is one such example, and there are towns with the same name in Indiana, Kentucky, West Virginia, Michigan and Kansas. Many more place names contain the word for "pawpaw" in various Native American languages. There is the Alcovy River in Georgia, which means "river among the pawpaw trees" in Muskogean, and the town of Natchitoches, Louisiana, named for the Native American tribe of the same name, is taken to mean "the pawpaw eaters."

The pawpaw ranges as far south as Florida, Louisiana and Texas, and as far north as Iowa, Michigan and New York. Ohio has proclaimed it to be the official state native fruit and also hosts the biggest pawpaw festival in the country. Someday I hope to taste the "Pawpaw Pale Ale" from the Zanesville, Ohio Weasel Boy Brewing Company!

Fossilized pawpaw seeds at the Meadowcroft site in Pennsylvania show that Native Americans were eating pawpaws over sixteen thousand years ago. Scientists believe that the pawpaw is a tropical species that spread north across half of the United States after the Ice Age, gradually becoming more resistant to the cold. It was dispersed by giant sloths and woolly mammoths at first, then later by human beings as the megafauna became extinct. Pawpaws will grow just about anywhere as far north as hardiness zone 6, but their preferred natural habitat is the forest understory in the deep, rich alluvial soils of river valleys.

The only wild pawpaw I ever saw in New York State, however, was along the trail to the outlet of Chautauqua Creek, also known as Peacock Point. It used to be "a thing" to have a pawpaw tree alongside your cottage on Lake Erie in Barcelona, but this custom has fallen into disuse. "Peacock's Grove," the last large tract of old-growth forest in the area, was reputed to be home to many wild pawpaw trees. Gages Gulf in nearby Ripley is also said to be home to wild pawpaw trees but I have never hiked in to see them.

It is believed that the Onondawaga (Seneca) and other Iroquoian groups extended the range of the pawpaw approximately two hundred miles along the lakes and into the Niagara River Valley in prehistoric times. Discontiguous pawpaw-growing areas of New Jersey, Delaware, Florida, Louisiana and the midwestern states may likewise represent agricultural efforts of other Native Americans. The Seneca Nation of today could have pawpaws on much of their Cattaraugus Territory, but the Allegany Territory is too cold.

❧

Each year I like to attend the Canandaigua Treaty Commemoration ceremony at the Treaty Rock by the Canandaigua courthouse on November 11. Americans meet citizens of the Six Nations and "polish the chain of friendship" between our peoples by telling stories about this 1794 treaty. We listen to the Thanksgiving Address in the Seneca language and view wampum belt reproductions of the treaty. The local historical museum is open and displays the parchment copy of the treaty in English. Afterwards we walk to the elementary school for craft sales and a dinner followed by more speaking and Iroquois social dancing. I've been bringing the same fruit salad there for about forty years and it is much appreciated. It's mostly apples and oranges but there is always a cup or two of frozen serviceberries, raspberries or blackberries from my farm to make it extra special on Treaty Day.

The Seneca are very proud of their treaty. It is still in force today and they continue to receive their calico treaty cloth each year as specified in it. There is barely a piece the size of a postage stamp for each citizen, but it is the guarantee and proof of Seneca sovereignty. The Seneca Nation is older than New York State. The Seneca may be surrounded by New York State but are, by treaty, not a part of it.

Though pawpaws do not look very nice by November 11, I took one to show to the nice lady at the Allegany Seneca Language Nest table. "What is that?!" she questioned me, impressed by the sweet smell. I explained how it would not grow on her reservation but that it could grow at Cattaraugus. She took it home and ate it anyway and said it was quite good. The flesh was still yellow orange but the skin had darkened to brown. The pawpaw was soft just like an overripe banana. I had read in a food list in *Iroquois Uses of Maize*, by Arthur Parker, that "*hadi'of*" is the Seneca word for pawpaw. Since Parker was a Tonawanda Seneca, I assume the pawpaw was once known at the Tonawanda Territory of the Seneca Nation as well.

On my next trip to Canandaigua, I took more overripe pawpaws and a bag of my entire year's crop of seeds. These I gifted to the Cattaraugus faithkeeper who had spoken the Thanksgiving Address. When he asked what they were I surprised him by saying in Seneca "*Hadi'ot gayasöh*," "Pawpaw it-is-called." This is one of the few times in my life that I have been able to say a sentence in Seneca. It surprised me too! When I saw the faithkeeper the next year he told me that some of the seeds had come up. The traditional foods are finding their way back to the Seneca people.

The Seneca language has words for all the native fruits, of course, of which the pawpaw is the largest. There are also words for quince, gooseberry and currant. The Iroquois enjoyed their fruits and had planted vast orchards of European fruits like peaches and apples. In 1779, the dreaded "Village Destroyer" (Hanondaga:nyas) ordered General Sullivan to destroy every Seneca, Cayuga and Onondaga village he could find, and the fruit orchards were burnt along with the cornfields. Hanondaga:nyas, or "Village Destroyer," is the Iroquois name for George Washington. The Canandaigua Treaty brought an end to this sad and violent chapter of our histories.

Pawpaws also hold a special historical significance for African-Americans. The fruits seemed familiar because Africa has hundreds of other fruits in the *Annonaceae* (Custard Apple) family of plants. The diet of slavery times could be augmented in fall by eating wild pawpaws and also by hunting the wild game that consumed them. The fruit also played a part in the story of the Underground Railroad. Fugitive slaves followed the river valleys on their trek north, hiding by day in swamps or forests where pawpaws were a significant source of food in the early autumn.

And what other fruit has its own butterfly? The zebra swallowtail *Protographium marcellus* lays its eggs only on the leaves of pawpaw. A few years after planting the trees at my farm I began to see zebra swallowtail butterflies around. The caterpillars eat pawpaw leaves but I have never noticed any harmful levels of defoliation in my patch.

In 1916 the American Genetics Association sponsored a contest for the best-tasting pawpaw. The purpose was to begin the breeding of improved pawpaw cultivars. The fifty dollar prize money for best fruit was won by Mrs. Frank Ketter of Lawrence County, Ohio, but this variety has been lost today. The development of improved pawpaw varieties and the hunt for the lost ones is told in Andrew Moore's fascinating book *Pawpaw*, Chelsea Green Publishing, 2015.

How can the pawpaw regain its place in modern agriculture after sixteen thousand years of pre-modern popularity? Its bark fibers were once used in production of ropes and clothing, but this usage is unlikely to return. There may be a niche market in use of its wood to smoke meats, imparting to them a unique flavor. Pawpaw beer is another growing market, but the most promising use for the fruit appears to be in the flavoring of ice cream products. Cooking may degrade the flavor of the fruit, but freezing does not. Frozen pawpaw pulp is now available year round from a number of companies. You can order pawpaw fruit itself in season from specialty farms at perhaps ten dollars per pound plus shipping. A few fancy restaurants may serve pawpaw salsa or other dishes. I have sold my meager crop at the Abundance Cooperative Market in Rochester, but never more than a few pounds. In the 1990s when the Ocean Spray company wanted to do a feasibility study on the development of pawpaw products, they needed one ton of fruit—but the amount was not available, and the study was abandoned.

Permaculturists note that pawpaws are immune to the allelopathic chemicals in black walnuts that inhibit the growth of so many plants. Pawpaws and black raspberries both can grow happily in the company of black walnuts. Pawpaws are high in niacin, which nutrient can sometimes be lacking in a corn-based diet. As they did with their corn, the Seneca treated pawpaws with wood ash as they dried the pulp into finger-sized loaves. This makes the niacin more available. They put dried pawpaw into soups and sauces and corncakes. Their only other sweetener of note was maple sugar.

Some modern researchers believe that dried pawpaw may actually cause illness but others say that the wood ash can moderate these negative effects. The jury is still out on this. I've heard that pawpaw is "an acquired taste." Others say that your body has to get used to this new fruit and may experience problems at first. This was my experience. I did have some minor intestinal unpleasantness after consuming my first pawpaw but never again thereafter.

❧

As a basket of pawpaws ripens the sweet smell comes to permeate the room. At first it is a pleasant experience, as with quince, but as the pawpaw gets riper the chemicals in the smell are changing, getting too strong or changing into less enjoyable forms. The smell can become heavy and oppressive.

To dry my pawpaws I peeled and seeded them, then mashed them in a bowl. I shaped them into loaves and dried them on a cookie sheet in a warm oven with the fire off. They dried in three or four dry heat treatments but never cooked. The smell was greatly diminished and the dried fruit was quite good in muesli and granola. The smell continued to develop and change in the tin I kept them in, but it never overwhelmed the room.

One February I had a bad bout with flu and didn't eat for a day or two. I staggered to the kitchen to drink some water and thought I could eat a bite of walnuts and dried pawpaw. I was wrong. In my sick state the smell of the dried fruit was beyond disgusting. Luckily I had not eaten anything in days because if I had, it would have ended up all over the floor. Ever since this incident I have been unable to tolerate the smell of dried pawpaw though I continue to enjoy the fresh ones.

My favorite pawpaw concoctions so far are a hot pawpaw-tomato-pepper salsa, and a pawpaw and orange smoothie. But right now I am imagining a pawpaw pie. It'll have a special pre-cooked crust with a bit of pecan meal. Into this I'll add uncooked pawpaw pulp mixed with whipped cream. I have not yet decided which spice I might add, perhaps orange zest and lemon juice.

Now who will make me some pawpaw ice cream?

# Pawpaw Recipes

## To Prepare Pawpaw

Select soft and aromatic fruit with blackish-brown stripes and splotches. Peel carefully and discard the skins. Slice the pawpaws the long way, then dig into them with a spoon or knife and remove the large, woody seeds. Usually just stirring with a spoon will make the pawpaw pulp smooth enough for you to work with, but if the pulp seems too "gloppy," use a masher or pulverize it in a food processor.

## Pawpaw Pie

1 1/2 cup pawpaw pulp
1 cup sugar
2 cups milk
2 eggs
1/4 teaspoon salt
2 tablespoons cornstarch

Purchase or prepare an open pie shell of choice. Cook this filling slowly in a double boiler until thickened, then pour into the piecrust. Chill and let set. If a meringue is desired, beat egg whites and a spoonful of sugar at high speed until stiff. Spoon this topping onto the warm pie filling, arrange artfully, then cook 10 minutes or until nicely brown at the edges in a pre-heated oven at 400°F. Chill and let set. The plain pie is particularly good served with ice cream.

## Pawpaw Cream Pie

1 cup pawpaw pulp
1 cup cream
1 cup milk
3 egg yolks
1/3 cup flour or 1/4 cup cornstarch
3/4 cup sugar
1 pre-baked pie shell

Cook the custard separately in a double boiler over a slow flame. When the custard has begun to thicken, pour it into the crust. Make meringue from the 3 egg whites, beat stiff, sweeten to taste, bake in a pre-heated oven at 400°F for 10 to 12 minutes until slightly browned. Let pie cool and set. Refrigerate before serving.

## Pawpaw Custard

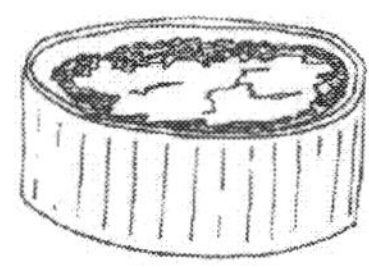

1 cup pawpaw pulp
2 ounces grated coconut
1 1/4 cup half-and-half
1 teaspoon vanilla
3 eggs, beaten
Pinch of salt
2 ounces superfine sugar
Orange zest

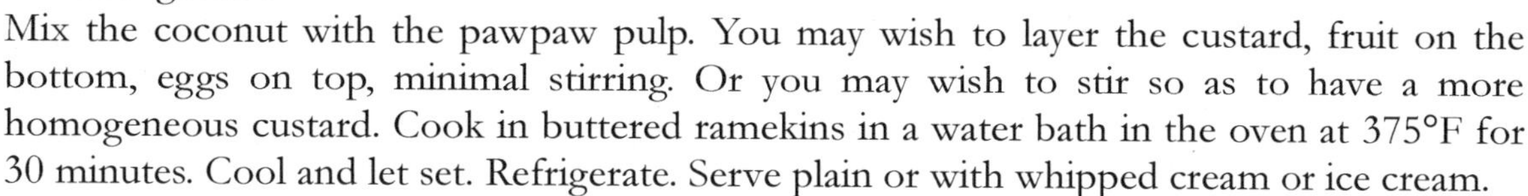

Mix the coconut with the pawpaw pulp. You may wish to layer the custard, fruit on the bottom, eggs on top, minimal stirring. Or you may wish to stir so as to have a more homogeneous custard. Cook in buttered ramekins in a water bath in the oven at 375°F for 30 minutes. Cool and let set. Refrigerate. Serve plain or with whipped cream or ice cream.

## Pawpaw Custard (by Billie Joe Tatum)

4 cups milk
4 egg yolks
1 teaspoon vanilla
1 tablespoon cornstarch mixed with 2 tablespoons milk
2 cups pawpaw pulp
1/2 cup confectioner's sugar
Pinch of salt

Warm the milk in a pan on the stove. Add the eggs and cornstarch and cook until thick. Don't boil. Let this cool, then add the pawpaw pulp, sugar and salt. Pour into individual serving glasses and refrigerate until firm.

## Barcelona Banana Butter

This recipe comes from an old Barcelona family. Barcelona, N.Y. is a small town located near where Chautauqua Creek flows into Lake Erie. Here there once was a huge tract of old-growth forest land called "Peacock's Grove" where pawpaws were common and referred to locally as "Barcelona Bananas." The grove is gone now but pawpaw trees persist along the creek path and in the yards of some cottages.

Several pawpaws peeled, seeded, and mashed
Scant spoonful of sugar
Nuts (Hickory are best)
Raisins

Gently heat the pawpaws and sugar as you continue to mash the "butter," adding nuts and raisins and whatever else may suit your fancy. Don't let it boil; only heat it briefly to incorporate the sugar. It keeps in a covered jar in the refrigerator for a week or two. Barcelona Pawpaw Butter is served for breakfast on toasted bead.

## Pawpaw Walnut Cookies

3/4 cup pawpaw pulp
1 cup flour
1/2 teaspoon baking powder
1/4 cup butter
1/2 cup brown sugar
1 egg
1/2 cup black walnuts

Be sure to roast the walnuts first. English walnuts are fine as well but black walnuts have a more distinctive taste. Try to mold the dough into smoother shapes. This is a very soft cookie. Drop by the spoonsful onto a greased cookie sheet. Bake 12 minutes at 350°F. You may want to try 375°F to brown them slightly, but then you will be sacrificing some of that distinctive pawpaw flavor. For a more Native American version, use the black walnuts and replace half of the flour with a fine corn meal.

## Pawpaw Cookies

1 1/2 cups pawpaw pulp
3/4 cup shortening of choice
1 cup sugar
1 egg
3 cups sifted flour
1 tablespoon baking soda
1 teaspoon salt
1/4 teaspoon ginger, 1/4 teaspoon allspice
1 teaspoon nutmeg, 1 teaspoon cinnamon

Form into balls. Press down with a greased glass to flatten. Cook on a greased cookie sheet for 15 minutes at 350°F.

## Pawpaw Fruit Cookies

1/2 cup raisins
1/2 cup dates
1 cup water
1/2 cup margarine or butter
1 cup oatmeal
1 cup flour
2 eggs
1/2 cup pawpaw pulp

1 teaspoon baking soda
1/2 cup nuts

Boil dried fruit for 3 minutes. Add shortening and other ingredients. Let the dough rest and cool in the refrigerator. Bake by spoonfuls, 10 minutes at 350°F on a greased cookie sheet.

## Pawpaw Cake

1/4 cup shortening
1 cup sugar
1 1/4 cup flour, sifted
1 teaspoon baking powder
1 cup pawpaw pulp
1 egg
1 teaspoon baking soda
1 teaspoon vanilla

Let bake at 350°F for 50 minutes. Frost with cream cheese thinned slightly with milk. Add pawpaw pulp, plus a bit of lemon juice, if you want to turn the frosting a slight yellow color.

## Pawpaw Cake II

1 3/4 cup flour
1 teaspoon baking soda
1 teaspoon baking powder
1/2 teaspoon salt
1/2 cup milk
1 tablespoon lemon juice
1/2 cup shortening
1 1/2 cup sugar
2 eggs
1 teaspoon vanilla
1/2 cup pawpaw pulp
1/2 cup nuts
3 eggs whites, beaten stiff

Grease and flour two 9-inch cake pans. Beat the egg whites stiff and fold in carefully at the end. Stir only until just combined. Bake at 350°F for 35 to 40 minutes. Let cool, then frost with Lemon Butter Frosting made with 1/2 cup butter, 1 tablespoon lemon juice, lemon rind, 1 pound confectioners sugar, and 6 tablespoons cream.

## Spiced Pawpaw Fruitcake

3 1/2 cup flour
4 teaspoons baking powder
1 teaspoon salt
1/2 teaspoon baking soda
2 teaspoon cinnamon
2 teaspoon ginger
1 teaspoon nutmeg
1 1/4 cup shortening
1 1/4 cup sugar
4 eggs
1 cup raisins
2 cups pawpaw pulp
1 1/2 cups nuts
3 cups candied fruit

Grease and flour two 9 by 5 by 3-inch loaf pans. Bake for 3 hours at 300°F in a water bath in the oven. Let cool, turn out of loaf pans and store in closed container.

## Pawpaw Ice Cream

1 quart milk
6 eggs
1/2 teaspoon salt
1 1/2 cup sugar
1 cup pawpaw pulp (or more)
1 lemon, juiced
1 quart heavy cream
2 tablespoons vanilla

Use this recipe in an ice cream maker.

## Pawpaw Bread

1 cup pawpaw pulp
1/3 cup shortening
2/3 cup sugar
2 eggs
1 ¾ cup flour
2 teaspoon baking powder
1/4 teaspoon baking soda

3/4 teaspoon salt

In a greased 8 by 4 by 3-inch loaf pan, bake 50 minutes at 350°F for a variation, try this recipe with candied orange peel or lemon peel.

## Pawpaw Muffins

1 pound pawpaw pulp
1 1/2 cup flour
1/2 cup white corn meal
1 tablespoon baking powder
1 egg
1/3 cup sweet sorghum syrup
1/4 cup oil
1 cup milk
1/2 cup nuts
1/2 cup raisins

Grease muffin tin or paper cups. Fill up about two-thirds of the way. Let bake for 18 minutes at 400°F.

## Pawpaw Preserves

12 pawpaws or about 5 pounds
2 cups water
3/4 cup sugar
1 lemon
1 orange

Skin and seed the pawpaws. Boil slowly then put in jars and process to preserve. The less you boil the mixture, the more pawpaw flavor you'll have. You must process the jars in boiling water to seal.

## Pawpaw Punch

1 pawpaw
1 1/2 pint cold water
1 strip lime peel
1 pinch salt
sugar to taste.

Or:

1 can of orange juice, prepared according to directions
2 cups pawpaw pulp

Process in the blender. Mix well, then strain.

## Pawpaw Smoothie

1/2 cup pawpaw pulp
1 cup yogurt
5 drops lemon juice
Pinch of nutmeg and cinnamon

Dilute with water to taste.

## Orange Pawpaw Juice

Juice and peel of 1/2 orange
Pulp of one pawpaw
1 pint of water
1 tablespoon agave nectar
1 teaspoon lemon juice

In a blender put the orange and its zest. Discard as much of the bitter white part of the peel as you can. Grate off the zest, then peel off the white before juicing the orange. Next add the seeded and peeled pawpaw. Add the water gradually. Filter and decant. You may wish to return some of the pulp to the juice. This juice will keep in the refrigerator for several days.

## Pawpaw Jello

Mix 2 cups of pawpaw pulp with one package of lemon jello ( 6 ounces).

## Pawpaw Salsa

2 yellow tomatoes
1 small orange pepper
handful of Italian parsley leaves
1 clove garlic
1/2 red onion, minced fine
1 avocado, diced
1 pawpaw, cubed
1 tablespoon lemon juice

1 small jalapeno pepper, seeded, diced fine

You may wish to add "the heat" by using 1 tablespoon of oriental chili paste or your hot sauce of choice al gusto instead of the fresh jalapeno pepper.

## Pawpaw Pasta Salad

100 g. prosciutto ham, sliced into small pieces
150 g. blue cheese, crumbled
2 tablespoons of a prepared Dijon mustard
1/2 lemon, juiced
300 ml cream
1 red onion, diced small
2 tablespoon melted butter
250 g pasta, cooked. (Spirals are particularly good!)
2 pawpaws, peeled, seeded and cubed

This recipe, which I found posted on the Internet by Terry Powell of the North American Pawpaw Growers Association, struck me as incredibly strange, but when I made it I found out that it is incredibly good! I increased the amount of pawpaw because I liked the way its sweet flavor balanced with the pungent onions and the salty ham and cheese. You may want to increase the amount of pawpaws yet again. This salad is best eaten fresh but will keep in the refrigerator for several days.

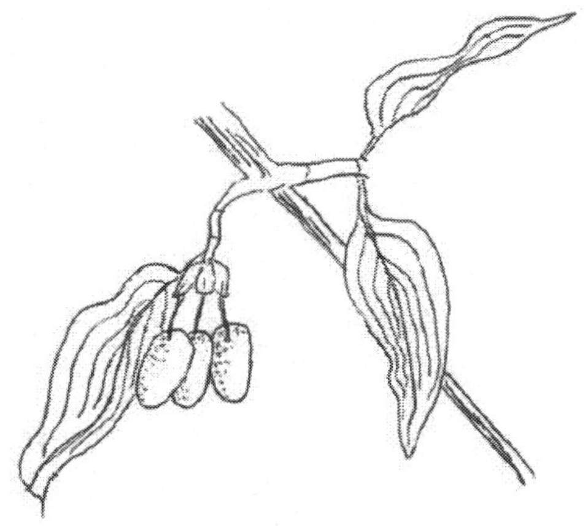

# Cornel

*Cornus mas*

Nobody seems to know what a "cornel" is anymore. No, it's not a university in Ithaca, New York. It's a fruit of a Eurasian tree in the dogwood family, *Cornus mas.* Some people call it "cornelian cherry," but the taste is totally different from cherries or any other fruit you have ever tasted. It has been described as being something like a cross between a plum and a tart cherry. There is probably one growing just a block or two from any urban location. It is widely planted in this country for its early spring yellow flowers, but not for its fruit. The fruit has long been used in Bosnia, Armenia, Turkey, the Ukraine, Russia—just not in America. That has got to change!

We didn't know what cornel was either until Jim Turner gifted us some of his "royal jelly." Jim worked at a garden with several cornel trees on the grounds planted for decoration. He took the fruit to clean up the sidewalk as well as to produce his jam. Mother proclaimed it was her new favorite jelly to put on toast in the morning.

My Turkish aunt came by and sampled the royal jelly, too. She was puzzled at first, perhaps expecting a bee product. (I did use to keep bees at her house.) When she tasted it, her face beamed in a broad smile. "This is *kizilcik!*" she said. "Back in Turkey we make a delicious red syrup from them. There is even a stoic old Turkish saying, 'If you cough up blood, just tell them you've been drinking *kizilcik* juice.'"

Each year after that Jim made a point of bringing more "royal jelly." Cornel jam or jelly is often called by this name, as in jelly "good enough to please a queen."

❧

Cornel is planted all across northeastern North America by the horticultural trade. These large bushes or small trees (They can be pruned to either.) are the first to flower in spring, usually even before saskatoon. Before there are any leaves out anywhere, the branches of cornel will be covered with swarms of small yellow blossoms. In earliest spring, these sparkling yellow trees stand out everywhere. The fruit becomes ripe by late August or early September. Trees planted in partial shade will ripen their fruit later. Cornel is a tough little dogwood that can survive dry soils better than any of the flowering dogwoods.

When we'd learned to tell the flower, Mother discovered that a specimen had been in the yard of an antique store on Main Street for all of her life. I found a variegated specimen within a block of my city home, but this one seems to bear fruit very sparsely, if at all. It seemed as if the cornel were growing everywhere. The selected cultivars have fruit larger than many cherries, perhaps even large enough to merit the occasional name "cornel plum." We once found several in a town park near Lake Ontario's southern shore.

The ornamental cultivars of *Cornus mas* would seem more numerous than those selected for fruit. I've seen "variegata" with elegant white-striped leaves but little or no fruit. "Elegantissima" is more yellowish with some pink-tinged leaves. "Golden glory" is columnar in form while "nana" is a dwarf. "Macrocarpa" has large fruit, "alba," white fruit and "flava," yellow.

*Cornus mas* was introduced to the Ukraine over nine hundred years ago by monks. There are specimens in the Kiev Botanical Gardens which are nearly two hundred years old and continue to bear fruit. Svetlana Klimenko of the Kiev Botanical Gardens has developed cultivars based on the fruit's culinary aspects—"Helen," "Pioneer," "Red Star." In my own six trees I can see quite a bit of genetic variation, subtle differences in fruit shape and ripening habits. In the wild, *Cornus mas* fruit may be white, yellow, orange or deep red. Of the available cultivars of cornel cherry, I had chosen to go with wild seedlings which I obtained from Jim. I planted these unselected seedlings and within five years they were in production. Now fifteen years later hyper-production is more like it! They are in a dry, sunny, stressful position along a road which is over-salted in winter, but the trees don't seem to care. Spruce in the same position have died. *Cornus mas* does not seem to be an overly invasive species in western New York, however. Most if not all of my unwanted "volunteers" are sweet cherries, not cornelian cherries.

You don't have to plant your own trees. Once you've noticed how common they are and how no one ever picks the fruit, you may fell tempted, even obligated, to consume some of this fruit which is going to waste. If you try to pick at a park or churchyard, I can see how this ought perhaps to be discouraged. The hanging of the berries on the tree is part of their beauty, their visual appeal, the horticultural effect of the planting.

What people worry about more than this is that there is a dangerous "wacko" making ready to consume poisonous berries in a public place. They will try to talk you out of it, as with juneberries. Watch the look of horror on their faces as you pop one of the fruits into your mouth! Your offering a taste of the fruit may not work because fresh cornel are extremely sour and not much good without added sugar unless they have gotten to the dark-red, gooshy-ripe stage, which is even more terrifying.

At first the fruit hangs well on the branch. The berries turn green, then yellow, then orange. But mine are only ripe when they finally become bright red in color and gooshy, just a day or two before birds start to focus on them or they fall off the tree and end up rotting on the ground. When the birds are suddenly into them, you know that the berries are at their softest and sweetest. The fruit falls off the branch at the slightest bump. Ripening is uneven, however. Soft-ripe berries can share the same branch with firm-ripe berries as well as green ones. You will have to return to pick the same tree again and again if you mean to get all of the fruit.

You can harvest cornel a bit early, when they still are firm and keep their shape, if you compensate for their bitterness by cooking and adding sugar. The earlier you pick them, the more sugar you must add. If you harvest them when they have sweetened themselves, the berries are very fragile and must be processed into jam or syrup immediately or they will mold. Fruit that is a bit hard and sour will continue to ripen, soften and sweeten if left alone for a few days. Cornels that are red but still unripe are sometimes mistaken for cranberries in a fruit salad. Just be sure to cut the pit out.

"*Cornus*" is the Latin for "horn," referring to the fact that the wood of the dogwood trees is as hard as horn. Cornel wood was used for wagon wheel spokes, spear shafts, wedges, pins and other difficult jobs requiring strength and durability. The sharpened wood alone can make a formidable spear. "Cornelian" is said probably to derive from the Greek for "cherry" which eventually came to mean red-colored, but originally referred to the pit of the cherry being as hard as horn. The wood is so hard and dense that it actually sinks in water.

A Neolithic site in the north of Greece revealed that the people long ago were eating einkorn wheat, barley, lentils, peas and cornelian cherries. The cornel was undoubtedly harvested from the wild by early man, and it is also one of our first domesticated fruit trees. It has been cultivated as a food crop for over 7,000 years. Two thousand years ago, Columella was writing of the cornelian cherry in his *On Agriculture*, advising that it be harvested at its firm-ripe stage. The cornel was grown in monastery gardens throughout the Middle Ages, although it didn't arrive in England until the 1500s. As stated, monks brought cornel to the Ukraine over nine hundred years ago, and the fruit is still very popular in that country today. It is used to flavor soft drinks, syrups, conserves, wines, liqueurs and as a fresh and a dried fruit. It is no surprise that the Ukraine is a world leader today in selection of cornelian cherry cultivars for agriculture. The fruit is also especially popular in Turkey, Bosnia, Moldova, Russia and other eastern European countries.

Now that my half dozen trees are producing considerable fruit (except for years when a late frost hits the blossoms), I decided to jump on the bandwagon to help repopularize the cornel. I have never seen any for sale in the United States except for preserves at the local Russian grocery store. I picked my crop and tried to sell it on consignment at my food co-op. They supported my efforts and donated several tubs of organic ice cream. I prepared a *rob de cornis* and served the syrup over vanilla ice cream to the delight of the customers. (*Rob de cornis* is the name for a French cornelian cherry syrup which was used to flavor apple or pear cider. "*Rob*" derives from the Arabic word "*sharab*" meaning "syrup.") Everyone liked it, and I sold about five pounds of tediously picked fruit the first year, though less and less in subsequent years. This year the cornel was discontinued. Clearly more work is needed to revive our knowledge and use of this venerable, ancient fruit.

In Turkey, "*serbert*" is an old-timey fruit juice drink often prepared with cornelian cherries. That is how "sorbet" became another name for the cornelian cherry in English. Add some precious ice and you have chilled fruit juices, then later frozen ones, hence the first "sherberts." Sherbert's first definition in my Webster's dictionary is a "refreshing drink, made of diluted fruit juice," although most of us would probably think first of the fruit ice version. *Sharbat* is the Persian word for a similar fruit drink. Cornel's intense color and flavor lends itself well to a whole class of liquid refreshments.

In the wild, cornel is native to eastern Europe and western Asia. The trees are small, twenty-five to thirty-five feet tall, with flaking bark. The leaves are about three inches long, vaguely oval in shape but with a slight point at the tips. They are easily recognized as dogwoods by the distinctive parallel venation pattern. The small yellow flowers are partially self-fertile and are the first to bloom in the spring. Young trees produce only male flowers and no fruit. Later the flowers become "perfect," which is a botanist's way of saying that the blossoms have both male and female parts. Although self-fertile at this point, the trees can still benefit from cross pollination. Mature trees can produce thirty to seventy pounds of fruit, ripening in late August or early September. To harvest, you can spread tarp or old sheets beneath your tree and shake down only the ripest berries, or you can pick by hand. Either way, your hands and your clothes will be cherry red by the time you are through. Dress accordingly! Overripe berries that burst when they fall into your shirt will make deep red stains and you must always sort through and discard any berries that are moldy. The reward will be fruit which can be used in many different recipes depending on the degree of ripeness it has achieved.

It is said that Romulus killed his brother Remus with a spear carved from the branch of a cornelian cherry tree. Ovid in the *Metamorphoses* recounts how Romulus cast a spear of cornel wood from the Aventine Hill. It sank deep into the ground, took root and grew into a tree. You might not have such luck yourself. It is possible to root softwood cuttings of cornel, but only about half of your cuttings will survive. Still it might be worth it. The cornel is the perfect small tree for the front yard. Just make sure to plant it a bit back from paths, sidewalks and entryways. This way, excess fruit that you don't want to make "royal jelly" with falls onto the ground and is quickly eaten by happy earthworms rather than becoming a royal pain that gets tracked into your house.

  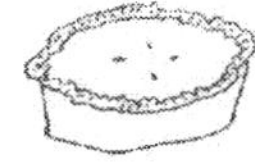

# Cornel Recipes

## Cornel Serving Suggestions

- Cornel juice
- Cornel syrup
- Cornel *lassi*
- Cornel cider
- As a tart addition to fruit salads
- Royal jelly (cornel preserves)
- Cornelian "thumbprint cookies"
- Vanilla cake with a stripe of cornel frosting
- Tapioca cornel swirl
- Dried cornel fruit leather
- *Lavashana* (dried and used to flavor main dishes)
- Cornel can find its way into a meal as fresh fruit, as part of the main course, as a drink or as a dessert.

## Cornelian Olives

Columella, the ancient Roman writer, describes in his treatise *On Agriculture* how to turn the green fruits into an olive substitute. Use must (a pulp of mashed grapes, especially the skins; origin of our word "mustard"—this is after the grapes have been pressed for wine) which has been boiled down and reduced by half. Plain crushed grapes would also be acceptable. To this add an equal part of wine vinegar and salt to taste. Into this brine go the green fruits which soon take on an olive-like character and keep for many months.

I didn't have any must so I kept my fruits in a 10 percent brine solution to which I gradually added wine vinegar. After a few weeks the fruits puffed up a bit and began to look the part of green olives. I sampled them after a month. Although they had none of olive's oiliness, they did taste a bit of olives, very meaty and a bit hard to get off the pit. They had lost most of that usual bitter aftertaste of the unripe fruit.

I picked my "olives" in late July before any sign of ripening. I washed them and removed the stems and made sure to discard the ugly ones. Then I used 1 cup salt, 9 cups water and 1 cup of wine vinegar, plus a token handful of crushed California green grapes, the better to approximate the must. Let sit in clean jars for a month

## Cornelian Cherry Pie

Prepare a pie crust with:

1 cup flour
5 tablespoons shortening
1/2 teaspoon salt
1 teaspoon sugar
2 tablespoons cold water to start (Add additional water a teaspoon at a time until your dough holds together.)

Prepare a filling with:

1 cup cornelian cherry paste, pre-sweetened to taste but still tart
1/2 cup cream
1 egg
1/8 teaspoon powdered clove
1/8 teaspoon cinnamon
2 tablespoons extra sugar
2 tablespoons cornstarch or other thickener

Bake at 375°F for 55 minutes or until set. Don't use a top crust; this pie will look like a "pumpkin" pie.

## Cornel Poppyseed Rolls

For your filling use:

3/4 cup cornel paste, sweetened to taste
1 twelve-ounce can poppyseed pastry filling
1/2 teaspoon ground cloves
1/2 teaspoon dried orange peel (or 1 teaspoon fresh orange zest)
1 tablespoon arrowroot flour

Prepare your dough with:

1/2 cup butter (1 stick), melted
1/3 cup milk
2 eggs
1 teaspoon sugar
Pinch of salt
1 teaspoon yeast
2 cups bread flour

Melt the butter on the stove, then add the milk to cool it down, followed by the other ingredients. Beat well, then add the flour last. Let this dough rise for half an hour, then knead it briefly and roll it out very thin. You will need to use another tablespoon or so of flour to prevent your dough from sticking to the table or rolling pin.

Spread the filling over the dough thinly, then roll it up and slice into 3/4-inch thick rounds. Place these on a greased baking sheet and let rise again. Bake at 375°F for 30 minutes. (These spiral rolls were good but messy. You could choose to seal the filling into triangles instead.)

## Cornelian Cherry Cheesecake

Prepare a cornel paste by cooking the flesh off the pits with minimal water. Add sugar to taste, probably about 1/2 cup sugar to each cup of fruit pulp. If your cornel was at the soft-ripe stage you can get by with less sugar.

8 ounces Neufchatel cheese
1/2 cup milk
2 eggs
4 tablespoons sugar (for the cheese and eggs)
1/4 teaspoon powdered clove
1/4 teaspoon cinnamon
1 cup pre-sweetened cornel paste

Bake at 375°F for one hour in your cheesecake crust of choice. Graham cracker crusts, nut meal crusts or even a simple pie crust will do.

## Cornel Fruit Salad

Orange sections, seeded and cut in half
Bananas, sliced
Pineapples, sliced
Melon, cut into bite-sized pieces
Cornel

Use cornel that is as soft-ripe and naturally sweet as you can get them. Pit the fruits by hand with a sharp knife. Soft fruits will break apart and disappear; firmer fruits will leave "cherry" like pieces but people will probably think that they are cranberries. Add a bit of yogurt or other dressing of choice.

## "Royal Jelly" (Cornel Preserves)

Pick your fruits as soft-ripe as you can, but be aware that they will not keep like this and demand your immediate attention. You can use berries not as ripe and compensate with more sugar if this is more convenient. Unripe uncooked fruits have a very astringent taste.

Add a small amount of water and slowly boil the fruits until the flesh is falling off the pits. Add more water as necessary. Continue boiling until the fruit easily passes though a food mill or applesauce spinner so that the pits may be discarded.

Add one cup of sugar for each cup of cornel pulp. Continue to boil and reduce the jelly until it will gel on its own or add your own commercial pectin to speed up the process. Pour into sterile jars and process in a boiling water bath for 15 minutes to seal.

Don't try to gel all of your cornel syrup. Try some as a drink flavoring. Sweeten to taste and add water and yogurt to create a cornel *lassi*. Try cornel-apple cider or cornel-orange juice. Process your cornel syrup well in a food processor to decrease the size of the pulp particles before adding the water, yogurt or fruit juice.

You may also choose to can your cornel syrup in a liquid form for later use in drinks, or cook it until it takes on a dry texture like apple butter and don't worry whether it gels or not.

## Cornel Marmalade / *Kizilcik Marmelati*

Prepare as for "Royal Jelly" but use orange juice instead of water. Add orange zest and small bits of candied orange peel. If you use strips of fresh orange peel, do be sure to remove as much of the pithy white flesh as possible. Spice the *marmelati* with a pinch of powdered clove, or try a whole clove at the bottom of each jelly jar. Pour into sterile jars and process in a boiling water bath for 15 minutes to seal.

## *Lavashana*

*Lavashana* is an Armenian fruit paste dried into sheets of "fruit leather" for storage. It's made from plums, barberries, cornel or other fruits singly or in combination for use in cooking.

Cook the cornel until the flesh separates from the pit easily. Use a food mill or press the fruit through a sieve to remove and discard the pits. Spread it out in a thin layer to dry in the hot Armenian sun, or dry it on waxed paper in the oven over a period of days. Preheat the oven, then turn it off as soon as you put your cookie sheets of *lavashana* in. Flip the fruit leather after a day or two and remove the paper. Give it more heat from time to time but only keep your product in the oven when it is off.

In Armenia the fruit is dried in the hot sun into paper-thin layers. These are rolled up for storage like a small scroll. Pieces of *lavashana* are added to the main dish to flavor the cooking liquid in place of fresh fruit. The fruit leather will "dissolve" in the warm dish, come apart and create a rich, dark sauce.

You may choose to sweeten your *lavashana* and eat it as "fruit leather" candy. Dry it very carefully, as it has a tendency to develop mold.

## Armenian Fish with Prunes

1 1/2 pounds fish in serving sized pieces (Try trout, red snapper, haddock or other fish.)
4 tablespoons butter

Sauté the fish in butter until nearly done, then set it aside. Make a sauce with:

2 tablespoons butter
1 onion, chopped fine
1 cup water
1 cup pitted prunes
1 roll of *lavashana*

Sauté the onion until golden. Add the water, prunes and *lavashana.* Boil and simmer the sauce until the prunes have plumped and the *lavashana* "dissolves." Add the fish gently to your boiling sauce. Turn off the heat and garnish with dill and cilantro. Serve with rice or potato or other vegetables at the side.

## Azeri-style Fruit-Stuffed Fish

Prepare sufficient stuffing to go into your fish. Fry one onion, chopped fine, in butter until golden. Add equal parts of walnuts and raisins, an "onion-sized" handful of each. Add half as much cornel paste as you did raisins. One additional tablespoon of melted butter. If you used dried *lavashana* or if your raisins don't seem to have plumped up, add a bit of additional water. Stuff your fish and bake it in the oven at 350°F for 20 minutes. Serve with rice.

# Elderberry

*Sambucus canadensis*

It was the 1930s, the middle of the Great Depression. Grandpa had been watching a certain elderberry bush all summer long with an eye for picking. It was located at the edge of a ditch, but still within the right-of-way for the road. Technically, it belonged to no one. He had noted from looking it up on a tax map that the farm land behind the elderberry bush was not associated with the farmhouse across the street from it. In other words, he felt he had just as good a claim to it as anyone else might have. It was mid-August, perhaps early September. The berries were as ripe as they could be, and the birds were starting to get them. It was elderberry time!

Grandpa loaded my mother and the three other kids into the car for a country ride whose true purpose was to lay in a supply of elderberry jelly for the winter and perhaps an elderberry pie or two for now. The children were armed with bags and scissors for the picking. They parked the car, crossed the ditch and began to bend the branches down and cut off the bulky berry clusters. The first bag wasn't even full before their unwelcome presence attracted the attention of the across-the-road residents who challenged the raiders with an emphatic, "You leave our elderberries alone!"

It turned out that this farmer had been watching the berry bushes even more closely than Grandpa had. There ensued an elderberry fight to end all elderberry fights. The children were deeply traumatized. The farmer was not impressed with Grandpa's knowledge of county rights-of-way and real estate law. At some point before the farmer fetched his shotgun Grandpa gave up, loaded the kids back into the car and drove on to another one of "his" elderberry patches that happened not to have a farmhouse within sight of it.

That's how we've done it ever since when we go elderberrying, thanks to this incident of long ago. The elderberry harvest becomes an excuse for extravagantly long country rides through wetlands and the thrill of sighting a great blue heron or a wood duck.

The foraging of food from the wilds is an important Scandinavian tradition, whether the times are hard or not. You would think that foraged foods would taste better because of all the extra attention they get. Was Grandpa getting in touch with his inner Swede or just his inner skinflint, eager to take advantage of free food? It was probably a little bit of both, plus he did like elderberries.

The lingonberry is the signature condiment of Swedish cuisine, but the traditions around the berry carried over to berry traditions here. Lingonberries are harvested from the wilds and are seldom grown as a "crop" on a farm. Swedish law has a concept called *allmänrätt* which means that all men have a right to the bounty of Mother Nature, women too. There is no such thing as "no trespassing" in Sweden. Anyone can fish a stream or pick berries in the forests. A land owner might post a sign reserving a certain field of berries near his home for his personal use and people would respect that, but there were always more berries over the next hill for the peasants to pick. The same would be true for elderberries. So, when Grandpa noticed some elderberries and would ask at the nearest house if anyone "fancied" them or if we could take them, he was just possibly acting out of *allmänrätt*. There are some people who don't fancy elderberries because they are so small and seedy and need to be cooked into something before eating, so he often got a "yes." And if he got a "no," there were still plenty of berry patches on the unpopulated roads.

The American elderberry *Sambucus canadensis* is a small shrub five to twelve feet tall. It grows almost anywhere sunny but it prefers it to be a bit damp, along the edge of a forest or ditch, at the edges of swamps or marshes but not out in the water. Botanists recognize over a dozen shrubs and small trees as being elderberries. They are classified as members of the Moschatel Family (*Adoxaceae*) but were formerly in the Honeysuckle Family *Caprifoliaceae*. Elderflowers do have a very sweet smell similar to honeysuckle.

All parts of the elder except for the fruits and flowers are poisonous! Leaves, twigs and bark of elderberry have cyanide-inducing compounds called glycosides, but poison is what you might want in an antiseptic wash for skin and wounds. Try one teaspoon of plant material steeped in one cup of boiling water for this purpose. Be sure NOT to use it internally. Cooking destroys the cyanide-based chemicals in the juice and makes it far more palatable but to be on the safe side, do not even eat fresh elderberries without cooking them. The berries won't kill you but they can cause diarrhea and vomiting. Cook them and sweeten them and they are safe and delicious. The flower of the elder is also used as a flavoring. This is sometimes called "elderblow" as in "elderberry blossoms." Elderberry syrups are both delicious and medicinal.

The European elder *Sambucus nigra* is more like a small tree growing ten to thirty feet tall. Its fruit can also be used for jelly. The European elder has stronger medicinal affects (and potentially more dangerous ones too) than the American elderberry does. The bark and roots are said to be diuretics (increasing the flow of urine), emetics (making you vomit) and purgatives (making it come out the other end). The fruit is an aperient (a laxative) and the flower is a diaphoretic (causing you to sweat).

*Sambucus racemosa*, the red elderberry, is a shrub up to fifteen feet in height. I have seen it infrequently and never in sufficient quantity to gather any berries. As a child I was told that the berries were poisonous. I later read that the berries are not poisonous and are perfectly good for making jelly, but the seeds can kill you and you have to filter them out. This hasn't made me want to run out and taste red elderberry jelly!

"Elderberry rob" is a delicious and medicinal syrup which you can prepare by crushing then cooking five pounds of black elderberries with one pound of sugar. Add a minimal amount of water. Filter the syrup and discard the seeds. Store it in a small bottle in the refrigerator and use it a spoonful at a time, or process and preserve larger amounts in sealed canning jars for later use.

Elderberry juice drinks and elderberry jelly would share, at least to some extent, the herbal and medicinal benefits of elderberry rob. It's just food that is also medicine. "Rob" is an old word for a medicinal syrup or conserve. There is even an old recipe for elderberry rob contained in *1001 Arabian Nights*.

A cordial is another route to take to imbibe elderberry in delicious sipfuls. Cordials include any number of herbal or fruity liqueurs taken in small amounts to revive, cheer and invigorate the body, the heart, the appetite—and the dinner party. The Swedes prepare an elderflower cordial by infusing the elder flowers in aquavit or schnapps. You could make your own cordial by infusing crushed elderberries in vodka, or use the blossoms for a more subtle and different flavor without the purple color. You can also use dried berries for this purpose.

Elder has been scientifically proven to have an anti-viral activity. The dried berries are high in vitamins A, B and C and are also high in anti-inflammatory compounds called flavonoids. Try steeping a spoonful of dried berries with your ordinary tea. Elder stimulates the immune system. A spoonful of syrup or a cordial taken at first onset of a cold or flu can make the illness of shorter duration. If elderberry rob is taken regularly, you can expect a lower incidence of viral infections. That piece of elderberry pie might be just as good for you. A spoonful of elderflower syrup in a small glass of warm milk makes for a soothing bedtime drink.

Appalachian folk use elderflower tea as a "nerve tonic" to treat conniptions and emotional upsets. The Meskwaki brewed a tea of elder bark to help with uterine contractions. The Onondaga make a poultice of elder bark with warm water to be applied to the forehead as a headache remedy. Compounds in the bark, such as rutin, quercetin and isoquercetin, are known to be capillary protectants and can pass through the skin. Delicate dosages of these compounds are to be found in the flowers and stems of the elders.

The Seneca and the Cayuga prepared an infusion of elderblossom and used this "tea" to sponge-bathe babies born prematurely, taking care not to get any of this medicine near the eyes, ears or nose.

Elderflowers are used to create elderflower syrups. Just infuse them in boiling sugar water and then let them sit for a day or longer. The flowers have a sweet fragrance that is easily lost, so don't over boil them. Elderflower infusions are also used in many sorts of cosmetic products. The most curious bit of lore that I found in my researches is that a shade-dried elderflower was formerly placed in baskets of apple varieties said to be "aromatic" so as better to preserve this quality of the fruit during long storage.

Elderberry juice concentrate is available at health food stores and food co-ops but it may be hard to locate at your ordinary supermarket. I purchased some grown in California and was amazed at how much sweeter it was than my own efforts using New York-grown berries. I chalked it up to that warm California sun, or perhaps the berries had been longer on the bush protected by netting, bird cannons or more dire measures.

Long, slow boiling during processing can also make your juice sweeter by concentrating what natural sugars are already there, although this is not appropriate for the delicate perfumed flavors of elderberry flowers.

Occasionally, you may encounter elderflower syrup or elderflower lemonade in commerce. In Europe, you are more likely to find the flavor of the flower used in recipes than the fruit. Elderflower water is a more ephemeral product with cosmetic and perfumery uses. Let your elderflowers steep long in hot water, then use this water to cleanse and clear you skin. Elderflower can be slowly dried and reserved for future uses. Use a comb to remove the flowers from the cluster.

❧

The elderberry is almost never seen in commerce today as fresh fruit. You will most often encounter it as jelly, less often as a juice concentrate or mixed in a fruit juice drink. Elderflower drinks are common in Europe but nearly unknown in America. Elderberry pies are well known in America, but they can be seedy. I prefer them as pies when combined with other fruits like apple, quince, peach or blackberry.

# Elderberry

There are several selected varieties of American elderberry available in the horticultural trade ("Adams," "York," "Nova," "Johns" and others) known for their larger-sized berries. The bare root plants were difficult for me to transplant because the buds or sprouting leaves break off so easily and often do not regrow. Many of the buds broke off during shipment as well. If you go this route, you will probably need protective fencing. One taste by a passing deer could finish them off. Because the selected cultivars are really just clones of one exceptional individual, you will need more than one variety to ensure pollination.

Elderberry is usually propagated by the removal of root suckers in the spring. You may also take softwood cuttings in April or May. Keep the cuttings damp for two days as they harden off, then plant them in pots and keep them in the shade, well watered. A dip in rooting hormone powder wouldn't hurt. After a month or so, move your plants into more direct sunlight. You'll soon see which cuttings show the most vigorous growth. Whether propagating by cutting or division, young elderberry bushes are extremely fragile and I have not had good luck with them.

Mature bushes can be stimulated to produce more fruit by rotational pruning every two to three years. The deer seem to love young elderberry sprouts before the mature leaves produce too much of their cyanide-based compounds. Be aware that cutting out of the dead wood may prove counterproductive. In nature the elder often dies back during winter, leaving a maze of dead branches. It sprouts again from buds hidden on the larger limbs. These contorted, dead branches serve to protect the young, tender sprouts from too much deer snacking. Let me tell you, I've lost many a young elderberry bush to the deer in spring.

Elderberry bushes need half to full sunlight in order to thrive. I discovered a number of elders in a patch of woods after it had been sustainably logged. They loved the rich dirt! It was a sure spot to find an ample harvest. The birds of the forest did not favor the berries as ravenously as did the birds of the open sunlight at my farm. As the forest grew back and the shade closed in, the bushes became taller and leggier. The berries were fewer and further between. After twenty years, they finally died out.

In Latin, elder is called "*ebulus*" from the verb *ebullire*, "to bubble out." The Celtic term for elder, "*crann troim*," translates as "the laden tree." These words obviously refer to elders grown in full sunlight where the panicles of berries are fully formed and close together. The beautiful creamy white flower clusters do look like waters at a roiling boil. So what will become of those elders in the deep woods? They will be back someday when the woods are logged again or a windstorm recreates areas of bright sunlight. The birds will seed them back in.

I put my bushes where I thought they would like it along the edge of my swamp but the deer ate most of them. Some did grow big enough to have berries and yes, the berries were noticeably larger than those on the wild bushes, but the birds make short work of them. I invested in bird netting and discovered that this was totally inappropriate for my naturalized plantings. Brambles and vines soon grew into the netting. I ended up destroying the bushes, the berry crop and the netting when I attempted to harvest.

And so it was that I reverted to my grandfather's habits and roamed the back country roads. I took frequent hikes into my swamp looking for the wild bushes. You need to check on the berries regularly once they begin to ripen or the birds will see to it that the fruit disappears rapidly. If you want to establish a new planting of these improved cultivars, my suggestion is to do it in an area that can be closely watched and intensely managed. Perhaps then the bird netting can give you greater advantage.

❧

I located a patch of bushes on a remote forested crossroads here in New York. For some reason these berries hung long on the bush, week after week, until they were almost as sweet as that California concentrate. The ditch provided irrigation; the roadways ensured ample sunlight. These berries actually began to ferment on the bush and would have made excellent elderberry wine. Their secret, I finally discovered, was the close proximity of a bald eagle nest! The berries on my farm were in an oasis of wildness surrounded by a vast monoculture of grapes. These berries had no chance of avoiding the songbirds and ripening to this degree of sweetness.

Elderberries like currants are said to be "twice picked." You can pick enough to make a few pies in mere minutes, as opposed to a half hour or longer in the raspberry patch or even longer if you are hunting down wild blackberries. The flat elderberry clusters can be a magnet for road dust or worse, so you will probably need to rinse them in water and set them aside to dry. If left unwashed on the cluster, the fresh berries will keep for a week or two in the refrigerator.

Now get ready for some purple fingers! The real work is the "second picking," the laborious process of "shucking" to separate the berries from their stems. Be sure to remove all stem remains from your finished product, as they can be distasteful or even toxic. The second picking is far more laborious than the first. Some folks use a "berry comb" sort of tool, or gently roll the clusters in a garbage bag to separate most of the berries from the stems. Whichever technique you choose to use, it is a tedious task. The twice-picked berries can be easily frozen for later use in pies and muffins. They can be easily dried on a cookie sheet in the oven and used later in good-tasting medicinal teas to help ward off winter colds and flu.

❧

Because elderberries are among the last berries to ripen in the summer, I long assumed that we are calling them "elder" as in "old." I was wrong. The etymological dictionary says that "elderberry" is related to an Anglo-Saxon word "*elloern*" which refers to the fact that the wood is hollow. The wood was once used for flutes, whistles, panpipes and blowguns to hunt small birds with darts. In America the branches were whittled into taps used in the collecting of maple sap for syrup.

Elder is also a wood of choice for the magic wand, so it is not surprising to find such a wealth of pagan lore associated with this plant. It wards off the evil eye and can protect you from witches. If you stand beneath an elder tree on Midsummer's Eve or Halloween, you will be able to see the Elf King or the Faerie Queen as they pass by with their retinue. Just as the elder is a source of dangerously potent herbal medicines, so too the wood of this plant is special and many are the warnings against using it improperly. The Wiccan Rede states:

*Elder be ye Lady's tree,*
*Burn it not or cursed be.*

The twigs of the elder tree were generally not burned. Some people believe that the souls of the dead were harbored in its branches. It was once the custom to pay homage to the tree or bush as you walked by, with a doff of the hat, a bow of the head, or a curtsy. This is a measure of the great respect which our ancestors once held for the elder.

Mother Hulda, Hermann Vogel (1854–1921)

The Elder Mother is a most ancient goddess known from England across Germany and north into Scandinavia. She is called Old Lady, Old Girl, Lady Ellhorn or Mother Holda in English. In Danish she is Hyldemoer. The elder tree is said to be her dwelling place. Holly and rowan trees are also sacred to her. If you ever glimpse by moonlight an older woman dressed in black hanging around an elder tree, that is she. Anyone who wants to make use of elder wood must first ask the Elder Mother for permission. You probably won't want to burn the wood when you find out how many other things it is good for.

There is a belief that witches, fairies and spirits live in the roots and hollows of the elder. Kneel before the plant and say:

*Lady Ellhorn, give me of thy wood,*
*And I will give thee of mine*
*When I become a tree.*

This gives the spirits time to move on before you cut any of the wood. Chewing on an elder twig can relieve a toothache, it is said. Carrying it in your pocket can relieve rheumatism. Growing an elderberry bush near your house can protect against lightning strikes and sorcery. It also repels snakes. Elderberry boughs were used to bless weddings. Pregnant women would kiss the tree to ensure health and good luck for their children. Elder leaves make a good poultice when boiled, cooled and wrapped around swellings, burns and infections. Steep the leaves in olive oil, then add beeswax to create a healing skin salve. Elder has been referred to as "the poor man's medicine chest."

In German, the Elder Mother is known as Frau Holle. She was associated with bears and lived in a cave at Hohlstein in the northern German state of Hessen. She appears as Mother Goose in the fairy tales of the Brothers Grimm. A snowstorm is said to be "Frau Holle shaking out her featherbeds." She is a studious and industrious winter goddess associated with women, childbirth, spinning, domestic animals, healing, death, rebirth, the household, the harvest, and of course the elder tree. That would be the elderberry bush in America.

Holda is said to be Woden's consort when he leads "the wild hunt" at the beginning of winter. Colds and flu begin to cull the human herd at this time, just as we cull our flocks of animals before the long winter to come. Wells, ponds, springs, fountains and elder trees are sacred to Holda. The Elder Mother is such a powerful ancient goddess that her attributes appear to have been distributed among the other, later goddesses Nerthus, Frigga, Freya and Hel.

Little else is known directly about the Elder Mother beyond some fairy tales and these botanical bits of pagan lore. But we can still see the linguistic evidence of Holda's power in Swedish. For instance, "*huld*" means benign and kindly, and "*hull*" denotes the flesh in good condition—as in "*ha gott hull*," meaning "to have good flesh." (To be plump and healthy.) "*Hyllan*" is a word used in the theater for "the gods," and "*hylla*" is a verb meaning "to applaud, congratulate or swear allegiance to." "Huldra" is also a siren, a female spirit who leads travelers off the beaten track to an uncertain fate. These words may well be related to Holda, the Elder Mother.

# Elderberry

Skogsfru, Hans Gude (1825–1903)

In Norway and Sweden the Elder Mother has given birth to a whole race of forest spirits. She is known as Skogsfru ("Forest Lady"), a beautiful woman from the front but with a hollow body and the tail of a cow or a fox. If you glimpse her from the back, you can see that she is hollow just like an old tree. Lesser male spirits devoted to her are called "*huldrekarl*," or sometimes referred to as "*hamadryads*" (tree spirits) in English, especially when in connection with Graeco-Roman tree spirits that are not quite as dangerous. As Huldra the siren, the "Lady of the Woods," she lures male travelers off the beaten track with many of her paramours meeting unfortunate ends in the forest. As Frau Holle, however, she is a kindly old woman who takes care of sickly or abandoned children, rewarding those who work for their keep in her household. The dual nature of the Elder Mother reflects the aspects of a powerful plant that can both harm and heal.

The elderberries ripened late in 1951, hanging heavy on the bush in western New York until the first week of September when I was born. Native Americans used elderberry root tea to induce labor, but my mother used jumping over a ditch to pick them. She was nine months pregnant and jumping over a ditch on Minton Road to get elderberries when her water broke and I started to come into the world. This patch of elderberry bushes was pointed out to me time and again over the years, and I picked elderberries there with great satisfaction knowing I was returning to my natal bush like some kind of foraging land salmon. This elderberry patch died out over the years due to overzealous mowing by the landowner, but I can see a few descendants poking their heads out of the woods further on down the road....

# Elderberry Recipes

## Elderberry Serving Suggestions

- Elderberry jelly
- Elderberry pie
- Apple-elderberry pie
- Elderberry cobblers
- Elderberry fruit soups
- Elderberry concentrate mixed with apple juice
- Elderberry juice drinks
- Elderberry muffins
- Elderberry bran muffins
- Elderberry tea
- Elderberry pancakes
- Elderberry wine
- Elderflower syrup
- Elderflower fritters
- Elderflower pancakes
- Elderflower lemonade and other drinks

Elderberry or elderflower syrup can be used to flavor a vast number of juice drinks, punches, desserts and salads. Elderflower is often used in alcoholic drinks as well as being used extensively in cosmetics which are not edible but often smell as good as if they are.

## Black-Elderberry Cobbler

1 cup elderberries
1 cup blackberries
Spread the berries into a buttered baking dish.
Sprinkle with 5 tablespoons sugar, or more to taste
Dot with 1 tablespoons extra butter

Prepare the batter:

1 beaten egg
1/2 cup milk
1/2 cup melted butter
1 1/2 cups flour
2 teaspoon baking powder
1/4 teaspoon salt
1/2 cup sugar

Mix the wet and dry ingredients well, then pour the batter over the uncooked berries. Bake at 400°F for 25 to 30 minutes until the berries are bubbling and the cobbler is starting to brown. Of course you can prepare a cobbler that is just elderberries, but I find that a bit too seedy for my taste and prefer to mix in blackberries. Another good choice is apples cut into small pieces.

## Elderberry Apple Crisp

Butter an 8 inch by 8 inch baking tin. Into it place:

2 cups apple pieces, peeled
1 cup elderberries

On top of this crumble the following:

1/2 cup brown sugar
1/2 cup rolled oats
1/4 cup flour
1/4 cup butter or margarine, cut in
1/4 teaspoon cinnamon
1/4 teaspoon allspice

Cut the butter into small pieces as you strew it across the top of the crisp. Bake at 400°F for 20 to 25 minutes. Serve warm with cream or ice cream on top. Vanilla yogurt is good too!

## *Holderschmarren*

This recipe is a cross between a fruit soup and a wet bread pudding. Fry the fruit in the butter first:

3 1/2 tablespoons butter
1 pound elderberries
1/2 pound pears, peeled
1/2 pound plums

Then add:

- 2 cups milk, mixed to a paste with
- 2 to 3 tablespoons flour
- Juice of 1/4 lemon
- Pinch of salt
- 1/4 pound of stale rye or French bread, crusts cut off

Cook until soft; add sugar to taste.

## Elder Fruit Soup

- 2 1/2 pounds elderberries
- 6 tablespoons water

Cook these together until the berries start to fall apart, then add:

- 3/4 cup sugar
- 2 tablespoons lemon juice
- Zest of one lemon
- 4 tablespoons cornstarch

Mix the cornstarch with a bit of the soup before adding to the pot. This will help to avoid clumps of flour in the soup.

More usual fruit soup recipes feature prunes, dried pears, raisins, apricots. A minority of elderberries would be welcome in other sorts of fruit soups. Spice with a cinnamon stick.

## Strawberry Elderflower Parfait

- 1 quart strawberries
- 3 tablespoons elderflower juice concentrate/syrup
- 2 egg yolks

Mash the berries well into the eggs and elderflower syrup. Then whip together:

- 3 tablespoons powdered sugar
- 2 egg whites, beaten
- 1 cup cream, whipped
- 2 tablespoons sugar or to taste

Mix these gently together, then freeze in a mold for 4 hours in the freezer. Place it in the refrigerator for one hour before serving, or let sit for 20 minutes at room temperature. Run hot water over the bottom of the mold to loosen, then turn out with a knife and serve in individual parfait glasses. Adapted from *Traditional Swedish Cooking* by Caroline Hofberg.

## Elderberry Flower Syrup

Gather 50 elderberry flower heads and using a fork carefully separate the fragrant flowers from the green stem. Discard the stems. Prepare a syrup:

12 cups of water
7 cups of sugar
3 lemons, juiced and zested
1 teaspoon citric acid

Boil the syrup and then pour it over the flowers and let it steep for 4 days. Strain and use. Elderflower syrup may also be canned for later use. Use 1 part syrup to 9 parts water to create an elderflower drink. You can add 2 tablespoons of elderflower syrup to a glass of soda water. Elderflower lemonade is also a very popular combination. Use the syrup also to flavor herbal teas, iced teas and even pancakes. Throw 1 tablespoon of elderflower syrup into your pancake recipe.

## Elderflower Champagne

4 large elderberry flower heads
2 1/2 pounds sugar
2 lemons (Use only the zest and the juice.)
4 tablespoons white wine vinegar
10 liters water (42.3 cups or 2.64 gallons)

Boil the water, then add the flowers, sugar, lemon juice, zest and vinegar. Let this steep for at least 24 hours. Use only the natural yeasts present in the flowers. Sterilize bottles, then strain the champagne into the bottles. Let sit for at least 2 weeks.

## Elderflower Fritters / *Holderkuechle*

Prepare a batter of:

1 3/4 cups flour
2 eggs
1/2 cup milk
Pinch of salt

Into this batter dip 16 elderflower bunches, stems and all. Deep fry in oil, then dust with powdered sugar and serve warm.

## Elder Blossom Skin Moisturizer

1/4 cup olive oil
2 tablespoons jojoba oil
1 tablespoon dried elderflower
1 tablespoon dried comfrey leaf
1 teaspoon beeswax

This is a cosmetic concoction that is good for your skin, not your stomach. Heat the oil and let the herbs steep in it as it cools. Let it sit for 3 days in the dark. Strain, then reheat, adding the beeswax. When the wax has melted, pour it all into containers and let it cool and set. This will keep for several months.

Elderflower Water was also once widely used as a rinse for the face. Boil a pot of water, then throw in one elderberry flower cluster. Take it off the stove and let it steep overnight. Take out the flower head before use.

## Elderberry Ginger Tea

Boil one or two inches of ginger root, cut into smaller pieces, with one tablespoon of dried elderberries. Boil briefly, then turn off the heat and let the tea steep. This tea has medicinal value as well as being delicious! Here is another version of the same with the addition of tea:

2 cups water
2 teabags (black or green) or 2 tablespoons loose tea
2 tablespoons dried elderberries
1 teaspoon minced ginger
1 teaspoon fennel seed

## Elderflower Chicken

Prepare a marinade:

1 cup elderberry flower syrup
3 tablespoons oil
2 tablespoons cider vinegar
1/3 cup fresh mint
1/3 cup fresh dill
Salt and pepper

Fry 1 pound of chicken in butter until it has browned, then bake it in the oven at 325°F for another 15 or 20 minutes until done. Let cool. Marinate the chicken pieces overnight in this elderflower marinade. Serve the chicken cold, thinly sliced, accompanied by pieces of red onion, cucumber and melon. Adapted from *Traditional Swedish Cooking* by Caroline Hofberg.

Yggdrasil (the World Tree), 1895, Lorenz Frølich (1820–1908)

# Epilogue

The more I worked on this book, the more fascinating and delicious were the tidbits assembled. It never stopped. I've put off publishing again and again because I hadn't baked this or brewed that or thoroughly investigated this or that pathway of lore that had been opened for me. The time approaches to finish this work before time finishes me! This epilogue is being written to explore the deficiencies in my work and to suggest new directions for future fruit explorers to travel.

For example, I have been unsuccessful in my efforts to curb fireblight and protect the medlars and quinces from insect damage. I own neither sprayer nor tractor. So there are many unresolved technical questions of an agricultural nature. Some answers are available just by contacting the County Co-operative Extension, while other answers are not available in English. For such technical questions regarding the growing of the medlar, try French or Italian agricultural sources. There is no commercial medlar production in America to speak of, but the preserves are still mass-produced in a number of European countries.

The doctrine of correspondences associates the medlar with anal and vaginal health based on the shape of the enlarged flower remains that persist on the bottom of the fruit. It looks vaguely like a bodily orifice, so that "must be" what this plant cures. Somehow this plant has been warped into some kind of "poster child" for concepts of "virginity" and "original sin." Behind this sex-negative brainwashing aspect, the medlar certainly had a more glorious past, yet I have been unable to find mention of any specific goddess lore linked to this fruit. Why is medlar wood so special for the Basque people? What sort of medlar lore could I find in the pre-Islamic traditions of Turkey or Persia? Quince seems to share a bit of this sexual/fertility aspect, as evidenced by the fact that the fruit appears in myths of Venus and Pomona, plus its use in modern-day Greek wedding traditions.

So, Venus and Pomona had their quinces, and Idunna had her apples. Pomona is also sometimes called the "Apple Mother." Huldra is associated with elderberries and was even said to dwell in the hollow wood. Hatho got his face full of hot blackberry syrup. Which goddess is associated with the medlar? That is what I want to find out. Modern day Wiccans need nothing more than to notice the pentagrams on the bottoms of this fruit to assert a special relationship with the Goddess.

Further researches in the old religions of Slavic areas and the agricultural practices of Russian "Old Way" believers may prove very fruitful in this regard, pun intended. Romulva (Lithuanian heathenism) has a long tradition of tree worship, but I have not yet had the time to investigate its stories about these old-time fruits.

Yggdrasil, the Tree of Life in the Nordic tradition, is said to be an ash, but at other times (like Yule) the tree seems more like an evergreen. Don't expect a mythical tree necessarily to be of one and only one species. The expanded view is that all of us plants and animals are growing like epiphytes on a cosmic world tree.

Fermentation is another surface barely scratched in this work. Certainly these fruits are still used in the production of specialty wines and meads. Vinegars are another related matter. Investigations of Turkish and Persian cuisines may tell us more about the use of quince and medlar vinegars. American regional cultural traditions can tell us more about persimmon beer. Seeing as it is so extremely sweet, how could the pawpaw not have been involved in fermentation? And I still haven't tried that pawpaw pale ale.

It is clear that there exists a world-wide antique fruit heritage that needs to be explored, documented and preserved. This in turn runs the gamut of ethnic cuisines, ancient mythology, agricultural practices in different cultures, amusing superstitions, botany, traditional and modern medicines, as well as much more.

So what was it that made me become an antique fruit missionary? I've been accused of being Amish because of my habits. I did live without electricity for periods in my life. It was a combination of choice and necessity, but I have always used mirrors, belt buckles and buttons. So, I'm not Amish. The Amish people I have met may sell blackberry or elderberry jam but lack traditional knowledge about other old-fashioned fruits. This was a surprise to me at first until I realized that the Amish are too busy making money to be able to keep up on labor intensive, minimally profitable fruits like gooseberries and medlars.

I have enjoyed meeting elders who remember these fruits from their youth. It brought a smile to family friend Col. Correl's face when I took him some pawpaws. He hadn't eaten any since the Great Depression when his (single) mother would procure some for them each fall. Pawpaws are very high in protein. Iron came from the weeds. The Colonel fondly remembered dining upon burdock greens, dandelions and lamb's quarters.

The first person I found to know medlars was my nonagenarian city neighbor Dottie.

"Oh, those. I haven't seen those in a long time!" she commented.

She spoke about them in exasperation, remembering all the tedious work involved in the preparation of a medlar sauce for the evening's roast pork. Then she was that three-year-old little girl again, sitting under the table out of the way, smiling, enjoying her medlar with a silver spoon while the women folk worked. It seemed like a rare happy moment in her long and difficult life. I seem to have incorporated that into my own memories as well, such is the magic of the medlar, that sense of hidden treasure.

Later I discovered that my much younger Bosnian neighbors also knew about medlars ("mušmula"). Hasan tells me that medlars aren't grown commercially in Bosnia, though you may sometimes see them in the markets. It seems that every other family has a medlar tree in their yard, rather like it was with quince trees in America when I was a child. It was Hasan who first demonstrated for me the eating of a medlar (in the out-of-doors) with no silver spoon.

Choose a well-bletted medlar and make a small tear in the skin using your fingernail or canine tooth. Press down on the pulp beneath the skin and direct it over top of the seeds towards the hole and into your mouth. As you finish, you may choose to suck the pulp off of each seed before spitting it, watermelon style, onto the ground. When Hasan gets a taste of frass, he spits it out and discards the fruit, then eagerly selects the next one.

"Yuck! Bugs got that one!"

Bosnians of all ages seem to know about cornel, quince and medlar. They use quince leaf tea and tea of the dried quince fruit (sliced) as a remedy for colds and coughs. Other countries have kept more of their traditional knowledge about these old-fashioned fruits than have we here in America.

I took my missionary work to the *Alliance Française Fête de Noël* with a basket of ripe medlars and a small poster of instructions on how to eat them with a spoon. I advertised them as "*le fruit de Noël du Moyen Age*" (the Christmas fruit of the Middle Ages). There were also thin pieces of medlar pie and a bowl of medlar yogurt with walnuts. Here the fruit did engender some excitement and more memories.

My friend Claire had not had medlars since her years in France during the Second World War. They brought a special smile to her face as well as memories of her uncle's medlar and pear trees, small joys for the children during horrible times.

"How do you say "*nèfles*" in English?" I heard younger people asking as they nibbled.

In French there is only one word for currants and gooseberries, "*groseilles*." If you really need to distinguish between the two, says Claire, you can call gooseberries "*groseilles maquereaux*" which means "mackerel currants." I asked her why and she presumed that the greenish color reminded people of the ocean or of fish. It is also possible that this word is a reflection of the culinary use of this berry with fish, as in the Bohuslän Gooseberry Fish Sauce recipe contained in this book. The Viking women may have brought their cooking style to Normandie.

Tail piece, Bewick British Birds, 1797, Thomas Bewick (1753–1828)

Now it is time for me to play my curmudgeon card. I may not be Amish but I do feel lucky to have been able to grow up in the country and to experience rural culture and village life. I remember an era before malls, computers and television. "But what did you do back then?" my students used to ask me. I still live this way, most of the time, without feeling poor or disadvantaged or deprived in any way.

I have observed disturbing changes in our society's food distribution system. Some foods have fallen out of fashion, especially my beloved old-fashioned fruits. Most foods come from afar and are so processed and chemical-filled that they hardly resemble food to me any more.

Back in the day we drank milk from cows that grazed within a mile of our house. Most of our food came from close to home. Certain staples like sugar, flour and coffee did come from afar, but the rest came more directly from the land. We bought our shoes and clothing in town from merchants who knew us by name. There were as many "mom and pop" grocery stores as there were supermarkets. Things are not like this any more.

# Epilogue

Refrigerators and freezers were not yet universal in my youth and we still used words like "icebox." Some families in Westfield kept their food at the "Locker Plant," a central facility that was really just a giant freezer divided into rental compartments. I'd hear comments like "Got me a side of beef for the winter." You'd head down to the Locker Plant while it was open during the day to saw off however much frozen meat you needed for the evening meal. Those carrots and potatoes and parsnips probably came from a farm right down the road whether you bought them at a supermarket or a farm stand. Our area had more fruit and vegetable processing plants in those days. Everyone used to grow everything back then. Today the land has become a monoculture of grapes in our area, for the most part.

Some families got all of their food off the land from hunting, fishing, foraging, gardening and animal husbandry. These were not trendy "locavores" like today, nor were they scrupulously principled rejectionist hippies. Hippies did not exist in the 1950s and the Amish had not yet spread into Chautauqua County (except for Cherry Creek). These were poor folks who had no access to stores or to money. There were no "food stamp" programs back then. These people were used to surviving long periods of time without money and without stores. Most people still had their "victory gardens" left over from the war. They could eat venison, trout and bullheads, as well as weeds and pawpaws.

Let me tell you about my grandfather's dear friend and neighbor, Edith Royce. She lived across the woodlot from Grandpa and had an old apple and pear orchard with many trees that were fun to climb. To us she was the "evil old witch" who came out and chased us off her property whenever we climbed the trees close to her house, but she was really not evil in any way. She looked at our intrusion as a visit and talked about Grandpa and how she had no insurance and how the lawyers would take away her house when a small boy would fall out of a tree on her property. Of course we did not understand this. She remembered that she had been our landlady when I was a baby. She offered us a taste of the ripening fruit but we had to go back into the woods to find a tree to climb where she could not see us. Who knows whose property it was on?

In her younger days Edith was certainly a suffragette and among the first women to graduate from Syracuse University. She would have been in her mid-twenties when women were first allowed to vote. Her family had an aristocratic outlook on life but that vanished along with most of their stocks and bonds during the Great Depression. Edith was too proud to go to the Poor Farm. She moved into a converted chicken coop at the edge of the farm and lived on next to nothing. Grandpa gave her rides in his car and knew when her checks came in from her meager surviving annuities. He took her to the bank, then shopping, then home. All she ever bought was flour, sugar, oatmeal, matches and saltine crackers. She picked wild strawberries in the fields around her home and put up as many glasses of jam as she could. Grandpa claimed that she lived off of wild strawberry jam and saltine crackers. By the 1950s she had inherited a house from family and moved into town. Now she lived just across the woodlot from my grandparents. Grandpa would take her onions and carrots from the garden; Grandma would send over wild cherry jelly or currant jam.

Grandpa was an insurance agent. In the 1930s and 1940s he was still letting a few people pay their insurance bills with butter or carrots or a side of pork. Do you know any insurance agent who would do that today?

I have used the old-fashioned fruits to paint a picture of a world that is very different from our world of today. I do not want to romanticize poverty or the eating of weeds and berries but to point out how greatly our system has changed in my 65 years. It frightens me when someone says to me "I don't think we can be friends. You don't have a cell phone or an answering machine." Yes, it's a brave new world out there!

I will conclude my work with a few stories about other old-fashioned fruits yet which I continue to investigate.

## Wild Black Cherry

The wild black cherry *Prunus serotina* is different from "black cherries" (a variety of "sweet cherries") and it was once widely used to flavor jelly, soda pops, candies and medicines. Wild black cherry trees are all over our area but you will want to find a younger one with low-hanging branches for easy picking. Grandma had a huge, low branch coming out of the woodlot near the driveway. It was easy for her to spread out an old sheet and shake the cherries down.

We claimed that Grandpa was so mean that he used to make Grandma pit each miniscule cherry by hand to make her jam or jelly. Truth is he wasn't quite that mean. Besides, it was easy to gather large amounts of fruit and boil them slowly for an hour or two adding a little water until the fruit is completely soft and the flesh is falling off the pits.

At this point you would add a bit more water so that you can more easily filter out and discard the pits. Sweeten your liquid to taste and continue to boil until you have reduced it to juice, jam, jelly or syrup. The liquid will get sweeter by itself as it reduces and the fruit sugars are concentrated, so don't sweeten it too much early on.

Wild black cherry was known to be good for cough drops, and it made a pretty good ice cream soda too. This was back when "dairy bars" served what they called "legal beverages."

# Epilogue

Where could you get a wild black cherry soda today? This meant two things. You take the bottle of soda pop. I'll go to the dairy bar and have an ice cream wild black cherry soda. This was a scoop of ice cream, a squirt of black cherry syrup and then soda water to top it off. It was wonderfully foamy, served in a tall crystal parfait glass and consumed with joint action of a spoon and a straw.

Since the ice cream soda was an attempt to recreate an alcoholic beverage and because it could only be served at a (dairy) bar, it was deemed to be too special a treat to be eaten on Sundays. A more mundane version was created by leaving out the sparkling soda water. This scoop of ice cream topped with fruit or syrup was served in a shorter parfait glass and consumed with a spoon, no straw. They called this a "sundae." Notice how the spelling was changed so as not to upset God on His day by naming an almost sinfully good dessert for it. At first sundaes were only served on Sunday but they proved to be so popular that they came to be served on other days as well.

We tend to forget that the reason soda pops have bubbles in them is to imitate champagne. At one time prohibition of alcohol was the progressive cause of the day and you could show your support by consuming an ice cream soda instead! You could only get this at a dairy bar for a price, unless your family was rich enough to afford enough ice to freeze the cream and also to have a soda bottle at home. Or perhaps you had one of those new-fangled electric ice boxes with a freezer? (The sundae was cheaper; it could also be more easily made at home if you had access to ice cream.)

This was the era of wild black-cherry syrup. Ice cream sodas aren't around any more, nor is the syrup. They gradually morphed into root-beer floats and whatnot, soda pop mixed with ice cream and no syrups and no fresh soda water. Today we have the "shake," although it is usually not clear what is being shaken.

Just imagine a scoop of ice cream from the cows on the hillside above town on a hot summer day, frozen with ice harvested last winter at Lake Chautauqua, sweetened with wild black cherry syrup from the trees of the forest and then made even more special by a shot of soda water to put bubbles in your nose so you'll have the illusion of champagne. This is a far more egalitarian vision than the black currant bomb!

We did not have a soda bottle. This was a thick glass bottle reinforced with wire mesh and topped by a compressor/sprayer apparatus. We did have a broken one with no sprayer which had been converted into a table lamp. Ice cream floats and sundaes were good enough for us. My father taught me these stories about sodas and sundaes while explaining our soda-bottle lamp.

## Chokecherry

Wild black cherry may grow to tremendous heights in the forest. Grandma was lucky to have one with a huge lower limb that sought out the light in the driveway. Chokecherry (*Prunus virginiana*) is a tree of more modest size up to twenty-five feet. The dark red or ruddy black fruit is the same size as the wild black cherry but it tastes slightly different, more astringent. As kids we joked that the fruits would make us choke if we ate them. We knew that they were good to whet your whistle if necessary but not as good as other fruits. We presumed that "choke" denoted a bad flavor and not its use to soothe choking and coughing. How wrong we were!

The chokeberry (*Aronia melanocarpa*) bush bears a bitter, astringent marginally edible but very healthy fruit that is sometimes also called a "chokecherry."

Last year I saw an interview on TV with a Native American chef telling about how he makes chokecherry sauce like his grandmother did. In August I noticed some beautiful chokecherries growing along the rails-to-trails path west of the Chautauqua Gorge and picked a bit of the fruit.

The secret is the long, slow boiling of the chokecherries in a bit of water. Watch it closely and add more water if it starts to get too thick. After an hour or two the pits separate so easily that you don't even need a food mill/applesauce spinner. You are left with a syrup so good that it scarcely needs any additional sweetening. The astringent taste has totally cooked away, or been hidden by the sweetness. This syrup was so good that I even hiked back to pick again and put up more of it.

Dried chokecherry is also used to make pemmican.

## Mayhaw

The small red fruit of the hawthorn tree is properly called a "haw." There are hundreds of species of hawthorns and just as many kinds of haws, most all of which are marginally edible and two species of which, the mayhaw, may actually be good. I've seen this tree advertised in catalogs but not yet grown one myself.

I wanted to try one of my own hawthorns. I'd been checking out a handsome, low tree on the path around the pond with large, attractive orange-red fruit. I nibbled a haw that I had picked up on the ground and it did not seem bad at all. I picked a mess of haws off the tree and made them into a jam so vile that no amount of sugar could make you want to eat it.

Perhaps I made my mistake when I judged the fruit hanging on the tree by a riper one that had fallen off. What if my haws needed to ripen unto softness in the same way as a medlar in order to be edible?

Maybe I just will have to get me a mayhaw.

*Crataegus aestivalis* and *Crataegus opaca* grow in zones 6 through 9 and are used for pies, preserves and wine. These fruits are better known in the South where they ripen by the end of May. That would probably be a bit later in the North. I don't like the sound of the word "junehaw" but I would probably like the fruit far more than I liked my hawthorns!

## Rosehips

For some reason roses have hips, not haws. A hip is the fruit of the rose. In Sweden rosehips are called "*nypon*" and are treated just like a normal fruit. The word sports an "-on" ending, as do so many of the Swedish words for the berries, witness "*lingon*" and "*smultron*" (wild strawberries). The singular form is the same as the plural. Does this mean that one is never enough? Rosehip preserves are common in Sweden. Pies and tarts are made with them as well. In America it is considered a bit strange to be eating rosehips. I fondly remember those rosehippy nut chews that were sold in health food stores during the 1970s but haven't seen them around since that time. Too bad.

Just as with haws, hips are "marginally edible." Some kinds are better than others. A few kinds of roses are grown especially for their hips, not their flowers. It seems that rosehips have an unusually high concentration of vitamin C.

I was in the process of extirpating the wild rosebush on my farm path (probably *Rosa eglanteria*) when I became fascinated by the huge crop of bright-orange rosehips, long and slender. It was late November and the fruit was soft and ripe. It seems the frosts only make the hip grow sweeter and gooier. I cut off the bush but didn't haul it away with the brush until after I had returned with a basket a week later to harvest a quart of fruit.

It was a bit tedious to remove the stem ends and floral tips but before long I had pure hips which I boiled slowly in a small amount of water. When the seeds separated easily from the hips I separated them out and discarded them by passing the goosh through the finest mesh on my food mill. The best was the thick sludge that clung to the back of the sieve. I put this back on a slow boil and added sugar and a spoonful of commercial pectin. I should have saved some of my quince seeds to help out with this! I ended up with the most delicious new discovery of the year—rosehip jam.

Next year there won't be a wild rosebush on the path where there was one this year, but that doesn't matter. I have dozens of these bushes spread around my farm, in the dry, sunny corners of the swamp. If I note their locations and return to harvest them next year, I'll have plenty of rosehip jam and perhaps even enough to reinvent the rosehippy nut chews.

Rosehip is another fruit which ripens like the medlar or the persimmon does. It is sweetest as it softens after the frost. It is not necessarily ripe just because it's orange in the summer. Wait until they start to soften, then pick them.

Unfortunately vitamin C degrades quickly at temperatures above 60° C, so my rosehip jam is probably not a vitamin source. It still tastes good!

*Nyponsoppa* (rosehip soup) is still popular in Scandinavia. The hips are harvested after the frost, then dried and used for tea or soup. To make soup, pulverize the hips and leave them to sit in some water. Liquefy the soup further in a blender. Pass it through a fine sieve to remove the seeds, then add sugar to sweeten and potato flour to thicken. Don't let it boil and you will be maximizing the vitamin C content of your soup. Serve it warm or cool with a bit of cream on the top.

Eglantine rosehips taste rather insipid in the summer but are quite good by late fall. Other rosehips are better.

In January I was brushing again and found another wild rose bush filled with fruit. In short order I picked another quart of hips. These I decided to process without heat so as to preserve the vitamins. I washed the fruit and snipped off all of the stem and floral remains. The hips were very soft and sweet but the seeds are incredibly hard. Make sure none of them get through your sieve. I put the wet hips through the finest mesh of my food mill and scraped up the paste. The slowness of the harvest of the pulp reminded me of medlars but the quart of hips soon produced a half cupful of mash. I added a spoonful of water to the food mill and was able to force even more of the pulp through the mesh. This I did twice for a total of three pressings. I added considerably more water to the mash left in the food mill and got a good half pint of rosehip juice which I reserved for other uses. I added a spoonful of sugar and small pieces of walnut but nothing else to my harvested pulp. I pressed this nutty paste out onto waxed papers and dried it in a hot oven, turned off. Rosehippy nut chews are reborn!

In conclusion rosehips are used in jams, preserves, pies, tarts, candies and even wines. "Rhodomel" is the word for mead flavored with rosehips. Do you remember the carnival novelty called "itching powder"? This was a malevolent powder designed to induce itching, not to cure it. One of the primary ingredients of this powder was the dried hairs from inside rosehips. Tarantula hairs were also used for these powders but the rosehip hairs must have been used to produce the cheaper versions!

## Rowanberry

In America we are more likely to call a rowan tree a "mountain ash" because of the similarities in the leaves, but this is superficial. Ash and mountain ash, the trees, are not close cousins like the words. Ash trees have "fruits" (in the botanical sense, not the culinary) called "samaras," papery helicopters with a single terminal wing. Rowan trees have beautiful orange-red clusters of berries. Ash leaves are "opposite," whereas rowan leaves are "alternate." The best rowan for berries is reputedly *Sorbus acuparia*, originally European but widely planted in America as well. There are a number of native *Sorbus* species here and also hybrid fruits of rowan combined with pear or hawthorn, but all the various sorts of rowan fruits are virtually unknown in America.

I purchased a German *Sorbus acuparia* selected for its fruit and soon had beautiful orange-red berry clusters all over. Every time I sampled a berry, it was horrible. The books said it's a fruit of late fall, so I waited and picked a mess of them at that time. Maybe they just needed sweetening? By the time I got back to my pickings, the berries had shriveled and the interior oxidized to a disagreeable brown color. I threw them out.

"Oh no!" said Hasan, my Bosnian neighbor. "The fruits get old, maybe they don't look so good, turned brown on the inside, but when you eat it, it's like brown sugar!" Stupid me.

I will have to try again, but now the tree has grown so high that I can't reach the berries easily.

Rowan is another one of those fruits that needs to "blet" like a medlar to become edible. The jelly is a brownish-amber color. It is strongly flavored, deep and earthy, the perfect accompaniment for meats, especially wild game.

Let's consider that old expression that I just used, "a mess of berries." Here "mess" is a collective noun designating some sort of food, lots of it, enough for a course at a meal if not a winter's supply, as in "She cooked up a mess of pancakes" or in the military expression "mess hall." Today the word "mess" has taken on some very unsavory connotations for the most part, as in "I sure did mess up when I threw away that mess of ripe rowanberries." How did having ample food supplies become something negative and disorderly?

"Mess" is also the word for my kitchen in both connotations. There's a mess of squash lying over there, a mess of apples on the floor, a mess of sunchokes and turnips waiting to have the dirt washed off them, a mess of medlars in baskets waiting for me to scoop them out, and a mess of berries in the freezer. It is too bad I threw out that mess of rowanberries last year because I didn't gather any this year. This experiment will have to be put off for another year.

It is always like this with different messes traveling through my kitchen at different times of the year. By now you've probably realized that I am somewhat of a squirrel myself, so yes, there's also a mess of nuts lying around—sacks of black walnuts, butterheartnuts (buartnuts), butternuts, gingko nuts, even a few pecans. The pecan trees grew for twenty five years before giving their first meager harvests. You can see that I have always lived this way.

Wonderfully magical foods come out of my messes, so many that I developed an alternate persona named "Mark Stewart." He is supposed to be a drag king pretending to be Martha Stewart's bastard half-brother, but really he is just me—serving gooseberry fools or medlar-butternut trifles on unmatched cracked china in the midst of squalor. Pay no attention to that mess of plastic containers in the corner, or to those dirty dishes in the sink!

There exists a great deal of heathen/pagan lore surrounding the rowan tree. Everyone knows that magic wands are made from the wood of rowan but nobody seems to know exactly why. Crosses of rowan wood tied in red thread are known to repel evil. The word "rowan" is etymologically related to our word for "red." There is no one myth that I have ever heard of which can explain the reason for rowan's overlying importance and sacredness. It would appear that the myth has been lost.

The flavor of rowanberry is said to be strong and gamey. Must gamey be bad? I find its flavor strong and different from other fruits, but not bad at all. Perhaps it is another form of honor for this fruit always to be paired with the wild game at the table, the "fruits" of the chase.

Here is a short alternative version of Aesop's fable of the sour grapes from Sweden. It goes "*Surt sa räven om rönnbären*" ("Sour said the fox about the rowanberries.") This old saying is open to various interpretations.

Rowan (*rönn*) is also known as *torshjälp* (Thor's help) in Swedish. This kenning is a reference to a myth in which Thor is almost killed in battle with a particularly bad giant. His exhausted body is floating downriver when a rowan tree extends its limbs into the water and catches him, enabling him to crawl back onto dry land and avoid drowning.

"Thor's help" may also be a kenning for Sif, his wife, as certainly she has helped Thor out many times in the past whereas the rowan tree is known to have done so only this once. Sif is also associated with the rowan tree because the Sami thundergod Horagalles has a consort named Ravdna who is herself strongly associated with the rowan tree.

Here I will cite and translate a bit about the rowan from Per Österman's book *Svenska jätteträd och deras mytologiska historia* (*Swedish Giant Trees and their Mythological History*), Artbooks, 2001.

> It is not particularly easy to find big rowan trees around today. They are regarded as a sort of junk wood without any commercial uses. This stands in sharp contrast to the huge significance which the rowan had back in the times of the peasant society when the tree was one of the most holy.
>
> This perception appears to have been spread all across northern Europe from Estonia through Scandinavia to England, Scotland, Ireland and the islands in the North Atlantic. In England the tree was called "witchen" or "witchwood," "häxträd" (hex tree). Today it is called the rowan. Thor's Finnish equivalent, Turisas, married Rauni—which is the Finnish word for rowan. In Estonia they would sometimes place a rowan wood cross on the chest of a dead man to prevent him from getting up again, which is a hilariously funny blending of heathen and Christian mythology. It was a question of protecting one's self in both systems.
>
> The mythological roots go even deeper than that. In India there are to be found myths and practices around trees very similar to the Nordic ones, which hint at a common Indo-European origin.
>
> We can only guess at what makes rowan so magically charged. The blood-red color of the berries and the shining trunk may have contributed. In addition the berries are rich in vitamin C and have been used in folk medicine to treat sicknesses associated with scarcity and deficiency. This in turn has strengthened the tree's holiness. The berries are also diuretic which was used to mitigate the affects of gout.
>
> If today's pasturelands are somewhat lacking in rowan trees, back in the day there must have been considerably more of them. Rowan was, as everyone knows, a powerful shield against evil spirits and supernatural beings. The custom of building bits of rowan wood into the plow was widespread, just like the habit of setting rowan twigs on things you wanted to protect, for example, all around newly sown fields.

> Rowan is also sometimes mentioned as a guardian tree. Since the tree was associated with Thor, the god of thunder, this may have been to protect the house from bolts of lightning. (Österman, page 86)

Rowan berries are produced in great profusion and are spread all around by the birds. The seeds fall everywhere and will grow, at least for a while, in the little soil accumulated in the crotches of trees and the crevices of boulders and cliffs. These so-called "flying rowan trees" (*flygrönner*) grow in all sorts of places almost like epiphytes and were regarded with particular respect and a sense of awe. These dwarf trees made the best dowsing rods to locate ground water for wells. (Witch-hazel twigs have a similar reputation but not the odd growth habit.)

Lastly, I will share with you something from my dream journal regarding the rowan tree. Yes, I am such a plant-faërie sort of person that I even dream about plants. Here is my "birthday-party rowan dream" which came six months before my 65th birthday.

# Epilogue

Thor with his hammer, Mårtin Eskil Winge (1825–1896)

## Rowan dream

It is late summer, and the people in my life are throwing me a retirement and 65th birthday party. Most of them are not really in my life but perhaps they ought to be. The guests are an odd collection of friends, family, high school classmates, townsfolk and work colleagues from school.

The party begins outside the back corner of the last school I taught at before my retirement. We are spread out picnic style on blankets on the grass. I never had a birthday party and am not enjoying this one. I notice a rowan tree growing at the corner of the building and go over to examine it.

The dream morphs now. It is still my birthday party but now they are holding it in the park around the historical museum in my hometown of Westfield. I overhear a teacher colleague and a high school classmate in the bushes comparing notes about their bipolar medications. All around me on the blankets is this same disparate collection of people, friends and family, pagans and faëries, teachers I taught with and members of my high school class. My deceased mother is sitting on a blanket next to my sister, nieces and cousins, beaming, smiling, laughing and listening as my colleagues share their memories of me at school. I do not remember these stories but I do remember thirty-five years of continuous sexual harassment, so I never enjoyed socializing with my colleagues and am not ready to do so now.

I return to the rowan tree, now growing at the corner of the museum. It sits on a little mound by the building a bit above the rest of the park. Where is Dave, my mate, someone whom I do want to see? There he is on the other side of the park, smiling, talking to a crowd of people. He loves birthdays, the more parties the merrier, but I do not, especially when it involves such a large number of people whom I really do not even want to see.

"Oh Jay," says one of the teachers. "Your sister is such an interesting person, so bright and creative, so artistic. . . and so proud of what you have done!" These words are particularly bitter for me because I know them to be largely untrue, though once they were.

The crowd moves to the kitchen door because Burger King is running the cafeteria just for the party. A shamanic drummer leatherman named River has demanded food for the crowds. The manager appears with a tray of still-frozen fast food so that we may make our selections.

Sister sidles up to me in line to order her food. "Oh, don't those chickens look good!" she says. This is the first time in three years that I have heard her voice. The chicken doesn't appeal to me but the potato-chive burger looks interesting. Suddenly I feel closed in and cannot make up my mind. There are too many people around me. I break out of line and head back outside onto the grounds to find again the rowan tree.

As is so often my wont, I feel more kinship with plants than I do with those human beings. The plants have always treated me right. I do dream of them often. Never have I dreamt of a rowan tree before but in this dream I am now returning to it for the third time.

I walk away from the crowd, up the mound and step into the branches of the tree. I climb up and up until I find some peace. I can see the entire park full of people who would not even be here if not for me. I realize now that I should rejoin my party, even though I am enjoying my time with the rowan tree far more.

I hold onto the branch above me and step out into space. I am too high off the ground now to dare to let go. The rowan tree branch does not bend as I had anticipated, not at all. The tree feels my apprehension and bends like a muscle down, down to deposit me gently on the ground. Then the branch moves slowly skyward back to its former position. I go back to the party.

I awaken with thoughts of *rönn* and *torshjälp* in my mind.

# Epilogue

Powerful dreams like this one only come rarely. What will I do about it?

If I am lucky, the party will end and I will head on out to my farm to spend another twenty-five or thirty years more with my quince and medlar trees. The rowan tree is planted up in front on the southeast corner, keeping the world at bay. Remember the old adage, "When the world wearies and society ceases to satisfy, there is always the garden."

You won't be able to find them in stores, most likely, but if you grow these plants on your own and eat their fruits you will learn to hear their stories. Perhaps you will find that you recognize old friends, as I did, and your memories will mix with mine.

# Acknowledgements

Some special thanks are in order to my editors, Andrew Rasanen and Mary Nagel, who have helped me to shape and publish this book. More thanks go out to Jim Turner, who helped me to plant my farm and did the photography on the cover. I would not have a farm to crow about without the help of my neighbor, Sam Walker, and my cousins Brent and Jordan Ellis. Their tractors and brush hogs have saved it from the wilderness of sumac and brambles that threatens it periodically.

# About the Author

Jay Stratton is a retired teacher and linguist as well as an amateur botanist and farmer who lives in Westfield and Rochester, New York. He graduated from Syracuse University and the University of Rochester. He also attended the State University of New York College of Forestry in Syracuse.

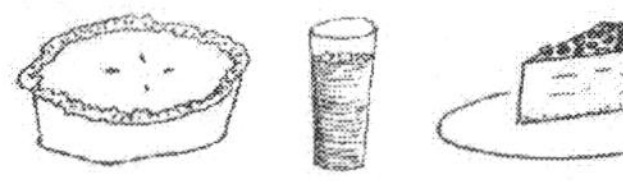

# Conversion Tables

Liquid measures

| **American** standard cup | | **metric equivalent** (approximately) |
|---|---|---|
| 1 cup = 1/2 pint | = 8 fl. oz. (fluid ounce) | = 2.37 dl (deciliter) |
| 1 tbs. (tablespoon) | = 1/2 fl. oz. | = 1.5 cl (centiliter) |
| 1 tsp. (teaspoon) | = 1/6 fl. oz. | = 0.5 cl |
| 1 pint | = 16 fl. oz. | = 4.73 dl |
| 1 quart = 2 pints | = 32 fl. oz. | = 9.46 dl |

| British standard cup | | metric equivalent (approximately) |
|---|---|---|
| 1 cup = 1/2 pint | = 10 fl. oz. | = 2.84 dl |
| 1 tbs. | = 0.55 fl. oz. | = 1.7 cl |
| 1 tsp. | = 1/5 fl. oz. | = 0.6 cl |
| 1 pint | = 20 fl. oz. | = 5.7 dl |
| 1 quart = 2 pints | = 40 fl. oz. | = 1.1 (liter) |

1 cup = 16 tablespoons
1 tablespoon = 3 teaspoons
1 liter = 10 deciliter = 100 centiliter

Solid measures

| **American/British** | | **metric equivalent** (approximately) |
|---|---|---|
| 1 lb. (pound) | = 16 oz. (ounces) | = 453 g (gram) |
| | 1 oz. | = 28 g |
| 2.2 lbs. | | = 1000 g = 1 kg (kilogram) |
| | 3 1/2 oz. | = 100 g |

Oven temperatures

| **Centigrade** | **Fahrenheit** | |
|---|---|---|
| up to 105°C | up to 225°F | cool |
| 105–135°C | 225–275°F | very slow |
| 135–160°C | 275–325°F | slow |
| 175–190°C | 350–375°F | moderate |
| 215–230°C | 400–450°F | hot |
| 230–260°C | 450–500°F | very hot |
| 260°C | 500°F | extremely hot |

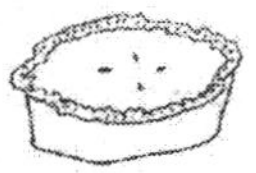

# Notes

# Notes

Made in the USA
Columbia, SC
16 November 2017